PEOPLE, MARKETS, GOODS:
ECONOMIES AND SOCIETIES IN HISTORY

Volume 22

Financial Failure in Early Modern England

T0311195

PEOPLE, MARKETS, GOODS:
ECONOMIES AND SOCIETIES IN HISTORY

ISSN: 2051-7467

Series editors
Marguerite Dupree – University of Glasgow
Steve Hindle – Washington University in St Louis
Jane Humphries – University of Oxford, London School of Economics
Willem M. Jongman – University of Groningen
John Turner – Queen's University Belfast
Jane Whittle – University of Exeter
Nuala Zahedieh – University of Cambridge

The interactions of economy and society, people and goods, transactions and actions are at the root of most human behaviours. Economic and social historians are participants in the same conversation about how markets have developed historically and how they have been constituted by economic actors and agencies in various social, institutional and geographical contexts. New debates now underpin much research in economic and social, cultural, demographic, urban and political history. Their themes have enduring resonance – financial stability and instability, the costs of health and welfare, the implications of poverty and riches, flows of trade and the centrality of communications. This paperback series aims to attract historians interested in economics and economists with an interest in history by publishing high quality, cutting edge academic research in the broad field of economic and social history from the late medieval/ early modern period to the present day. It encourages the interaction of qualitative and quantitative methods through both excellent monographs and collections offering path-breaking overviews of key research concerns. Taking as its benchmark international relevance and excellence it is open to scholars and subjects of any geographical areas from the case study to the multi-nation comparison.

PREVIOUSLY PUBLISHED TITLES IN THE SERIES ARE
LISTED AT THE BACK OF THIS VOLUME

Financial Failure in Early Modern England

Aidan Collins

THE BOYDELL PRESS

First published 2024
The Boydell Press, Woodbridge

ISBN 978-1-83765-190-0

The Boydell Press is an imprint of Boydell & Brewer Ltd
PO Box 9, Woodbridge, Suffolk IP12 3DF, UK
and of Boydell & Brewer Inc.
668 Mt Hope Avenue, Rochester, NY 14620-2731, USA
website: www.boydellandbrewer.com

A catalogue record for this book is available
from the British Library

The publisher has no responsibility for the continued existence or accuracy of URLs for
external or third-party internet websites referred to in this book, and does not guarantee
that any content on such websites is, or will remain, accurate or appropriate

Contents

Contents

Preface and Acknowledgements

I left school at sixteen to begin a career in professional football. After a few successful years playing in England – winning the FA Youth Cup, representing England at U18 level, and making several appearances in the old Division One, the Championship, and League Two – I had some money sitting in a savings account. My agent, solicitor, and many more experienced people around me advised me not to waste it, and instead to buy a house. I took their advice and in 2005 at the age of eighteen I entered the property market. A few years later, I was told by a surgeon that I would have to retire due to persistent knee injuries. With the insurance company rejecting my claim, and my workers' union – the Professional Footballers' Association – refusing to provide any financial support, the 2008 financial crisis struck the global economy. With no money and no job, I decided to go back to college to undertake my A-levels and eventually went on to complete an Undergraduate Degree in History at Goldsmiths, University of London. I thoroughly enjoyed my degree and when I looked into potential sources of funding to begin an MA in early modern history, I discovered that these were few and far between. As such, I decided to sell my house to pay for my MA, which I hoped would lead to a PhD and – eventually – a career in academia.

When the house was eventually sold, I was left with just about enough to cover the cost of tuition. I asked myself some obvious questions: How could the same physical building be worth so much less in such a short period of time? Why had no one warned me of the potential downside to owning property? How could so many experts not see this coming? To what extent was this my fault and due to my own failings? In thinking about these questions, I realised that when I bought the house I had never asked some less obvious questions: Where did the bank get the money to grant me a mortgage? How could I so easily get a mortgage in the first place? And perhaps most perplexing, if the bank had failed, what gave them the right – morally and legally – to continue to demand repayment? This book has emerged from my initial interest in these questions, and the ways in which people continue to describe, debate, and discuss financial and personal failures – such as my own – both in the past and in contemporary society.

While the interest in the themes of the book has a longer history, the substantial research for the project began at the University of York, and I am grateful for the support provided by the Department of History, the Department of Economics, and the Humanities Research Centre. My biggest thanks go to Natasha Glaisyer for her continued advice, encouragement, and good humour throughout the project. For their invaluable comments on earlier drafts, I am indebted to Mark Jenner, Judith Spicksley, Amanda Capern, Laura Stewart, the anonymous readers of the manuscript, the series editors, and the editorial director, Michael Middeke.

The majority of this research was supported by the Arts and Humanities Research Council (grant number AH/L503848/1). Further financial support for the completion of the book came from a Scouloudi Research Award in association with the Institute of Historical Research, and a Fellowship with the Royal Historical Society. I would like to thank Liz Hore and Amanda Bevan at The National Archives for their patience in explaining the complicated cataloguing of Chancery documents. Chapter four has been developed from an earlier version which was published in *Cultural and Social History* and is reproduced here with the following permission: 'Narratives of Bankruptcy, Failure, and Decline in the Court of Chancery, 1678–1750' by Aidan Collins © 2022 The Author(s), taken from *Cultural and Social History* 2022, Vol: 19 Iss:1, © Informa UK Limited, trading as Taylor & Francis Group 2022, reprinted by permission of Taylor & Francis Ltd.

Since the beginning of this project and the publication of the book, I have held various temporary contracts at the universities of York, Lincoln, Teesside, Sheffield, Keele, Manchester, Lancaster, Goldsmiths, and Newcastle. I would like to thank the following colleagues for their help, support, and advice on research, writing, and navigating an academic career: Amy Creighton, Megan Henvey, Chris Renwick, Oleg Benesch, Simon Ditchfield, Harry Munt, Lucy Sackville, Nick Seager, Siobhan Talbott, Ian Atherton, Luke Davies, Alannah Tomkins, Robert Nantes, Erin Bell, Emily Ireland, Stuart Gorse, Alexia Yates, and Hannah Barker. A version of chapter three was presented at 'The Temporalities of Capitalism' conference in association with the University of Bern, and I wish to thank the conference organisers and participants for their detailed feedback which helped to strengthen the chapter.

Finally, having written a book about financial failure, it would be remiss of me not to thank those who kept me in employment and my neck above water throughout my undergraduate, postgraduate, and postdoctoral career. I would like to thank Karen, Stu, Jo – and to a much lesser extent – Don, for employing me and providing friendship for several summers, and the Peckham branch of the Post Office for giving me two weeks off – either side of Christmas of course – to complete the final manuscript.

Abbreviations

AALT	University of Houston: Anglo-American Legal Tradition
EHR	Economic History Review
LHR	Law and History Review
LX	Lexis+ UK
ODNB	Oxford Dictionary of National Biography (Oxford University Press), online edition
TNA	The National Archives, Kew

Conventions and Monetary Values

Original spelling and punctuation in all primary sources have been reproduced throughout and my own insertions have been made in square brackets. Unless otherwise stated, all emphasis – italics and capital letters – was found in the original texts. In some instances, the spelling of a particular name can vary within the same case. As such, the short titles of cases are reproduced as they are found on TNA or the AALT website. The name of any individual in a case is spelt according to the first reference in the original document. For example, in *Metcalfe v Letchmere* (1720), the plaintiff would be referred to as 'Richard Lechmere', but the short title of the case — *Metcalfe v Letchmere* (1720) — is reproduced as it is found on The National Archives' website.

In the currency used throughout, £1 is made up of 20s (shillings), and 1s is made up of 12d (pence). Attempting to provide details of the changes in monetary value from the seventeenth century to the modern day is a difficult task. For example, £100 in 1700 could be worth between £10,698.33 and £2,562,000.00 in 2017, depending on how it was calculated.[1] Perhaps a more effective way to think about £100 in 1700 is to compare it to living standards and annual income, as it has been estimated that an income of £50 per annum was the entry point for the middle rank of society.[2] Therefore, £100 would be twice the annual income for those on the threshold of the middling sort in 1700.

Though sources from before 1752 use Lady Day dating, I have taken the year to begin on 1 January and end on 31 December.

---

1   TNA, 'Currency converter: 1270–2017', estimates £10,698.33 in purchasing power, Stable URL: https://www.nationalarchives.gov.uk/currency-converter/ (accessed 29/03/2024); 'Purchasing Power of British Pounds from 1270 to Present', MeasuringWorth, 2024, estimates between £14,270.00 and £2,562,000.00 in purchasing power, Stable URL: www.measuring-worth.com/ppoweruk/ (accessed 29/03/2024).

2   Peter Earle, *The Making of the English Middle Class: Business, Society, and Family Life in London, 1660–1730* (Berkeley, 1989), pp. 14–15.

Introduction

On 4 March 1729, the creditors of Jeremiah Faulkner – a flax dresser and rope maker from Willersey, Gloucestershire – petitioned the Lord Chancellor to execute a commission of bankruptcy. Faulkner was found to have owed 'several Hundreds of pounds' to numerous creditors 'before he failed in the world and became a Bankrupt'. A meeting of the creditors was arranged and James Church and Joseph Withers – merchants from London – were nominated 'assignees' to collect and distribute Faulkner's estate to satisfy his debts. On 27 March 1729, the assignees travelled 100 miles to Gloucestershire to take an inventory of Faulkner's goods, claiming they made, 'the best Enquiry they were able into the Estate and Effects of the said Jeremiah Faulkner', which they believed would be sufficient to repay the entire debt.[1]

If the commission of bankruptcy went smoothly, then the entire procedure would have been conducted and completed without recourse to any other legal jurisdiction. However, in the example of Jeremiah Faulkner, the assignees claimed that the bankrupt 'hath not thought fitt to attend the said Commissioners or submitt to be examined or make any Discovery of his Estate and Effects'. Instead, Faulkner 'retired into some secret Place in the Country with the Privity of the said Elizabeth his Wife' and continued to abscond 'from his normal place of Habitation and abode'. As Faulkner had refused to cooperate with the commission of bankruptcy, Church and Withers submitted a bill of complaint in Chancery on 30 April 1730 and sought the assistance of the court to gain a full discovery of Faulkner's estate.[2] Ultimately, the assignees needed the overarching authority of the court of Chancery to complete or repair the ongoing debt-recovery process.

This book is about failure. In bankruptcy proceedings, failure has a legal definition: Jeremiah Faulkner – and many others like him – had failed to repay a debt within a specified time. Because they had not fulfilled their responsibilities and behaved in a trustworthy and credible manner, bankrupt individuals were seen to be immoral. In the example above, the assignees claimed that Faulkner was continuing to act in an untrustworthy way by concealing assets and refusing to cooperate with the ongoing debt-recovery process. However, this notion of failure became increasingly complex because bankruptcy cases

1   TNA, C11/365/89, 'Church v Faulkner' (1730), Bill of Complaint.
2   Ibid.

involved an interconnected network of indebtedness, which often included close relatives, neighbours, and traders from the local community. Conceptions of failure filtered outwards into wider society and implicated individuals beyond just the bankrupt. As people began to look back and appraise the actions and words of those involved in trade, a far wider network of creditors, debtors, and middlemen was blamed for the knock-on effect of an individual financial failure. As these complexities grew, the simplicity of the bankruptcy system began to be tested and the procedure itself can be seen to have broken down and have failed to come to a satisfactory conclusion.

Failure has been discussed in other economic and legal contexts, most notably imprisonment for debt. Tawny Paul has argued that debt insecurity was a 'defining feature of commercial experience' in eighteenth-century Britain. While approximately 33,000 businesses went bankrupt throughout the eighteenth century, some 3.3 million individuals were imprisoned for debt.[3] As such, Paul recognises that an analysis of failure is central to 'understanding commercial culture, business practices and economic change in the British and Atlantic worlds'.[4] Similarly, Alexander Wakelam has examined how traders used imprisonment for debt as a coercive tool to enforce contracts. For Wakelam, debtors' prisons were an effective and persuasive part of early modern life as they incentivised cooperation and provided definitive consequences for purchases on security.[5] Elsewhere, scholars have used the term failure as a synonym for bankruptcy, and have analysed business failure, the collapse of banks and institutions, the downfall of goldsmith bankers after the Stop of the Exchequer of 1672, and well-known or spectacular bankruptcies.[6]

---

3   Tawny Paul, *The Poverty of Disaster: Debt and Insecurity in Eighteenth-Century Britain* (Cambridge, 2019), pp. 1–6; the figure of 33,000 bankrupts is taken from Julian Hoppit, *Risk and Failure in English Business 1700–1800* (Cambridge, 1987), p. 42.
4   Paul, *The Poverty of Disaster*, p. 5.
5   Alexander Wakelam, *Credit and Debt in Eighteenth Century England: An Economic History of Debtors' Prisons* (London, 2020), p. 30.
6   J. Keith Horsefield, 'The "Stop of the Exchequer" Revisited', *EHR*, 35 (1982), pp. 511–528; Barbara J. Todd, 'Fiscal Citizens: Female Investors in Public Finance Before the South Sea Bubble', in Sigrun Haude and Melinda S. Zook (eds), *Challenging Orthodoxies: The Social and Cultural Worlds of Early Modern Women* (Surrey, 2014); pp. 53–74; Rowena Dudley, 'The Failure of Burton's Bank and its Aftermath', *Irish Economic and Social History* 40 (2013), pp. 1–30; Seán Kenny and John D. Turner, 'Wildcat Bankers or Political Failure? The Irish Financial Pantomime, 1797–1826', *European Review of Economic History*, 24 (2020), pp. 522–577; K. H. Burley, 'An Essex Clothier of the Eighteenth Century', *EHR*, 11 (1958), pp. 289–301; Michael Quilter, 'Daniel Defoe: Bankrupt and Bankruptcy Reformer', *The Journal of Legal History*, 25 (2004), pp. 53–73; Ann M. Carlos and Larry Neal, 'Women Investors in Early Capital Markets, 1720–1725', *Financial History Review*, 11 (2004), pp. 197–224; John Paul, 'Bankruptcy and Capital Punishment in the 18th and 19th Centuries' (16 January 2009). Available at SSRN: https://ssrn.com/abstract=1329067

The seminal work on English bankruptcy was conducted by Julian Hoppit in 1987. In *Risk and Failure in English Business 1700–1800*, Hoppit takes a quantitative approach to bankruptcy, examining the significance and causes of bankruptcy throughout the eighteenth century and attempting to track changes in the numbers of bankrupts between periods, regions, and occupations. Hoppit attributes failure to unforeseen crises and the bigger picture of business cycles, war, local economic conditions, and bad weather.[7] Over the first half of the century, the number of bankrupts was 'relatively low and steady … before rising very steeply and continuously thereafter'.[8] In contrast, Paul concludes that middling people of the period were 'subjected to sustained structural insecurities, punctuated by life events and short-term economic fluctuations, and grounded in a growing and fragile credit market'.[9] Studies of bankruptcy have provided crucial insights into economic and legal failure, highlighting the necessity of paying close attention to the mechanisms for dealing with debt and how this links to macro-economic change, commercial culture, and business practices throughout the early modern period. This book adds a new dimension to existing scholarship by focusing on bankruptcy as a social construct, which needs to be understood – rather than measured – in order to highlight changing attitudes, assumptions, and narratives concerning economic and social failure. Focusing on individual instances and particular moments of failure will refocus attention on everyday actions and people's interactions with the court.

But of course, there is a more complex notion of failure that is at play in bankruptcy proceedings, one that links to wider notions of credibility, trustworthiness, and morality. Craig Muldrew has shown how credit and capital came to depend on the public means of social communication and circulating judgements about the value of other members of communities. For Muldrew, 'the stress on trust as a necessary social bond meant that increasingly a good reputation for honesty and reliability in obligations was of great social importance'.[10] As the main economic unit of assessment, it became essential for households to be able to judge the trustworthiness of one another before extending credit or entering into contracts. Such bonds of trust would

(accessed 25/03/2024); George Selgin, 'Those Dishonest Goldsmiths', *Financial History Review*, 19 (2012), pp. 269–288; Nicola Phillips, *The Profligate Son: Or, a True Story of Family Conflict, Fashionable Vice, and Financial Ruin in Regency England* (Oxford, 2013); Peter Brealey, 'The Charitable Corporation for the Relief of Industrious Poor: Philanthropy, Profit and Sleaze in London, 1707–1733', *History*, 98 (2013), pp. 708–729.

7   Hoppit, *Risk and Failure in English Business*; see also Louis Levinthal, 'The Early History of Bankruptcy Law', *University of Pennsylvania Law Review*, 66 (1918), pp. 223–250.

8   Hoppit, *Risk and Failure in English Business*, p. 46.

9   Paul, *The Poverty of Disaster*, p. 90.

10 Craig Muldrew, *The Economy of Obligation: The Culture of Credit and Social Relations in Early Modern England* (Basingstoke, 1998), p. 148.

have acted to bind communities together, as they were based upon 'moral knowledge about others'. As such, a 'culture of credit' became understood and reinforced through social communication and circulating judgements about other members of the community, seen in the development of what Muldrew calls a sort of 'competitive piety'.[11] Building on the work of Muldrew, scholars such as Alexandra Shepard and Judith Spicksley have explored the language of self-description, as a range of men and women appeared as witnesses in ecclesiastical courts, responding to the question of their worth. As appearing in court was a routine activity, there was an expectation of plausibility in such assessments, which can provide valuable insights into the processes of social estimation in which witnesses themselves held a stake.[12]

Lena Liapi has used printed pamphlets alongside local court proceedings to demonstrate the ambivalence of trust in the urban environment and the precarious link between distrust and sociability. As Liapi concludes, 'in a city full of strangers, people were aware of the risk involved in trusting others, while at the same time found it impossible – and undesirable – to trust no one'. Pamphlets warned of the dangers of criminals feigning friendship, familiarity, or distant family relations in order to gain an individual's trust.[13] Margot Finn has shown how individuals involved in credit networks were regularly reminded of the importance of honouring contracts and repaying debts, whether that be from the pulpit, contemporary literature, or simply from their local shopkeepers and neighbours. As the relationship between status and wealth became increasingly difficult to quantify throughout the early modern period, Finn argues that interpersonal credit remained insecure well into the twentieth century.[14] While these works address the many ways in which credit, worth, and trustworthiness were conceptualised – and how this changed over time – they do not explicitly engage with debates surrounding how this was seen to have broken down, and the complexities involved in attempting to repair this process.

In contrast, there is a burgeoning scholarship by business historians which analyses family business strategies, and what the sociologist Yoram Ben-Porath

11   Ibid., pp. 148–150.
12   Alexandra Shepard, *Accounting For Oneself: Worth, Status, and the Social Order in Early Modern England* (Oxford, 2015), p. 36; see also Alexandra Shepard and Judith Spicksley, 'Worth, Age, and Social Status in Early Modern England', *EHR*, 64 (2011), pp. 493–530; Alexandra Shepard, 'The Worth of Married Women Witnesses in the English Church Courts, 1550-1730', in Cordelia Beattie and Matthew Frank Stevens (eds), *Married Women and the Law in Premodern Northwest Europe* (Woodbridge, 2013), pp. 191–212.
13   Lena Liapi, *Roguery in Print: Crime and Culture in Early Modern London* (Woodbridge, 2019), pp. 93–94.
14   Margot Finn, *The Character of Credit: Personal Debt in English Culture, 1740–1914* (Cambridge, 2003).

has termed the 'implicit contract' of family.[15] Increasingly, success and failure are being analysed in the context of the family, demonstrating the extent to which family, kin, and perceived likeness – ethnic identity, religion, and natural allegiances – created bonds of trust that enabled a competitive advantage in trade.[16] Elsewhere, I have argued that rather than seeing the family as a homogenous economic unit, scholars should continue to explore the divisions within families, which will highlight the interconnected nature of failure within family units and close-knit networks.[17] In a similar manner, Mabel Winter has undertaken a microstudy of the failure of the institution Thompson and Company. Winter analyses the interconnected nature of seventeenth-century finance, commerce, and politics, showing how the partners' multifaceted careers – as merchants, bankers, and politicians – effected their ability to maintain their reputations and satisfy obligations. For Winter, the collapse of the company 'appears to have been politically motivated', as the partners' social and political reputations collapsed before their economic failure.[18] Such analysis demonstrates how failure in the political, social, or familial sphere could lead to an economic collapse, providing a more nuanced interpretation of merchant and financial networks.

15   Hannah Barker, *Family and Business During the Industrial Revolution* (Oxford, 2017); Yoram Ben-Porath, 'The F-Connection: Families, Friends, and Firms and the Organization of Exchange', *Population and Development Review*, 6 (1980), pp. 1–30.

16   Francesca Trivellato, *The Familiarity of Strangers: The Sephardic Diaspora, Livorno, and Cross-Cultural Trade in the Early Modern Period* (New Haven, 2009), pp. 3–4; Naomi Tadmor, *Family and Friends in Eighteenth-Century England: Household, Kinship and Patronage* (Cambridge, 2001); Margaret Hunt, *The Middling Sort: Commerce, Gender, and the Family in England, 1680–1780* (London, 1996), pp. 19–22; Sophie H. Jones and Siobhan Talbott, 'Sole Traders? The Role of the Extended Family in Eighteenth-Century Atlantic Business Networks', *Enterprise and Society*, 23 (2021), pp. 1–30; Douglas Hamilton, 'Local Connections, Global Ambitions: Creating a Transoceanic Network in the Eighteenth-Century British Atlantic Empire', *International Journal of Maritime History*, 23 (2011), pp. 283–300.

17   Aidan Collins, 'The Interconnected Nature of Family Indebtedness: The Halliday Family of Frome, Somerset (1733–1752)', *Enterprise and Society* (open access online, 2023), pp. 1–27; see also Sheryllynne Haggerty, '"You Promise Well and Perform as Badly:" The Failure of the "Implicit Contract of Family" in the Scottish Atlantic', *International Journal of Maritime History*, 23 (2011), pp. 267–282; David Hancock, 'The Trouble with Networks; Managing the Scots' Early Modern Madeira Trade', *Business History Review* 79 (2005), pp. 467–491.

18   Mabel Winter, *Banking, Projecting and Politicking in Early Modern England: The Rise and Fall of Thompson and Company 1671–1678* (Cham, 2022), pp. 13–14; Mabel Winter, 'The Collapse of Thompson and Company: Credit, Reputation and Risk in Early Modern England', *Social History*, 45 (2020), pp. 145–166.

Discussing narratives and representations of failure in eighteenth-century Philadelphia, Toby Ditz has argued that most merchants saw business reversals as the result of 'personal failure rather than social forces ... merchants ascribed failures to the character flaws and immoral conduct of others, or, much less frequently, to their own moral shortcomings'. Such narratives tended to 'focus on the plight of the failed merchant at the moment of his defeat and exposure'.[19] Bruce Mann has argued that the redefinition of debt from sin to risk was still not complete in America by the end of the eighteenth century.[20] In the context of the boom-and-bust era in nineteenth-century America, Scott Sandage has argued that 'success or failure often depended on the story that a man could tell about his own life – or that others could tell about him'.[21] While discussed in greater detail below, parallels can be drawn with English bankruptcy, as individuals sought to identify and clarify the exact moment a debtor failed in their obligations. A range of individuals attempted to look back and appraise the actions or words of debtors and their trading partners in an attempt to establish dishonesty. Analysing the numerous meanings and conceptualisations of failure will show how the complexities of bankruptcy procedure upset the flow of knowledge and circulating judgements about others in the trading environment. Failure was described and debated not just in economic terms, but also came to rely on a combination of social, community, and religious values which led to individual bankruptcies.

The difficulty in identifying dishonest and untrustworthy behaviour led to the final manifestation and interpretation of failure which is addressed in the book: the inability of those involved in a commission of bankruptcy – bankruptcy commissioners, assignees, creditors, debtors, trading partners, family members, legal experts, etc. – to effectively conclude and complete the debt-recovery process. All sources utilised in the book were where the bankruptcy process had somehow gone wrong, and certain individuals required the overarching authority of the court to repair, or complete, the procedure.[22] As such, the book is the first substantial work to analyse how the procedure of bankruptcy was litigated in the court of Chancery, demonstrating the complex and multifaceted nature of debt recovery, and increasing our knowledge of the various meanings attached to failure throughout early modern England.

---

19   Toby Ditz, 'Shipwrecked; or, Masculinity Imperiled: Mercantile Representations of Failure and the Gendered Self in Eighteenth-Century Philadelphia', *The Journal of American History*, 81 (1994), pp. 51–80, p. 58, p. 70.
20   Bruce H. Mann, *Republic of Debtors: Bankruptcy in the Age of American Independence* (Cambridge, 2002), p. 5.
21   Scott A. Sandage, *Born Losers: A History of Failure in America* (Cambridge, 2005), p. 9.
22   A breakdown of the source material used for each chapter can be found in Appendix One.

Bankruptcy as a Legal Status

While any individual could become insolvent, bankruptcy was a legal category which was assigned to a debtor through a procedure established in early modern statutes.[23] As Bruce Mann has shown, insolvency can be calculated in numerous ways based upon the sole criterion of failure. For example, insolvency can occur when a debtor's liabilities exceed their assets, or when the assets available to creditors are insufficient to pay the debt, or when a debtor cannot pay their debts when they come due. In this manner, insolvency is a question of fact, whereas bankruptcy is a legal status.[24]

As a creation of parliament, bankruptcy first entered the statute books in 1543 as, 'An Act Against Such Persons as do Make Bankrupt'.[25] However, the specific wording of the act was so vague as to make its practical application unworkable, and between 1571 and 1624 further legislation was enacted which established the fundamental early modern principles of bankruptcy law.[26] Within these acts certain stipulations applied, restricting who could become a bankrupt. Firstly, certain trades and professions were excluded. A person could only become a bankrupt if they were, 'a Merchant or other Person using or exercising the Trade of Merchandize by way of Bargaining, Exchange, Rechange, Bartry, Chevisance, or otherwise, in Gross or by Retail, or seeking his or her Trade of Living by Buying and Selling'.[27] Put simply, only merchants or traders making their living through 'Buying and Selling' could become a bankrupt, a stipulation that remained a part of English law until 1861.[28] The early statutes were intended to limit the jurisdiction of bankruptcy to the business world and protect the landowning and farming community. However, social and economic changes over the next two centuries made this stipulation difficult to implement practically.[29]

---

23 For the law of insolvency, see Ian F. Fletcher, *The Law of Insolvency*, 5th edn (London, 2017).

24 Mann, *Republic of Debtors*, pp. 44–46.

25 34 & 35 Henry VIII c.4 (1543).

26 The full list of statutes concerning bankruptcy for this period are, 34 & 35 Henry VIII c.4 (1543); 13 Elizabeth I c.7 (1571); 1 James I c.15 (1603); 21 James I c.19 (1624); 4 & 5 Anne I c.4 (1706); 6 Anne c.22 (1707); 10 Anne c.15 (1711); 7 Geo 1 c.31 (1720); 5 Geo 2 c.30 (1731); 19 Geo 2 c.32 (1745).

27 13 Elizabeth I c.7 (1571).

28 24 & 25 Vict c.134 (1861), s.69; 13 Elizabeth. I c.7 (1571); Several European countries – such as France, Spain, Belgium, Greece, Luxembourg, Italy, and Portugal – maintained the trading distinction into the twenty-first century; Fletcher, *The Law of Insolvency*, pp. 7–8.

29 For the political and economic rationale of this distinction, see Hoppit, *Risk and Failure in English Business*, p. 24; W. S. Holdsworth, *A History of English Law* (16 vols, London, 1926–1966), vol. 8, p. 237, n. 4; Ian P. H. Duffy, 'English Bankrupts, 1571–1861', *The American*

The term 'merchant' referred to a long-distance wholesale trader. The assumption at the time was that only overseas merchants – who were seen as a distinct class – had the ability to utilise credit to such an extent as to contract great debts. As Thomas Nowlan explained to a select committee in 1818, the bankruptcy laws were created at a period when, 'comparatively speaking, trade was in its infancy, and credit very limited'.[30] The short-term nature of borrowing and the simplicity of credit instruments limited the ability of credit to circulate.[31] Between 1571 and 1825, only minor statutory modifications were made to the operative definition found in the original description of a trader.[32] For example, the preoccupation of the sixteenth-century statutes with fraud led to scriveners, who were described as any person who receives 'other Mens Monies or Estates into his Trust or Custody', being brought within the scope of bankruptcy in 1624.[33] As William Jones explains, these men were important because like brokers – familiar in the world of finance but not mentioned in the statute – they engaged in 'incipient forms of banking'. Scriveners traded in money, and their failure or dishonesty held the potential to have 'widespread repercussions'.[34]

Over a century later, this concept was extended to include 'Bankers, Brokers and Factors' who were 'frequently intrusted with great Sums of Money, and with Goods and Effects of very great Value belonging to other Persons', entering the statute books in 1731.[35] In contrast, a statute of 1662 exempted share-holders in the East India and Guinea Companies and the Royal Fishing Trade from becoming bankrupt. This was done so that 'divers Noblemen, Gentlemen and Persons of Quality, no ways bred up to Trade or Merchandize … may not be discouraged in those honourable Endeavours for promoting publick Undertakings'.[36] As Ian Duffy explains, these provisions were enacted so that parliament could ensure that commercial non-traders did not expose their property to seizure and sale in bankruptcy proceedings.[37] Similar protection was extended to subscribers in other joint-stock companies, such as the Bank of

---

Journal of Legal History, 24 (1980), pp. 283–305; Aidan Collins, 'Bankrupt Traders in the Court of Chancery, 1674–1750', *Eighteenth-Century Studies*, 55 (2021), pp. 65–82.

30   Further Report of Minutes of Evidence Taken Before the Select Committee Appointed to Consider of the Bankrupt Laws, testimony of Thomas Nowlan, vol. 6 (House of Commons, 1818), p. 2.

31   Muldrew, *The Economy of Obligation*.

32   See Duffy, 'English Bankrupts, 1571–1861', pp. 283–305.

33   21 Ja. 1, c. 19 (1624), s.2; see Duffy, 'English Bankrupts', pp. 283–305.

34   W. J. Jones, 'The Foundations of English Bankruptcy: Statutes and Commissions in the Early Modern Period', *Transactions of the American Philosophical Society*, 69 (1979), pp. 1–63, p. 21.

35   5 Geo. 2, c.30 (1731) s.39.

36   14 Cha. 2, c.24 (1662) s.1–2.

37   Duffy, 'English Bankrupts, 1571–1861', p. 292.

England (1697), the New East India Company (1698), the South Sea Company (1711), the Royal Exchange and London Assurance Companies (1720), and the English Linen Company (1764).[38]

As parliament had not explicitly explained why bankruptcy was restricted to merchants or traders – and had only made minor statutory alterations to the definitions of a trader – it fell to the courts to decide which occupations fell within the scope of the statutes.[39] This process became increasingly complex over the next two centuries as the economy expanded and the distinction between traders and non-traders began to erode. The Commercial Revolution and the expansion of overseas trade in the seventeenth and eighteenth centuries coincided with structural transformations associated with the Financial Revolution: the establishment of a national debt, the foundation of the Bank of England, the emergence of a stock market, the expansion of paper instruments of exchange, the origins of the insurance industry, and the efficient administration of taxation and debt collection.[40] Merchants and other distinguished trading groups – such as sailors and mariners – saw a deterioration in their wealth and status, which reflected the political, commercial, and financial transformation of the state.[41] The legislature failed to keep up with these changes, reflecting a larger change in the economy which is particularly highlighted in bankruptcy proceedings.[42] During the seventeenth and eighteenth centuries, groups that were categorically excluded from the jurisdiction of bankruptcy – such as farmers and innkeepers – began to be subjected to litigation in Chancery, demonstrating that the earlier notion that bankruptcy should be limited to overseas traders had broadened to include all those who were engaged in the widespread use of credit.[43] By the nineteenth century it was proposed that bankruptcy should apply to all those who used bills of exchange, as this was the most common paper instrument used in trade.[44]

Secondly, an individual must have committed an 'act of bankruptcy' which sought to deny a creditor the satisfaction of their claim; being defined as 'any

38   8, 9 William III c.20 (1697), s.47; 9, 10 William III c.44 (1698), s.74; 9 Anne c.21 (1711), s.42; 6 George I c.18 (1720), s.10; 4 George III c.37 (1764) s.13.

39   Lawrence M. Friedman, and Thadeus F. Niemira, 'The Concept of the "Trader" in Early Bankruptcy Law', *Saint Louis University Law Journal*, 5 (1958), pp. 223–249.

40   Peter Dickson, *The Financial Revolution in England: A Study in the Development of Public Credit, 1688–1756* (London, 1967); Henry Roseveare, *The Financial Revolution 1660–1750* (London, 1991).

41   Perry Gauci, *The Politics of Trade: The Overseas Merchant in State and Society, 1660–1720* (Oxford, 2001); Eleanor Hubbard, *Englishmen at Sea: Labor and the Nation at the Dawn of Empire, 1570–1630* (New Haven, 2021); Peter Earle, *Sailors: English Merchant Seamen 1650–1775* (London, 1998).

42   Gauci, *The Politics of Trade*.

43   Collins, 'Bankrupt Traders in the Court of Chancery', pp. 65–82.

44   Hoppit, *Risk and Failure*, pp. 24–25.

such Person … which shall keep his or their Houses, or flee to Parts unknown, as is aforesaid, or intent to delay or defraud their Creditors deceitfully by Covin or Collusion'.[45] These statutory defined acts demonstrated the debtor's intent to delay, obstruct, or defraud their creditors, and can be seen as the law's attempt to identify failure. Throughout the seventeenth and eighteenth centuries, bankruptcy statutes provided a growing list of specific acts that would be considered actionable. The statute of 5 Geo 2 (1731) described sixteen ways in which a debtor could evade a creditor's demands, the most common of which were absconding or keeping house.[46] It was from this point that an individual became a bankrupt in the eyes of the law and the wider community, as they were seen to have disturbed the social order by removing themselves from public view and concealing their activities. Committing an act of bankruptcy was a definitive sign that a debtor could no longer maintain their economic commitments. As such, absconding was simultaneously a criminal act, as well as a way in which traders established that an individual was no longer creditworthy.

The 1543 act was intended to improve the efficiency of debt collection. The act took aim at 'divers and sundry Persons', who 'craftily obtaining into their Hands Mens Goods, do suddenly flee to Parts unknown, or keep their Houses, not minding to pay or restore to any their Creditors, their Debts and Duties'. Such action was seen to be, 'against all Reason, Equity and good Conscience'.[47] While there are several accounts of the etymology of the word 'bankruptcy', they all suggest that it was initially used around the Mediterranean to refer to traders who ran away from their debts.[48] Similarly, while the modern use of the word 'absconding' is rare, during the early modern period it was employed widely to connote being hidden from view, or to flee into hiding or an inaccessible place, 'typically to elude a creditor, escape from custody, or avoid arrest'.[49] Absconding and the inability to force debtors into the repayment of debts was a global issue that persisted until the modern period. Discussing the campaign against imprisonment for debt in Upper Canada during the nineteenth century, Jeffrey McNairn has shown how debtors' bodies were taken to prevent the individual from absconding, rather than to punish default.[50] From its very

---

45   34 & 35 Henry VIII c.4 (1543).
46   5 Geo 2 c.30 (1731); 16 acts of bankruptcy are listed in the following publication, Edward Green, *The Spirit of the Bankrupt Laws Wherein are Principally Considered, the Authority and Power of the Commissioners* (London, 1767), pp. 37–38; see Emily Kadens, 'The Last Bankrupt Hanged: Balancing Incentives in the Development of Bankruptcy Law', *Duke Law Journal*, 59 (2010), pp. 1229–1319, p. 1241.
47   34 & 35 Henry VIII c.4 (1543).
48   Jukka Kilpi, *The Ethics of Bankruptcy* (London, 1998), p. 10.
49   OED.
50   Jeffrey L. McNairn, '"The Common Sympathies of our Nature": Moral Sentiments, Emotional Economies, and Imprisonment for Debt in Upper Canada', *Social History*, 49 (2016), pp. 49–71.

creation as a legal principle, bankruptcy was associated with the criminal act of absconding in an attempt to avoid the repayment of just debts. Finally, a debtor had to have owed more than £100 to one creditor, £150 to two or more creditors, or £200 to three or more creditors.[51] Again, this stipulation was straightforward in theory, but as the economy expanded this threshold became easier to meet. Often, this benchmark was declared as a legal fiction to initiate proceedings, and could include the total value of penalties as well as the actual capital debt.[52]

When discussing the implementation of these statutes, Robert Weisberg has claimed that the coverage of the 1543 statute was hopelessly vague, based as much on 'literary sentiment' as on legislation. In contrast, the 1571 statute became so rigidly defined that it demanded the attention of parliament and the courts for the next three centuries. Weisberg has argued that any further 'legislative tinkering' only worsened the already established mechanical flaws.[53] Because of the restrictions established in the statutes, Jones has stated that 'debtors were many but bankrupts few', while Wakelam describes bankruptcy procedure as 'restrictive, arbitrary, and ineffective'.[54] While these were the three main stipulations which applied to bankruptcy, in their day-to-day implementation they were far more complicated and a commission of bankruptcy was largely a private affair, conducted with little oversight from state authorities.

Bankruptcy Procedure

The statute of 13 Elizabeth I (1571) created the position of bankruptcy commissioner, and any creditor could petition the Lord Chancellor and a commission of bankruptcy would be granted as a matter of course upon their *ex parte* [with respect to or in the interests of one side only] evidence.[55] This meant that a debtor was forced into bankruptcy proceedings and modern notions of voluntary bankruptcy did not appear in England until the middle of the nineteenth century.[56] The Chancellor directed each bankruptcy to a group of

---

51   21 James I c.19 (1624).
52   Jones, 'The Foundations of English Bankruptcy', p. 31.
53   Robert Weisberg, 'Commercial Morality, the Merchant Character, and the History of the Voidable Preference', *Stanford Law Review*, 39 (1986) pp. 3–138, pp. 21–27.
54   Jones, 'The Foundations of English Bankruptcy', p. 5.
55   13 Elizabeth I c.7 (1571); this process has been referred to in numerous ways, but for clarity and consistency, the process will be referred to as a commission of bankruptcy throughout. For example, both Thomas Goodinge and Thomas Davies refer to 'commission of bankrupts' and a 'commission of bankruptcy' throughout their publications, Thomas Goodinge, *The Law Against Bankrupts*, 5th edn (London, 1726); Thomas Davies, *The Laws Relating to Bankrupts* (London, 1744).
56   Voluntary bankruptcy was introduced for merchants in 1841, 7 & 8 Victoria c.96 (1841), and for non-merchants in 1861, 24 & 25 Victoria c.134 (1861); voluntariness was abolished

five individuals, although only three needed to sit to be quorate. The statute specified that these individuals were expected to be 'wise and honest discreet persons'.[57] In 1619, Francis Bacon ordered that at least one commissioner must be someone learned in the law, and William Jones has stated that 'this became more or less the rule'.[58] Commissioners were not government officials, but private individuals – usually solicitors or barristers – paid out of the proceeds of the bankrupt's estate.[59]

It has been estimated that a commissioner during this period could earn around £300 per year in fees, which by 1831 had only risen to £380.[60] William Holdsworth has suggested that such a sum could not secure capable individuals to deal with a business as difficult as that of bankruptcy, as commissioners 'were either young men who might be competent, but who were inexperienced, or old men who were experienced, but incompetent'.[61] Similarly, Hoppit has claimed that accusations of inefficiency were commonplace, as commissioners 'were either young, lively, and inexperienced or old, pedestrian and experienced'.[62] By the nineteenth century, Joshua Getzler has argued that commissioners had garnered 'an infamous reputation for being venal, vicious, and incompetent'.[63] The success of any insolvency or bankruptcy procedure, at any time in history, is largely dependent upon those who administer it.[64] Because commissioners were not paid the going rate for professional barristers and were private citizens paid from the bankrupt's estate – and the assignees who collected and distributed the estate were also creditors – bankruptcy largely remained a private matter, undertaken by those who held a vested interest in the outcome. As such, accusations of incompetence and corruption were commonplace.[65]

During the reign of Charles I, professional commissioners in London began to execute bankruptcy proceedings, and the practice had become so familiar throughout the eighteenth century that permanent lists of commissioners

---

in 32 & 33 Victoria c.71 (1869), but was restored in 46 & 47 Victoria c.52 (1883).
57   13 Elizabeth I c.7 (1571); Jones, 'The Foundations of English Bankruptcy', p. 25.
58   Ibid., p. 26.
59   Gerard Malynes, *Consuetudo, Vel, Lex Mercatoria: Or, The Ancient Law-Merchant*, 3rd edn (London, 1686), p. 158.
60   Ian P. H. Duffy, *Bankruptcy and Insolvency in London During the Industrial Revolution* (London, 1985), p. 35.
61   Holdsworth, *A History of English Law*, vol. 1, p. 472.
62   Hoppit, *Risk and Failure in English Business*, p. 37.
63   Joshua Getzler, 'Chancery Reform and Law Reform', *LHR*, 22 (2004), pp. 601–608, p. 605.
64   Ulrich Falk and Christoph Kling, 'The Regulatory Concept of Compulsory Composition in the German Bankruptcy Act', in Albrecht Cordes and Margit Schulte Beerbühl (eds), *Dealing With Economic Failure: Between Norm and Practice (15th to 21st Century)* (New York, 2016), pp. 215–242.
65   Kadens, 'The Last Bankrupt Hanged', p. 1243.

existed. By the late eighteenth century, one publication listed sixty-five commissioners, who were separated into thirteen lists of five.[66] Outside of London, there were no set lists and the petitioning creditor's solicitor usually nominated commissioners from the local community, who would be confirmed by the court.[67] In 1743, *The Law For and Against Bankrupts*, published by a 'Commissioner of Bankrupts', stated that the cost of opening a commission was at least £50.[68] This process would obviously decrease the bankrupt's estate and any subsequent payments made to creditors.

Once the Lord Chancellor had assigned commissioners, then the substantial work of the commission could begin. Commissioners were tasked with investigating whether a debtor could be declared a bankrupt within the legal stipulations outlined above. Only if, and when, these three conditions had been met was a debtor declared a bankrupt in the legal sense of the word. Hoppit has estimated that throughout the eighteenth century, this process of investigation confirmed that a debtor was a bankrupt in four out of every five instances. Therefore, in 20 per cent of cases, the commissioners could not satisfy the legal criteria and the debtor was not considered a bankrupt within the true intent and meaning of the statutes.[69] In order to give notice to the debtor that a commission had been taken out, the 1571 statute required commissioners to ensure that a proclamation was made in the appropriate marketplace on five market days. Under the statute of 1 James I (1604), lawful warning was to be left in writing on three occasions where the bankrupt had lived the previous year.[70] It became established that commissioners notified the debtor through an advertisement in the *London Gazette*, ordering them to surrender for investigation. In theory, these notifications made a commission of bankruptcy a 'matter of record', meaning it was the responsibility of the community to take notice of the proceedings. At this stage, all creditors with a legitimate claim would need to come forward and pay their contribution money towards the running of the commission.[71]

When the commissioners had made their declaration, they placed a further notification in the *London Gazette*, ordering the bankrupt to surrender their property. Their place of residence and place of work would be searched, and all goods seized. A meeting of the creditors would be arranged, whereby assignees

---

66   *A Succinct Digest of the Laws Relating to Bankrupts* (Dublin, 1791), p. 3.
67   Michael Lobban, 'Bankruptcy and Insolvency', in John Baker (ed.), *The Oxford History of the Laws of England*, vol. 12 (Oxford, 2010), pp. 786–787.
68   *The Law For and Against Bankrupts* (York, 1743), p. 166.
69   Hoppit, *Risk and Failure in English Business*, p. 36.
70   1 James I c.15 (1603); Jones, 'The Foundations of English Bankruptcy', p. 26.
71   Ibid., p. 34. The extent to which a commission was known to the public, and the degree to which creditors voluntarily paid and entered the commission, is examined in greater detail in chapter three.

would be elected – usually the largest creditors – to collect and distribute the bankrupt's estate. Simultaneously, creditors would prove their debts to the commissioners as assignees collected, appraised, and sold the bankrupt's estate. Depending on the circumstances, this could be a lengthy and complicated affair, especially when there were multiple claims on issues such as property, inheritance, and marriage contracts. As such, it was not uncommon for multiple dividends to be issued.[72] As well as the bankrupt's property, assignees were able to take anything they held in their 'possession, order and disposition' which belonged to another person at the time of their bankruptcy.[73] This rule was designed to ensure that secret creditors would not maintain the bankrupt's solvency, deceiving others and giving credit to someone who appeared to have more assets than they held in reality. For example, if a debtor sold his goods to another under a bill of sale, but kept possession of them, then the goods would be liable to the commission of bankruptcy.[74]

Commissioners' statutory power greatly increased throughout the seventeenth century. The sixteenth-century statutes granted commissioners authority to call before them and examine under oath any person who may be indebted to the bankrupt, or have any of the bankrupt's goods in their possession. This could be done by any means the commissioners 'shall think meet and convenient'.[75] The 1604 act clarified that commissioners could examine the bankrupt himself, while the 1624 statute extended their authority to examining the wife of the bankrupt, as well as allowing commissioners to break down the door and forcibly enter the house of a bankrupt, something which had previously been forbidden under common law.[76] As witnesses were sworn under oath, they were subject to the same charges of perjury as if they were giving evidence in any other court of the realm, while those failing to attend could be imprisoned.[77] If the bankrupt was found guilty of concealing goods or behaving in a fraudulent manner, then they could be sentenced to stand in the pillory for two hours, and have one of their ears nailed to the pillory, and subsequently removed.[78] As one commentator summarised in 1678, commissioners 'have power to administer an Oath, to send to Prison, to release out of Prison; they can break open Houses, seize Goods, sell them, extend Lands, and in short, do

---

72 Hoppit, *Risk and Failure in English Business*, p. 37.
73 21 Jac. I c.19 (1624).
74 Lobban, 'Bankruptcy and Insolvency', p. 789.
75 34 & 35 Henry VIII c.4 (1543); quote at 13 Elizabeth I c.7 (1571).
76 1 James I c.15 (1603); 21 James I c.19 (1624); the statute of 4 & 5 Anne I c.4 (1706) further extended the commissioners' authority to examine any person who may have information about the bankrupt's estate, or any acts of bankruptcy committed.
77 Goodinge, *The Law Against Bankrupts*, p. 69.
78 21 James I c.19 (1624); Kadens, 'The Last Bankrupt Hanged', p. 1247.

any thing for the advantage of the Creditors'.[79] Ultimately, the aim of legislation throughout the sixteenth and early seventeenth centuries was to increase the coercive powers of commissioners in an attempt to prevent fraud and abuse of the legal system.[80]

The early statutes were created to increase the collection powers of creditors over fraudulent debtors. The bankrupt was viewed as a criminal, with the 1543 statute referring to the debtor as an 'offender'.[81] As Emily Kadens concludes, 'the law's sole concern was that creditors should be repaid, while the interests of the debtor were ignored'.[82] The main characteristic of bankruptcy procedure was that all creditors would join together in a single action, whereby the entirety of the bankrupt's goods and estate would be collected and evenly distributed according to each creditor's individual claim. Creditors retained a legal right to the bankrupt's future earnings until their debts had been satisfied in full, meaning that the collection and distribution of the bankrupt's estate continued while the commission remained in force. After completion, it was also theoretically possible for individual creditors to pursue other legal avenues, including suing the bankrupt in the common law courts, or keeping the bankrupt in prison until the entirety of the debt was repaid.[83] The law made no distinction between the criminal, fraudulent bankrupt, and the unfortunate insolvent who had failed due to loss or misfortune. While it was necessary to have the bankrupt cooperate in the legal process, it was assumed throughout the seventeenth century that the simple threat of punishment would coerce the debtor into compliance.[84]

In 1706, the statute of 4 & 5 Anne – and the clarifying act of 6 Anne (1707) – dramatically altered bankruptcy law in England, as for the first time it enabled creditors to discharge a bankrupt from future liability, as long as four fifths by number and value agreed.[85] If the estate paid eight shillings in the pound, a

79 John Vernon, *The Compleat Comptinghouse* (London, 1678), p. 185.
80 Duffy, *Bankruptcy and Insolvency*, p. 9.
81 34 & 35 Henry VIII c.4 (1543).
82 Kadens, 'The Last Bankrupt Hanged', p. 1236; see also Emily Kadens, 'The Pitkin Affair: A Study of Fraud in Early English Bankruptcy', *American Bankruptcy Law Journal*, 84 (2010), pp. 483–570.
83 Kadens, 'The Last Bankrupt Hanged', pp. 1242–1243.
84 Ibid., p.1235.
85 4 & 5 Anne allowed the commission to decide on discharge, 6 Anne made this a decision of the creditors, 4 & 5 Anne I c.4 (1706); 6 Anne c.22 (1707). There has been some confusion in the existing literature on the dating of this act, as an English statute was dated according to the year of the first day of the parliamentary session. This began in October 1705, but the act only passed the two houses of parliament and received royal assent in March 1706. Thus, the act is commonly referred to as either 1705 or 1706, but for historical accuracy it is necessary to understand that the act did not come into force until 1706. For a discussion of such confusion, see Kadens, 'The Last Bankrupt Hanged', p. 1237.

further provision entitled the bankrupt to 5 per cent of the estate recovered – provided this did not exceed £200 in value – so as not to leave them destitute throughout the proceeding.[86] Essentially, a discharge meant that creditors were not only abrogating their legal right to full repayment but also giving part of the estate back to the debtor.[87] However, the four fifths provision led to significant barriers to the granting of discharge. As one commentator stated, this left bankrupts:

> to the Mercy of a very few or one single Creditor, and made his Liberty, and Freedom of Setling again, very uncertain; for if *two* Creditors of *Twenty Pounds* each, were to oppose his Certificate against *Seven*, willing to discharge him, to whom he owed as many *Thousand Pounds* each, he could not obtain his Discharge for Want of *Four Fifths* in *Number*; or if *Four* Creditors, to whom he was indebted *One Thousand Pounds* each, were inclined to Lenity, yet was another single Creditor, whose Demands should be but *One Penny* above *One Thousand Pounds*, to withstand the rest, His Case would be the same, for Want of *Four Fifths* in *Value*.[88]

Modern historians have seen the introduction of discharge as a monumental evolution of the bankruptcy laws. John C. McCoid II has suggested that the discharge provision, 'ranks ahead in importance of all others in Anglo-American bankruptcy history', as it was 'the ultimate instrument of the transformation of bankruptcy from a creditors' collection remedy to a system of statutorily mandated composition mutually beneficial to debtors and creditors'.[89] Similarly, Charles Jordan Tabb has shown how 4 & 5 Anne became a model for American legislation after independence.[90]

The 1706 act was the first juncture whereby the law sought to obtain the assistance of a debtor in their financial dismantling, by simultaneously incentivising and coercing debtors into cooperation. Discharge was intended to entice the debtor to be honest, while fraudulent bankruptcy – defined as a

86   4 & 5 Anne I c.4 (1706).
87   Ann M. Carlos, Edward Kosack, and Luis Castro Penarrieta, 'Bankruptcy Discharge and the Emergence of Debtor Rights in Eighteenth Century England', *Enterprise & Society*, 20 (2019), pp. 475–506.
88   Philanthropos, *Proposals for Promoting Industry and Advancing Proper Credit* (London, 1732), p. 30.
89   John C. McCoid II, 'Discharge: The Most Important Development in Bankruptcy History', *American Bankruptcy Law Journal*, 70 (1996), pp. 163–193; p. 164, p. 192; see also Margit Schulte Beerbühl, who claims that the discharge provision can be seen as a turning point in the history of bankruptcy legislation, as it 'introduced for the first time the possibility of a discharge from debt and a debt-free fresh start for the honest traders', 'Introduction', in Cordes and Beerbühl (eds), *Dealing With Economic Failure*, pp. 9–26, p. 17.
90   Charles Jordan Tabb, 'The Historical Evolution of the Bankruptcy Discharge', *American Bankruptcy Law Journal*, 65 (1991), pp. 325–371.

debtor's failure to fully disclose assets before a commission of bankruptcy – was made a capital offence. For Kadens, coercing the debtor to be honest proved a failure, whereas the beginning of 'incentivised cooperation' went on to have a 'fruitful future'.[91] Despite the alterations in the law, Kadens concludes that fraud continued to occur, partly because 'the benefits promised by discharge were too often unobtainable', leading to what she describes as 'a fraudulent debtors' playground'.[92] The practical implementation of the four fifths stipulation – in both value and number – remained a serious obstacle to the ability to produce a satisfactory outcome.

Finally, in official bankruptcy records – notices in the *London Gazette*, bankruptcy commissioners' files, and Chancery proceedings – debtors were not required to explain how and why they had failed.[93] Bankruptcy commissioners tended to focus their attention on the procedural elements of their examination, deciding whether the debtor could be declared a bankrupt according to the stipulations outlined in the statutes, and attempting to locate assets.[94] As Margaret Hunt has shown, there is little evidence that the average trader was able to separate economic theory and the working of the market from the 'human and social context'.[95] Bankrupts themselves tended to blame misfortunes, uncertainties, the failure of other individuals, and the inability to recover debts due to themselves. Often, bankrupts pleaded for more time to satisfy the demands being made upon them. On the other hand, creditors blamed bankrupts for moral shortcomings and personal deficiencies: inattention to financial accounts, lack of industry, inexperience, domestic extravagance, deficiencies in character, greed, fraud, and incompetence. As Robert Nantes has shown, it was creditors' actions that 'directly caused individual bankruptcies'.[96] Overall, to speak about direct causes is problematic, as they were specific to individual traders and their relationship to others. However, it is possible to discuss how and why the commission of bankruptcy failed. Inefficiencies in procedure, coupled with the complex nature of untangling multiple debts, led to several suits initiated in Chancery which took direct aim at the manner in which the commission itself had carried out its business. Such cases highlight specific aspects of the failure of the debt-recovery process.

91   Kadens, 'The Last Bankrupt Hanged', p. 1229.
92   Ibid., p. 1289, p. 1272.
93   Hoppit, *Risk and Failure in English Business*, p. 43.
94   Robert Nantes, 'English Bankrupts 1732–1831: A Social Account' (unpublished PhD dissertation, University of Exeter, 2020), pp. 115–116.
95   Margaret Hunt, 'Time-Management, Writing, and Accounting in the Eighteenth-Century English Trading Family: A Bourgeois Enlightenment', *Business and Economic History*, 18 (1989), pp. 150–159, p. 152; see also Joyce Appleby, *Economic Thought and Ideology in Seventeenth-Century England* (New Jersey, 1978), pp. 242–279.
96   Nantes, 'English Bankrupts', p. 113.

Alternate Forms of Debt Recovery

Official bankruptcy procedure was just one of several routes available to early modern creditors. In 1786, Josiah Dornford outlined the three classes of debtors that were established in the law: 'The first under the description of Merchants and capital Traders. The second of Tradesmen, Mechanics, and Artificers, in the middle walk of life. The third, of the lower orders of Journeymen, of Laborers, and Domestics.'[97] These three distinctions were intended to distinguish the size of indebtedness, from the largest to the smallest. In theory, the debts of the first class of debtor were recovered through bankruptcy proceedings, the second through the insolvency process, and the third via small debt courts. However, growing economic activity and the expansion in the use of credit meant that occupational boundaries and classifications had become obsolete.[98]

The avenues available to creditors can be separated into unofficial recovery outside of the law, and official legal procedures. Outside of the law, failure could be dealt with via numerous agreements between debtors and creditors. In seventeenth-century rural communities, creditors could come together to swap and cancel debts in a system known as 'reckoning'. While the depersonalised nature of credit relations made this system difficult to implement – especially in urban areas – debt swapping still occurred in a less formal manner.[99] Alternatively, a creditor could grant a debtor a letter of licence to carry on their business in order to repay debts, or could issue a deed of inspection, whereby the debtor continued in business under the control of creditors. In both examples, creditors did not think the debtor had permanently failed, or else it would be in their interest to seize and release their assets as quickly as possible. If this were the case, then a composition could be enacted, whereby the debtor's assets were placed in the possession of trustees, acting on behalf of all of the creditors.[100] While this took place outside official bankruptcy procedure, many early modern contemporaries praised compositions for being cheap and efficient, with one suggesting that compositions were themselves 'private bankruptcies'.[101] But as Hoppit has concluded, while unofficial means of dealing

---

97   Josiah Dornford, *Seven Letters to the Lords and Commons of Great Britain, Upon the Impolicy, Inhumanity, and Injustice, of Our Present Mode of Arresting the Bodies of Debtors* (London, 1786), p. 9.
98   Duffy, *Bankruptcy and Insolvency*, p. 56.
99   Craig Muldrew, 'Interpreting the Market: The Ethics of Credit Community Relations in Early Modern England', *Social History*, 18 (1993), pp. 163–183; Wakelam, *Credit and Debt*, pp. 26–28.
100   Hoppit, *Risk and Failure in English Business*, pp. 29–30.
101   B. Montagu, *A Summary of the Law of Composition with Creditors* (London, 1823), p. 39.

with failure 'were superficially attractive they were of limited applicability'.[102] One crucial weakness of this mode of debt recovery was that it depended on the full cooperation of all creditors. If one creditor stood out against a composition – for example, because they felt they deserved or could gain repayment in full – then the only recourse for the remaining creditors was through official bankruptcy proceedings.[103]

Bankruptcy procedure offered greater authority and a more certain outcome, as it 'was the only legally constituted method that put all creditors on an equal footing, forced the debtor to comply and acknowledged a permanent inability on his part to meet all his obligations'. Furthermore, bankruptcy was the only process that investigated the debtor closely about their effects, assets, and personal circumstances.[104] As one anonymous tract surmised, 'The common End of all the Laws relating to Bankrupts, is to discover and collect the Estate of the Debtor, in the best and speediest Manner, in order to make an equal Distribution of it among all Creditors'.[105] In Thomas Goodinge's *The Law Against Bankrupts*, the author concludes 'He that is a Bankrupt to one Creditor, is a Bankrupt to all'.[106] Early modern contemporaries understood the statutes were intended to be interpreted for the benefit of all of the creditors.

Outside of official bankruptcy procedure, a creditor could seek recovery through the common law courts. Debt collection in the three main jurisdictions – King's Bench, Common Pleas, and Exchequer of Pleas – offered plaintiff-creditors the prospect of potentially low-cost, quick, and predictable recovery. Clinton Francis has suggested that creditors were attracted to common law litigation for three reasons: 'a predictable jury outcome, a "loser-pays-all-costs" rule, and a system of pretrial and posttrial process enforced by arrest and imprisonment'.[107] In contrast to the bankruptcy system, a few points are worth making. Firstly, a common feature of this form of debt recovery is that creditors acted individually, without joining other creditors in a collective action. Secondly, this approach would only be attractive if the debtor was seen to be solvent, as the common law viewed the debtor as being recalcitrant, rather than being unable to repay. A creditor could utilise the force of the law to proceed against either the debtor's property or their body by incarceration

---

102 Hoppit, *Risk and Failure in English Business*, p. 32.
103 Ibid., pp. 30–31.
104 Ibid., p. 34.
105 *Considerations Upon Commissions of Bankrupts* (London, 1727), p. 4.
106 Goodinge, *The Law Against Bankrupts*, pp. 145–146; Peter Earl calls this 'the standard contemporary textbook', *The Making of the English Middle Class: Business, Society and Family Life in London, 1660–1730* (London, 1989), p. 363, n. 32.
107 Clinton W. Francis, 'Practice, Strategy, and Institution: Debt Collection in the English Common-Law Courts, 1740–1840', *Northwestern University Law Review*, 80 (1986), pp. 807–955, p. 811.

to encourage repayment. Thirdly, the vast majority of common law cases concerned either proof of contract or the issue of a defendant's satisfaction of the debt claimed. If a creditor could 'prove their debt' in the form of a written obligation – especially bonds, bills of exchange, and promissory notes – then they held a high probability of recovering their debt in full.[108]

Finally, a creditor could order a debtor to be brought before one of the common law courts to attend a hearing of a suit, either by a simple summons or by having them arrested and held to bail. If they defaulted on bail, then they could be imprisoned. If the debt was subsequently proved to be good the creditor could choose to proceed 'in execution', either against the property of the debtor or against their body by detaining them in prison, almost as an insurance policy or assurance against future repayment.[109] This meant that two types of imprisonment were possible, on mesne process – pre-trial – or on final process – post-trial – until the debt was repaid or a composition made. Critics of this procedure singled it out as providing extraordinary discretionary powers to creditors, in what Joanna Innes has described as a form of 'legalized bullying'.[110] In this manner, debt imprisonment was about finding a way to incentivise debtors to fulfil their financial agreements, rather than punishing them for non-payment. As Wakelam has argued, it 'coerced debtors to find a solution to obstacles of repayment by giving them something tangible to lose if they did not'.[111] What is clear is that such an oppressive and capricious legal system provided creditors with a vast array of powers, while simultaneously presenting several opportunities and motivations for debtors to avoid arrest. There were several options available to both creditors and debtors within this system, ranging from mutually beneficial agreements to outright fraud. While bankruptcy procedure was just one of the available avenues, it was common for individuals to have been involved in several procedures at any given moment. As such, bankruptcy suits in Chancery frequently referred to previous and ongoing attempts to recoup debts.

In theory, bankrupts were safeguarded from imprisonment. For example, once a bankrupt received an order to appear before the commission, they could not be arrested for the next forty-two days. If a debtor was still fearful of arrest, they could gain a 'warrant of protection for his person' which could be produced to prove their status as a bankrupt.[112] The theoretical position of bankrupts in relation to imprisonment has been presented in a rather

---

108   Francis, 'Practice, Strategy, and Institution', p. 812.
109   Wakelam, *Credit and Debt*.
110   Jonna Innes, *Inferior Politics: Social Problems and Social Policies in Eighteenth-Century Britain* (Oxford, 2009), p. 229.
111   Wakelam, *Credit and Debt*, p. 35.
112   Anon., *Solicitor's Guide* (London, 1768), pp. 17–18.

straightforward and simplistic manner in the existing historiography.[113] More recent scholarship by Tawny Paul and Alexander Wakelam recognises that in reality imprisonment was a fate that rarely affected bankrupts, rather than not at all.[114] Indeed, Paul has shown how between 1736 and 1772, roughly 1 per cent of debtors in the Fleet and King's Bench prisons were discharged and underwent the bankruptcy process.[115] For several bankrupts, imprisonment appears to be the start of their personal failure, as lying in prison for two months or more was a definitive act of bankruptcy. For example, in *Dod v Robson* (1745), John Whitehead, a grocer and chapman from Darlington, was arrested on 27 November 1745, after Thomas Wakeling initiated a suit in King's Bench for £80. Unable to make bail, or repay the debt, Whitehead remained in Durham gaol for over two months and as such committed an act of bankruptcy. On 26 March 1745, a commission of bankruptcy was taken out against him, and in February the following year the two assignees initiated a bill in Chancery to discover any goods that were still in the four defendants' possession.[116]

One final complication arose when debts were due to the crown on a writ of extent. As one nineteenth-century commentator explained, a 'writ of extent, or *extendi facias*, is a writ of execution against the body lands and goods, or the lands and goods, or the lands only, of the debtor: and it is either for the *king*, or the *subject*'.[117] Crucially, writs of extent took precedence over bankruptcy proceedings, as the king was not bound by the laws of bankruptcy. This meant that while creditors in a commission of bankruptcy received a proportion of their debt – so many pence in the pound – on a pro rata basis, debts to the crown still needed to be satisfied in full. While bankruptcy procedure protected the bankrupt from imprisonment, an extent could override this privilege and imprison the bankrupt until repayment was made.[118]

---

113   Markham V. Lester has stated that 'a bankrupt could not be imprisoned', Markham V. Lester, *Victorian Insolvency: Bankruptcy, Imprisonment for Debt, and Company Winding-up in Nineteenth-Century England* (Oxford, 1995), p. 88; Margot Finn has stated, 'bankruptcy proceedings, restricted by law to merchants and traders who owed substantial sums, allowed substantial commercial men both to avoid imprisonment and to extinguish their debts in full', *Character of Credit*, pp. 110–111; Jerry White states that bankrupts could continue 'without any humiliations of arrest or imprisonment that less wealthy people suffered', *Mansions of Misery: A Biography of the Marshalsea Debtors' Prison* (London, 2016), p. 2.

114   Paul, *Poverty of Disaster*, p. 37, p. 65; Wakelam, *Credit and Debt*, pp. 34–37.

115   Paul, *Poverty of Disaster*, pp. 104–108.

116   TNA, C11/380/5, 'Dod v Robson' (1745), Bill of Complaint.

117   William Tidd, *The Practice of the Courts of King's Bench and Common Pleas in Personal Actions and Ejectment*, 8th edn (Philadelphia, 1828), vol. 2, pp. 1088–1089.

118   Alexander Burrill, *A Law Dictionary and Glossary* (New York, 1859), pp. 591–92; William Blackstone, *Commentaries on the Laws of England* (4 vols, London, 1794), vol. 3, pp. 419–20.

The legislation and procedure outlined above meant that the vast majority of debtors would not fall under the jurisdiction of bankruptcy. Wakelam describes bankruptcy as an 'extreme measure', which was 'insufficient for the purpose of enforcing everyday contracts'.[119] Similarly, Jones clarifies that 'all sorts of men were debtors, but only a tiny fraction could be bankrupts'.[120] The individual routes to debt recovery have usually been discussed in isolation, but it is important to have a firm understanding of the complexities and interconnected nature of these avenues which form part of the overarching experience of credit and debt in early modern England.

The Historiography of Bankruptcy and Chancery

Historians of pre-modern England have tended to treat bankruptcy and Chancery as two distinct areas of scholarly research, meaning that Chancery has largely been overlooked in the existing historiography of early modern bankruptcy. Similarly, the scholarship on the equitable jurisdiction of Chancery has failed to account for the manner in which the procedure of bankruptcy was litigated within the court. This is a strange omission, as under the stewardship of Heneage Finch, the first Earl of Nottingham – who presided as Lord Keeper of the Great Seal and later as Lord Chancellor between 1673 and 1682 – the court took a more active role in bankruptcy proceedings, being established as the sole appellate jurisdiction.[121] Put simply, under the tenure of Nottingham, any person involved in a commission could submit a bill and have their specific claim investigated by the court.

While bankruptcy maintains economic relevance in contemporary society, and certain institutions – particularly the mass media – hold a mild fascination with the topic, its early modern past has received far less attention. Writing in 2010, Kadens stated that 'despite the current and historical importance of bankruptcy, its pre-modern past has barely been investigated'.[122] Somewhat unsurprisingly, much of the focus on bankruptcy has come from legal scholars, who have attempted to understand the evolution of bankruptcy laws and their subsequent implementation in modern societies.[123] Broadly speaking, legal

---

119   Wakelam, *Credit and Debt*, p. 34.
120   Jones, 'The Foundations of English Bankruptcy', p. 36.
121   D. E. C. Yale (ed.), *Lord Chancellor Nottingham's Chancery Cases* (2 vols, London, 1957), vol. 1, pp. cxiv–cxx.
122   Kadens, 'The Last Bankrupt Hanged', p. 1235.
123   See Duffy, *Bankruptcy and Insolvency*; Duffy, 'English Bankrupts, 1571–1861', pp. 283–305; Jay Cohen, 'The History of Imprisonment for Debt and its Relation to the Development of Discharge in Bankruptcy', *The Journal of Legal History*, 3 (1982), pp. 153–171; Thomas E. Plank, 'The Constitutional Limits of Bankruptcy', *Tennessee Law*

historians who approach the topic of bankruptcy do so in an attempt to outline alterations of the law and the circumstances behind the introduction of new legislation. In a lengthy article, William Jones provides a detailed summary of each bankruptcy statute from 1543 to 1706, attempting to establish the political, economic, and social circumstances which led to their creation. Jones views these statutes as 'mundane attempts to establish new rules within the limited field of debt', suggesting that they were 'intended to provide solutions to a selection of immediate problems'.[124] Further attention has focused on the legal creation of discharge in 1706, and scholars have attempted to understand how this statutory alteration impacted bankruptcy proceedings. For example, between 1757 and 1759 only 48 per cent of bankrupts received a discharge, which had only risen to roughly 60 per cent by the end of the century. Kadens has argued that because discharge was relatively unobtainable, fraud continued to flourish.[125] In contrast, Ann Carlos, Edward Kosack, and Luis Castro Penarrieta argue that similar statistics – whereby over half of all bankrupts received a discharge between 1730 and 1750 – demonstrate the willingness of creditors to grant discharge, which encouraged future investment by returning creditor assets and entrepreneurial talent to the economy.[126]

Several edited collections have approached bankruptcy from an international perspective, providing detailed chapters on a single country or geographic location, before attempting to draw together conclusions in a global context. While providing insights into specific case studies, these collections largely attempt to explain the evolution of bankruptcy law in relation to large-scale developments, such as institutional change, the rise of capitalism, the role of the state in managing failure, colonial expansion, and the desire to see entrepreneurial spirit returned to the wider economy.[127] These publications represent a significant contribution to the field, and have provided a more nuanced understanding of international bankruptcy. Such scholarship has greatly enhanced our understanding of how – and very often why – the law developed in such

Review, 63 (1996), pp. 487–584; Mann, _Republic of Debtors_; McNairn, '"The Common Sympathies of our Nature"', pp. 49–72.

124 Jones, 'The Foundations of English Bankruptcy', p. 7; see also Jérôme Sgard, 'Courts at Work: Bankruptcy Statutes, Majority Rule and Private Contracting in England (17th–18th Century)', _Journal of Comparative Economics_, 44 (2016), pp. 450–460.

125 Kadens, 'The Last Bankrupt Hanged', p. 1290.

126 Carlos, Kosack and Penarrieta, 'Bankruptcy Discharge and the Emergence of Debtor Rights', pp. 475–506.

127 Thomas Max Safley (ed.), _The History of Bankruptcy: Economic, Social and Cultural Implications in Early Modern England_ (London, 2013); Cordes and Beerbühl (eds), _Dealing With Economic Failure_; Karl Gratzer and Dieter Stiefel (eds), _History of Insolvency and Bankruptcy From an International Perspective_ (Huddinge, 2008); Cátia Antunes and Susana Münch Miranda, 'Going Bust: Some Reflections on Colonial Bankruptcies', _Itinerario_, 43 (2019), pp. 47–62.

a fashion, and has illustrated the difficulties in its practical implementation throughout the early modern period.[128] But again, these studies have focused on macro-economic elements of failure, rather than individual instances and social constructions.

In relation to Chancery, legal scholars often utilise the records of the court to demonstrate how a particular topic developed within the equitable jurisdiction. Several examples of this approach can be seen in publications discussing how the court dealt with copyright injunction, trusts litigation, patent law, and the interests of parents, children, and property.[129] However, few scholars have sought to combine the study of bankruptcy and Chancery in their analysis. One notable exception can be seen in the work of David Smith, who looks at a number of cases in Chancery which specifically dealt with the sole issue of bills of conformity – a remedy for insolvent debtors in courts of equity – between 1603 and James I's eventual abolition of conformity in 1624. Smith charts the growth of conformity and its eventual defeat within the context of charity and property, which 'mediated ideas of kingship with hard economic and legal realities'. Ultimately, Smith's use of Chancery records is placed within the wider context of the role of equitable jurisdictions, the limitations of the common law, and the development of an effective law of insolvency.[130] As such, Smith's concern is less with the specificities of bankruptcy procedure, and more with broad economic and legal developments relating to debt recovery in the early seventeenth century. But again, few scholars have extensively utilised Chancery materials in their research, meaning that the records of the court are

128   David A. Smith has utilised Chancery records in relation to bankruptcy and bills of conformity but only states that bankruptcy 'was limited to English subjects who made their living by buying and selling ("traders") ... until 1861', 'The Error of Young Cyrus: The Bill of Conformity and Jacobean Kingship, 1603–1624', *LHR*, 28 (2010), pp. 307–341; Emily Kadens has used Chancery sources to reconstruct the eighteenth-century bankruptcy scandal, the Pitkin Affair, 'The Pitkin Affair', pp. 483–570; William Jones and Sheila Marriner have made limited use of Chancery material in their research; Jones, 'The Foundations of English Bankruptcy', pp. 1–63; Sheila Marriner, 'English Bankruptcy Records and Statistics Before 1850', *EHR*, 33 (1980), pp. 351–366.

129   H. Tomás Gómez-Arostegui, 'What History Teaches Us About Copyright Injunctions and the Inadequate- Remedy-at-Law Requirement', *Southern California Law Review*, 81 (2008), pp. 1197–1280; N. G. Jones, 'Trusts Litigation in Chancery After the Statute of Uses: The First Fifty Years', in Matthew Dyson and David Ibbetson (eds), *Law and Legal Process: Substantive Law and Procedure in English Legal History* (Cambridge, 2013), pp. 103–125; N. G. Jones, 'Trusts for Secrecy: The Case of John Dudley, Duke of Northumberland', *The Cambridge Law Journal*, 54 (1995), pp. 545–551; Bottomley, 'Patent Cases in the Court of Chancery', pp. 27–43; Adam Hofri-Winogradow, 'Parents, Children and Property in Late Eighteenth-Century Chancery', *Oxford Journal of Legal Studies*, 32 (2012), pp. 741–769.

130   Smith, 'The Error of Young Cyrus', pp. 307–341.

dramatically underused as a source for the social and economic understanding of pre-modern bankruptcy.[131]

The scholarship outlined above provides insights into the attitudes and motivations of the legislature, as well as creditors within the debt-recovery process. It does not, however, grant us access to the complexities and specificities of the ongoing bankruptcy procedure, and the problems, issues, and obstacles that needed to be overcome in order to successfully complete this process. This book seeks to bridge the gap by analysing the manner in which cases involving bankruptcy were litigated in the court. This will enhance our historical understanding of the topic of bankruptcy by analysing how this initially autonomous legal procedure came to rely on Chancery to maintain and oversee the process. I argue that the level of complexity and the multifaceted nature of bankruptcy procedure – and credit networks more generally – has been overlooked, and misunderstood, in the historiography.

Chapter Outlines

The book is loosely organised around the stage of proceeding in Chancery – which forms the basis of the chapter structure – and pays close attention to the types of documentation created and presented to the court at these different phases in the legal process. Because every critical stage of a proceeding was recorded in written form, it is essential to pay close attention to the procedure of the court, and the people and processes that went into creating the written documents which have survived. As each stage of proceeding required a different ordering of language in order to conform to the legal requirements of the court, I argue that scholars can only understand how bankruptcy – or indeed any type of suit – was litigated by providing background and context to the jurisdiction under discussion, the type of document being used, and finally, the stage of proceeding from which these sources have been analysed. Using Chancery sources to reconstruct the operation of bankruptcy will provide new evidence

---

131   Mabel Winter has incorporated Chancery material alongside other sources to reconstruct the failure of Thompson and Company, *Banking, Projecting and Politicking in Early Modern England*. Aaron Graham has undertaken three case studies in Chancery to demonstrate how the development of the British fiscal-military state was still underpinned by commercial entrepreneurs utilising informal credit, 'Military Contractors and the Money Markets, 1700–15', in Aaron Graham and Patrick Walsh (eds), *The British Fiscal-Military States, 1660–c.1783* (London, 2016), pp. 81–112. Emily Kadens has used Chancery sources to reconstruct the eighteenth-century bankruptcy scandal, the Pitkin Affair, 'The Pitkin Affair', pp. 483–570. William Jones and Sheila Marriner have made limited use of Chancery material in their research, Jones, 'The Foundations of English Bankruptcy'; Sheila Marriner, 'English Bankruptcy Records and Statistics Before 1850', *EHR*, vol. 33, no. 3 (1980), pp. 351–366.

of the numerous meanings associated with economic and personal failure in early modern society. As such, each chapter provides a different perspective on credit and debt to enhance our understanding of the multiple meanings attached to failure within bankruptcy proceedings.

The first chapter provides a historiographical account of the ways in which social historians of the law have utilised legal records in their research, and how this has evolved over the past fifty years. Social historians have often been criticised for taking evidence out of context, and I argue that it is crucial that scholars have a fundamental understanding of the court's process and procedures in order to understand the evidence that has emerged from that context. The following sections provide a detailed overview of the operation of the court and the development of its equitable jurisdiction. Throughout the book, close attention is paid to the people involved in the legal process: litigants, defendants, witnesses, debtors, creditors, bankruptcy officials, court officials, and legal experts. Coupled with the introduction above, the first chapter provides an analysis of the roles and duties of officers of the court and legal experts, as well as how the court was used by a range of individuals entangled in a complex and ongoing process of debt recovery. Focusing on evidence and methodology provides a conceptual framework for the themes of failure which appear in each chapter, while also providing preliminary details of the way in which failure was established as a social construct within the court to mediate in social and financial affairs.

Chapters two and three are based upon the pleadings – bills of complaint and their subsequent answers – stage of proceeding.[132] Chapter two examines the manner in which cases were initiated in Chancery, illustrating the reasons why those involved in a commission of bankruptcy sought redress from the court. This chapter shows the degree to which the interconnected and overlapping principles of debt recovery upset the expected path of a commission. The failure to come to a satisfactory conclusion meant that individuals needed to circum-navigate specific issues within the overarching authority of the court. In doing so, we see how the ideals established in the statutes and legal commentary did not conform to day-to-day legality in practice, as the multifaceted nature of failure is demonstrated through individuals manipulating the legal process for their future benefit. The third chapter discusses the degree to which the commission and knowledge of the individual actions of a bankrupt were widely known to those within the trading community. Particular attention is paid to the timing of specific events as those within the legal process sought to establish a coherent timeline of failure. Analysing the flow of information, and

---

132   A search for the term 'bankrupt' on TNA online Discovery returns 971 cases between 1674 and 1750. A five-year sample – beginning at 1700 and ending at 1750 – was undertaken in order to reduce the number of cases to a manageable total of 228, an overview of which is provided in Appendix Two.

the transfer of knowledge, will provide new evidence relating to how, why, and when individuals made circulating judgements about a bankrupt's failure. This chapter seeks to analyse multiple aspects of the temporality of trade, both in the past and opportunities in the future.

Chapter four turns to the evidentiary stage of proceeding and analyses the specific and evaluative language utilised in depositions, as a wide range of witnesses were interrogated on aspects of an individual failure. This stage of proceeding provided a platform for a range of witnesses to comment on an individual bankruptcy, and by analysing the specific words and phrases used in the formulation of narratives concerning bankruptcy, we can illuminate wider social attitudes towards failure. Focusing on the collaborative nature of witness testimony will show how individuals fell from an initially respectable and credible position to that of a bankrupt, mirroring wider conceptions of credibility. The chapter illuminates the way in which Chancery helped to inflect social narratives of failure, demonstrating how economic knowledge was created, shared, and disseminated within the wider community.

Chapter five focuses on the final stage of proceeding in Chancery by analysing a set of enrolled decrees. In contrast to legal scholars – who have used the records of the court to establish how the substantive context of the law developed over time – this chapter focuses on how the judges came to interpret and understand failure in order to render appropriate relief. Despite being the final stage of the legal process, this chapter shows that the court rarely offered a definitive conclusion to the wider economic dispute, as the collection and redistribution of the bankrupt's estate could occur in numerous ways. In this sense, the judges acted as arbitrators, and we can see the practical implementation of equitable principles of justice being applied to complex and multifaceted disputes relating to debt recovery. Ultimately, this chapter is a departure from the previous analysis, as the focus is placed firmly on the narratives created by the judges as they grappled with interpreting the social construction of failure within the court.

By undertaking such a methodological approach and paying close attention to the processes and procedures of the court at different stages of proceeding, the book informs our historical understanding of the social and cultural meanings of debt collection. As Chancery was an institution which helped to create legal narratives, the book provides evidence of the manner in which the court mediated social and financial affairs. This can inform us of how economic knowledge was disseminated and shared within the trading community. As well as containing strategic constructions created to conform to the legal requirements of the court, Chancery documents were contingent upon the memory, interpretation, and moral judgements of a range of individuals who utilised the court for their own benefit. Throughout, we will see how creditors, debtors, bankrupts, and witnesses expected others to act – both in the past and in the future – highlighting the norms and values of wider society. However, because of the complexities and interconnected nature of bankruptcy suits, we also see how such concepts interacted with the court's conception of conscience as a juristic principle. In several instances, it was not just the bankrupt's actions that were scrutinised, but other members of the process, further complicating our historical understanding of how an equitable court came to make decisions based upon the concepts of fairness and justice.

As the first major study to analyse how cases involving bankruptcy were litigated within the court, the book refocuses attention on the importance of Chancery records in the history of pre-modern bankruptcy. Particular attention is paid to the specific and evaluative language utilised in relation to fraud, creditworthiness, honesty, and sincerity, and how these can inform us of wider social perceptions of failure.

I

The Court of Chancery

Social Historians of the Law

In the past fifty years, the methodology employed by social historians of the law has undergone a dramatic adjustment. Beginning in the 1970s and 1980s, scholars turned their attention towards a statistical understanding of crime and criminal proceedings. As archival material became more readily available, historians analysed the proceedings of the criminal courts – partly because of the sheer size and scale of available material in civil jurisdictions – to comment on the history of crime, law and order, and other related topics. With English records being more laconic than their European counterparts – containing fewer depositions and often simply documenting the final stages of a proceeding – the focus turned towards attempting a quantitative understanding of English law, due to the perceived limitations inhibiting a qualitative interpretation.[1] As James Sharpe stated in 1984, 'the most useful' approach to the history of crime, is the 'systematic study of court archives, usually with some notion of statistical analysis in mind'.[2] While such studies provided an insight into changes in the criminal system, they told us little about the reasons behind such changes, or about the people involved in illicit and illegal behaviour. Ultimately, only a small

---

1   The list of prominent works is too long to effectively list here, but perhaps the most notable are J. M. Beattie, *Crime and the Courts in England 1660–1800* (Oxford, 1986); J. S. Cockburn (ed.), *Crime in England 1550–1800* (London, 1977); Alan Macfarlane, *Witchcraft in Tudor and Stuart England: A Regional and Comparative Study* (London, 1970); J. A Sharpe, *Crime in Seventeenth-Century England* (Cambridge, 1983); Joel Samaha, *Law and Order in Historical Perspective: The Case of Elizabethan Essex* (New York, 1974). The early progress of the history of crime in early modern England can also be found in a number of review articles, see Victor Bailey, 'Bibliographical Essay: Crime, Criminal Justice and Authority in England', *Bulletin of the Society for the Study of Labour History*, 40 (1980), pp. 36–46; E. W. Ives, 'English Law and English Society', *History*, 61 (1981), pp. 50–60; J. A. Sharpe, 'The History of Crime in Late Medieval and Early Modern England: A Review of the Field', *Social History*, 7 (1982), pp. 187–203; Joanna Innes and John Styles, 'The Crime Wave: Writing on Crime and Criminal Justice in England', *Journal of British Studies*, 25 (1988), pp. 380–435.
2   J. A. Sharpe, *Crime in Early Modern England 1550–1750* (London, 1999), pp. 13–14.

minority of individuals found themselves involved in criminal proceedings, and as Sharpe concludes, quantification provided 'a framework for future research, and a starting point for future debate about the history of crime'.[3]

The most influential scholar to build on such a framework was Christopher Brooks, who demonstrated that between 1200 and 1700, 'ordinary people were in court more often, and knew more about "law" (however defined), than they have at any time subsequently'.[4] One of Brooks' major contributions to our understanding of legal institutions was his analysis of the previously overlooked fluctuations in the volume of litigation initiated in the central courts of Westminster, both in common law and equity. Broadly speaking, Brooks' findings can be summarised as follows: the sixteenth century saw a rapid expansion of business, before growth slowed in the seventeenth century and levelled out towards its end. During the late seventeenth century there began a contraction in the level of business, which subsequently became far more pronounced in the middle decades of the eighteenth century. Finally, there was a limited revival during the first three decades of the nineteenth century.[5] In attempting to explain this phenomenon, Brooks suggests that it was now possible to see a society whereby 'the rule of law was replacing individual action'.[6] Brooks helped to show how the law – and especially the central courts at Westminster – became a mechanism for resolving disputes in a progressively better way. Ultimately, Brooks reset the focus of social historians of the law towards access to justice and court usage by ordinary people.[7]

The overwhelming majority of cases brought before every court and jurisdiction in early modern England concerned debt recovery.[8] In attempting to understand the nature of this phenomenon, scholars began to pay closer attention to local courts. Craig Muldrew analysed the local records of King's Lynn in an attempt to discover not only who was suing whom, but just as

---

3   Sharpe, *Crime in Early Modern England*, pp. 61–62.
4   Christopher W. Brooks, *Lawyers, Litigation and English Society Since 1450* (London, 1998), p. 128.
5   Brooks, 'Interpersonal Conflict and Social Tension', pp. 357–399; Brooks, *Pettyfoggers and Vipers of the Commonwealth*, pp. 54–55.
6   Brooks, *Lawyers, Litigation and English Society Since 1450*, p. 19.
7   Brooks, Christopher W., *Law, Politics and Society in Early Modern England* (Cambridge, 2008); Brooks, *Pettyfoggers and Vipers of the Commonwealth*; Brooks, *Lawyers, Litigation and English Society Since 1450*; see also Michael Lobban, Joanne Begiato, Adrian Green (eds), *Law, Lawyers, and Litigants in Early Modern England: Essays in Memory of Christopher W. Brooks* (Cambridge, 2019).
8   For example, 90 per cent of all suits brought before the King's Bench and the Court of Common Pleas between 1490 and 1640 concerned action for debt and property, Bruce Lenman and Geoffrey Parker, 'The State, the Community and the Criminal Law in Early Modern Europe', in V. A. C. Gatrell, Bruce Lenman and Geoffrey Parker (eds), *Crime and the Law: The Social History of Crime in Western Europe Since 1500* (London, 1980), pp. 11–48.

importantly, 'who was lending to whom'.[9] Muldrew's work has greatly enhanced our understanding of credit networks and the role that local jurisdictions played as an institution which aided debt recovery.[10] However, Muldrew utilised relatively straightforward suits – concerning a single debt and only one lender and one borrower – to conduct a quantitative analysis of the socio-economic background of debtors and creditors, particularly in relation to social standing, occupation, and income. For example, 85 per cent of all cases brought before the borough court of King's Lynn concerned sales credit, or credit extended for services rendered, or for work done.[11] In order to understand how assessments of credibility and trustworthiness were made, Muldrew relied on the 'comments' of as many historical agents as possible, which were taken largely from letters, diaries, autobiographies, and printed instruction pamphlets. Thus, while Muldrew's quantitative analysis of debt recovery comes from legal records, the qualitative study of mutual surveillance comes from outside the legal setting.[12]

Building on the work of Muldrew, Alexandra Shepard has suggested that rather than constituting the basis of credit, such bonds of trust, 'merely overlaid their more concrete foundations in the goods that both represented wealth and provided security against default'.[13] Utilising over 13,500 testimonials, Shepard explores the language of self-description, as a broad range of men and women appeared as witnesses in ecclesiastical courts, responding to the question of their worth. The monetary values provided by witnesses 'were at the heart of a *qualitative* frame of reference for the quantification of status', in what Shepard terms a 'culture of appraisal'.[14] The assessment of moveable

9   Craig Muldrew, 'Credit and the Courts: Debt Litigation in a Seventeenth-Century Urban Community', *EHR*, 6 (1993), pp. 23–38, p. 36.

10   See Muldrew, 'Credit and the Courts', pp. 23–38; Craig Muldrew, 'The Culture of Reconciliation: Community and the Settlement of Economic Disputes in Early Modern England', *The Historical Journal*, 39 (1996), pp. 915–942; Craig Muldrew, 'Rural Credit, Market Areas and Legal Institutions in the Countryside in England, 1550–1700', in Christopher Brooks and Michael Lobban (eds), *Communities and Courts in Britain, 1150-1900* (London, 1997), pp. 155–178; for later publications see Craig Muldrew, '"Hard food for Midas": Cash and its Social Value in Early Modern England', *Past & Present*, 170 (2001), pp. 78–120; Craig Muldrew, '"A Mutual Assent of Her Mind"?: Women, Debt, Litigation and Contract in Early Modern England', *History Workshop Journal*, 55 (2003), pp. 47–71; Craig Muldrew, 'Class and Credit: Social Identity, Wealth and the Life Course in Early Modern England', in Henry French and Jonathan Barry (eds), *Identity and Agency in England, 1500–1800* (Basingstoke, 2004), pp. 147–177.

11   Muldrew, *The Economy of Obligation*, p. 204.

12   Ibid., pp. 1–8.

13   Shepard, *Accounting For Oneself*, p. 36; see also Shepard and Spicksley, 'Worth, Age, and Social Status in Early Modern England', pp. 493–530; Shepard, 'The Worth of Married Women Witnesses in the English Church Courts', pp. 191–212.

14   Shepard, *Accounting For Oneself*, p. 28.

property was essential to successful social estimation, as 'the evaluation of goods served as the foundation for interpersonal credit relations', which meant that individuals were, 'adept at judging the value of each other's goods'.[15] However, from the late seventeenth century, both the nature of responses from witnesses, as well as the frequency of inquiries relating to worth, declined dramatically. As Shepard argues, these changes were 'indicative of a gradual yet profound transition in the calculus of esteem and the operation of credit across the long seventeenth century'.[16] Between 1550 and 1650, physical markers of worth became limited, and were 'more likely to involve the appraisal of the *flow* rather than the *stock* of goods, thereby forming a less stable foundation for the brokerage of credit'.[17] Entering the late seventeenth century, interpersonal credit was becoming insecure as the relationship between status and wealth became increasingly difficult to quantify.[18] According to Margot Finn, this trend continued well into the twentieth century.[19]

The work of these scholars has greatly enhanced our understanding of the levels and fluctuations of litigation, the way in which individuals utilised the legal system, the interconnected nature of credit networks, and the importance of trust and reputation in the early modern economy. However, analysing the way in which bankruptcy cases were litigated in the court complicates our under-standing of credit and failure. For example, Muldrew presents debt recovery in too simplistic a manner, largely relying on the quantitative aspects of legal records. Shepard's work has emphasised the qualitative side of legal sources, paying closer attention to the individuals involved in the legal process. But perhaps more importantly, Shepard demonstrates that entering the late seven-teenth century the assessment of worth based upon reputation, and even goods, was unstable and becoming difficult to judge. The insecurity and inability to effectively judge an individual's credibility and worth can be seen in Chancery suits involving bankruptcy, which were extremely complex, often involving numerous creditors, debtors, and claims on a single – or even multiple – estates. The levels of debt involved far outstripped anything that could be litigated in a local jurisdiction.

A statistical understanding of outcome – as seen in homicide rates, conviction rates, levels of crime, etc. – is again unhelpful. While there was obviously a spectrum of success and failure throughout Chancery, the concept of a 'winning' or 'losing' party cannot be clarified and quantified to any sufficient degree.[20] Because of the complex and multi-layered nature of

15   Ibid., p. 303, p. 45.
16   Ibid., p. 277.
17   Ibid., p. 2.
18   Ibid., p. 301.
19   Finn, *The Character of Credit*.
20   This concept is analysed in detail in chapter five.

bankruptcy suits, the 'success' of the outcome would vary dramatically from one individual to the next, even within a defined party, such as 'plaintiffs' or 'defendants'. For example, while the assignees of a bankrupt may have initiated a suit in Chancery, they were doing so for the benefit of *all* of the creditors of the bankrupt, some of whom may not yet have come forward and proven their debts. Furthermore, they were doing so on behalf of the existing commission of bankruptcy, a legal procedure in its own right. While we might expect legal proceedings to be straightforward, or at least initiated with a sole purpose in mind, this is simply not the case. These suits were far more contested than the existing scholarship has recognised.

Turning to the use of language in legal documents, the manner in which scholars have analysed the concepts of narrative and storytelling, particularly in relation to how these were constructed and turned into legal evidence, has again undergone a dramatic re-evaluation. The first scholars to utilise legal evidence in a substantial manner took their lead from anthropology, and can be seen in classical texts such as Carlo Ginzburg's *The Cheese and the Worms* and Emmanuel Le Roy Ladurie's *Montaillou*.[21] Within these examples, the legal case acts as the central source, from which a type of narrative reconstruction of a set of events, ideologies, or historical insights broadens outwards.[22] More recent scholarship has attempted to shift the focus away from attempting to ascertain fact or fiction, innocence or guilt, while several other scholarly works have focused upon one trial, one case, or one dispute within a legal setting.[23] However, the focus remains firmly placed on the trial itself, and the reconstruction of any subsequent narrative by historians has been developed from this focal point.

21   Carlo Ginzburg, *The Cheese and the Worms: The Cosmos of a Sixteenth-Century Miller*, trans. John and Anne Tedeschi (London, 1976); Emmanuel Le Roy Ladurie, *Montaillou: Cathars and Catholics in a French Village*, trans. Barbara Bray (New York, 1978).
22   Thomas Kuen, 'Reading Microhistory: The Example of Giovanni and Lusanna', *Journal of Modern History*, 61 (1989), pp. 512–535, p. 523.
23   Alastair Bellany and Thomas Cogswell, *The Murder of King James I* (New Haven, 2015); see Joanne Bailey, 'Voices in Court: Lawyers' or Litigants'?', *Historical Research*, 74 (2001), pp. 392–408; Donna T. Andrew and Randall McGowen, *The Perreaus and Mrs. Rudd: Forgery and Betrayal in Eighteenth-Century London* (Berkeley, 2001); Andrew Hadfield and Simon Healy, 'Edmund Spenser and Chancery in 1597', *Law and Humanities*, 6 (2012), pp. 57–64; Larry Neal, *'I Am Not Master of Events': The Speculations of John Law and Lord Londonerry in the Mississippi and South Sea Bubbles* (New Haven, 2012); Clive Holmes, 'The Case of Joan Peterson: Witchcraft, Family Conflict, Legal Invention, and Constitutional Theory', in Dyson and Ibbetson (eds), *Law and Legal Process*, pp. 148–166; Sadie Jarrett, 'Credibility in the Court of Chancery: Salesbury v Bagot, 1671–1677', *The Seventeenth Century*, 36 (2019), pp. 1–26; Hannah Worthen, Briony McDonagh, and Amanda Capern, 'Gender, Property and Succession in the Early Modern English Aristocracy: The Case of Martha Janes and her Illegitimate Children', *Women's History Review*, 30 (2019), pp. 1–20.

However, there are other approaches to narrative and legal records. Joanne Bailey has suggested that there have been two broad approaches to the interpretation of legal evidence. The first set of historians 'act as "story-tellers", constructing stories of individuals, relationships and communities from legal testimony'. For Bailey this approach is flawed, as litigation does not provide a 'candid window' through which to view early modern society. Instead, litigation has more in common with fairground mirrors, 'reflecting back images distorted by several factors'. The second, and perhaps more nuanced approach, tends to focus on 'discourse', as scholars undertake the role of 'translators', who seek to 'decode the symbol and form' of the language presented in legal evidence. Yet, Bailey claims that this approach is similarly flawed, as it 'fails to differentiate between ideology and day-to-day experience, eliding the two without explaining how the former acted upon the latter'.[24] As Tom Johnson has bluntly put it, 'the old, empiricist quest for "real voices" in testimonies has to some extent been replaced by a contemporary quest for "real discourses"'.[25] For Johnson, this approach is problematic, as it assumes that witnesses were passive, and the legal narrative was largely shaped by legal experts. As such, Johnson hopes to return a degree of agency to witnesses, by giving them 'some of their critical faculties back'.[26] While much of this analysis has been reserved for discussions of witness testimony as a form of evidence – which is analysed in greater detail in chapter four relating to depositions – there are broader issues relating to the construction of narrative within a legal setting.

Tim Stretton has claimed that it is 'perhaps unfortunate that Natalie Davis used the term *fiction* rather than *narratives* in the title of her influential book about archives, leading many readers to think of invention rather than creative structuring in legal testimonies'.[27] As the individuals creating legal discourse sought to be plausible and persuasive to the authority of the court, the resulting evidence therefore allows us to 'reconstruct norms, conventions, and moral benchmarks or templates by comparing multiple documents to determine which content was shared and which unique'.[28] While certain scholars continue to focus on the narrative or 'story' of a case, others have moved away from the legal dispute itself, and have instead turned their attention towards the narratives of individuals within legal arenas. As Stretton concludes, while the context of the dispute outside of the courtroom can be of great importance, this 'is matched by the need to understand the context of the courtroom itself'.

24   Bailey, 'Voices in Court', pp. 406–407.
25   Tom Johnson, 'The Preconstruction of Witness Testimony: Law and Social Discourse in England before the Reformation', *LHR*, 32 (2014), pp. 127–147, pp. 127–128.
26   Ibid., p. 146.
27   Tim Stretton, 'Women, Legal Records, and the Problem of the Lawyer's Hand', *Journal of British Studies*, 58 (2019), pp. 684–700, p. 696.
28   Ibid., p. 696.

In this manner, the creation, form, and utilisation of narrative 'were shaped according to the demands of the legal institution in which it was heard'.[29] This approach is further extended and broken down in subsequent chapters, not only by analysing the narratives of individuals but also by analysing the presentation of such narratives at each separate stage of proceeding. Each chapter pauses and concentrates on similar types of documents found at each phase of the legal process, zooming in on the construction of narrative, as specific documents contained a distinct and purposeful use of language, which had been utilised to conform to the legal requirements of the court.

In terms of Chancery material, medieval scholars are restricted in the types of documents they can use, as prior to the fifteenth century only petitions or bills of complaint survive. From around the 1450s, a limited number of defendants' answers survived and the court began to formally record its decisions from about the 1530s.[30] Nevertheless, scholars of the medieval period have imaginatively utilised these documents in order to discuss a range of topics, including but not limited to, marriage disputes, testamentary cases, single working women, urban merchant identities, the involvement of legal experts in the creation of bills of complaint, and the presence of emotional discourse in such bills.[31] Because of such limitations, medieval historians have paid closer attention to how these documents were created, as well as the form and type of narrative presented in Chancery petitions.

For example, Timothy Haskett has investigated the 'conditions and aspirations' of parties involved in initiating suits from the late fourteenth to the early

---

29   Tim Stretton, 'Social Historians and the Records of Litigation', in Sølvi Sogner (ed.), *Fact, Fiction and Forensic Evidence* (Oslo, 1997), pp. 15–34, p. 18.

30   Merridee L. Bailey, 'Shaping London Merchant Identities: Emotions, Reputation and Power in the Court of Chancery', in Deborah Simonton (ed.), *The Routledge History Handbook of Gender and the Urban Experience* (London, 2017), pp. 327–337, p. 330; Haskett, 'The Medieval English Court of Chancery', p. 281.

31   Sara M. Butler, 'The Law as a Weapon in Marital Disputes: Evidence from the Late Medieval Court of Chancery, 1424–1529', *Journal of British Studies*, 43 (2004), pp. 291–316; Joseph Biancalana, 'Testamentary Cases in Fifteenth-Century Chancery', *LHR*, 76 (2008), pp. 283–306; Cordelia Beattie, 'Single Women, Work, and Family: The Chancery Dispute of Jane Wynde and Margaret Clerk' in Michael Goodich (ed.), *Voices From the Bench: the Narratives of Lesser Folk in Medieval Trials* (Basingstoke, 2006), pp. 177–202; Bailey, 'Shaping London Merchant Identities', pp. 327–337; Timothy S. Haskett, 'Country Lawyers? The Composers of English Chancery Bills', in Peter Birks (ed.), *The Life of the Law: Proceedings of the Tenth British Legal History Conference, Oxford 1991* (London, 1993), pp. 9–24; Timothy S. Haskett, 'The Presentation of Cases in Medieval Chancery Bills', in W. M. Gordon and T. D. Fergus (eds), *Legal History in the Making: Proceedings of the Ninth British Legal History Conference, Glasgow 1989* (London, 1991), pp. 11–28; Merridee L. Bailey, '"Most Hevynesse and Sorowe": The Presence of Emotions in the Late Medieval and Early Modern Court of Chancery', *LHR*, 37 (2019), pp. 1–28.

sixteenth century.[32] In numerous articles, Haskett analyses the composition of Chancery bills by asking the seemingly simple, but often overlooked, questions of how complainants proceeded in initiating suits, who they turned to for help, and how the final documents were created.[33] Haskett claims that the written English within bills shows their origin to have occurred outside of the court, 'indicating the activity in the country of men – very probably lawyers – who knew well the proper form with which to approach the court of chancery, and who used it skilfully to present cases in a clear and forceful manner'.[34] Haskett distinguishes these 'country' products from the more common language and style of bills written in 'Chancery English'.[35] The use of unusual, distinct, and colloquial language, coupled with the varied nature of handwriting – and the fact that more than one scribe wrote on each document – meant that several bills were in fact composed outside Westminster and brought to Chancery to initiate a suit.[36] Such research illuminates the people and the processes that went into creating Chancery documents, and such a careful and considered approach must be applied to the surviving documentation when we attempt to reconstruct narratives and utilise them as evidence.

Cordelia Beattie analyses fifteenth-century Chancery bills to illustrate how women were engaged in multiple suits across a range of jurisdictions in order to negotiate solutions to a single social or economic issue. As Beattie explains, 'Chancery is only one piece of the puzzle of how women negotiated justice in late medieval England, but its records can also shed light on some of the missing pieces'.[37] Because Chancery bills often detailed the background to a social dispute, this could bring into view other courts, demonstrating 'how litigants might pursue justice in a number of arenas, consecutively or concurrently'.[38] As such, the specific social, economic, or legal disagreement may have begun prior to the initiation of a bill of complaint being submitted in Chancery. Yet, what is crucial in Beattie's analysis, is that we can reconstruct a narrative timeline of events from Chancery material alone. Bills of complaint:

> might give us only the start of a case in Chancery, but by necessity they almost always refer to a legal dispute already in process elsewhere and sometimes to the backstory to the dispute. While such narratives were

32   Haskett, 'Country Lawyers?', pp. 9–24; Timothy S. Haskett, 'Conscience, Justice and Authority in the Late-Medieval English Court of Chancery', in Anthony Musson (ed.), *Expectations of the Law in the Middle Ages* (Woodbridge, 2001), pp. 151–164.
33   Haskett, 'Country Lawyers?', pp. 9–24.
34   Haskett, 'The Presentation of Cases in Medieval Chancery Bills', p. 13.
35   Haskett, 'Country Lawyers?', p. 12.
36   Ibid., p. 15.
37   Cordelia Beattie, 'A Piece of the Puzzle: Women and the Law as Viewed from the Late Medieval Court of Chancery', *Journal of British Studies*, 58 (2019), pp. 751–767, p. 751.
38   Ibid., p. 766.

clearly constructed to advantage petitioners in their requests to Chancery, the bills were only necessary because the petitioners were running the risk of losing in another court.[39]

The information gathered from Chancery bills can demonstrate how individual parties were involved in multiple jurisdictions, for 'what was essentially one dispute'.[40] As such, the Chancery case is only a small part of a much broader dispute, and the rationale for the case coming to Chancery could be manifold. In this manner, it is possible to utilise Chancery cases in isolation, while at the same time placing the dispute within a broader framework of debt recovery.

Tim Stretton has argued that while historians must remain vigilant in their approach to archival material, 'they do not have to settle on a single unified approach to all legal records'.[41] While this is certainly true, certain methodological approaches to early modern legal records can be problematic. In terms of Chancery, scholars have tended to dip into the records and discuss a specific topic, without paying close attention to the process, procedures, and individuals involved in creating and using the documents which have survived. Perhaps the most obvious example of such an approach can be seen in the work of Andy Wood who, across several publications, draws from a range of legal sources, and multiple jurisdictions, to comment on specific aspects of social history. In an article discussing the 'mechanics of social subordination' and plebeian solidarity in an early modern Yorkshire village, Wood draws the majority of his archival sources from the court of Star Chamber, explaining that Star Chamber complaints, 'remain notorious for their highly constructed, rhetorical nature'.[42] Across a wide range of documentation – including complaints, answers, rejoinders, and depositions – Wood claims that disputants 'consistently questioned the testimony of their opponents'.[43] Wood follows several disputes concerning a leaseholder – Sir Stephen Proctor – through the court. However, Wood seamlessly quotes from these various stages of the legal process, with little or no background or context to the specific details of each stage of proceeding, or to the processes that went into creating the surviving documentation.

Wood builds on this approach in subsequent work. In 'Fear, Hatred and the Hidden Injuries of Class in Early Modern England', Wood comments on the relationship between deference and defiance within the context of class and social relations. In this article, Wood not only quotes from different

---

39   Ibid., p. 753.
40   Ibid., p. 754.
41   Stretton, 'Women, Legal Records, and the Problem of the Lawyer's Hand', p. 687.
42   Andy Wood, 'Subordination, Solidarity and the Limits of Popular Agency in a Yorkshire Valley, c.1596–1615', *Past and Present*, 193 (2006), pp. 41–72, p. 49.
43   Ibid., p. 49.

stages of the legal process, but also references a wide range of courts. This includes drawing on the central courts of Westminster – such as the courts of Exchequer, Chancery, and Star Chamber – as well as the court of the Duchy of Lancaster.[44] When discussing attempts to defend common rights and oppose enclosure in legal sources, Wood utilises three quotes all discussing the village of Malmesbury – in modern-day Wiltshire – in 1609, within a single endnote:

> Here, the 'poor inhabitants' were set against opponents who were variously described as 'some of the wealthier sorte'; 'men of great estate' and as 'some persons that have bene of the Richar Sort'. These powerful individuals had enclosed Malmesbury's common 'to theire owne private use and have denied the resydue of the Inhabitants householders theire common'. Again, therefore, we see the identification of the enemies of plebeian community.[45]

While Wood does explain that this example has been 'culled from complaints addressed to Westminster equity courts', which were, 'usually somewhat exaggerated and rhetorical', a closer analysis of the endnote shows that these quotes have been taken from Star Chamber bills, Chancery decree rolls, and finally, Star Chamber proceedings.[46] While Wood has provided coherent and convincing arguments relating to numerous aspects of social activity from legal records, I would argue that this approach is problematic, as he fails to pay attention to the variations in process and procedure between jurisdictions, as well as the differences between the types of documents found at each stage of proceeding. Indeed, other scholars have failed to pay close attention to the specific details surrounding the court which produced the documentation that survives.[47] As such, this book sets out to highlight the issues with such an approach, and promulgates a more compelling methodology for utilising legal records in order to foreground the multiple meanings associated with failure as cases progressed through the legal framework of the court.

Another approach scholars take when utilising Chancery records is to supplement this material with other – usually local – sources in order to gain a greater understanding of the background details of the individuals involved in suits. Christine Churches, for example, has undertaken a case study of several legal disputes involving two merchants – Thomas and Walter Lutwidge – during

---

44   Andy Wood, 'Fear, Hatred and the Hidden Injuries of Class in Early Modern England', *Journal of Social History*, 39 (2006), pp. 803–826; a similar methodological approach is taken in Andy Wood, '"Some Banglyng About the Customes": Popular Memory and the Experience of Defeat in a Sussex Village, 1549–1640', *Rural History*, 25 (2014), pp. 1–14.
45   Wood, 'Fear, Hatred and the Hidden Injuries of Class', p. 811.
46   Ibid., p. 811, n. 37.
47   See Nicola Whyte, 'Landscape, Memory and Custom: Parish Identities c.1550–1700', *Social History*, 32 (2007), pp. 166–186.

the first half of the eighteenth century. Having consulted a range of supplementary evidence – including private correspondence and business papers – Churches successfully shows how these cases were initiated with the intent to delay the proceedings, and 'weaken the opponent through legal costs or loss of reputation and credit or simply to evade temporarily (or even permanently) the terms of an agreement, the payment of wages or customs duties, and the repayment of debts'.[48] As Chancery could grant an injunction to stop proceedings at common law, Churches claims that these bills were initiated out of 'prevarication or spite ... with the sole purpose of staving off execution of judgement already given against them at common law'.[49] Similarly, Amanda Capern has utilised supplementary material alongside the full range of Chancery records, in order to discuss the capacity of rumour to be transformed into legal evidence. Explaining that physical evidence – such as covenants, titles, loans, and mortgages – was presented to the court alongside the pleadings and depositions, Capern states that it was 'memory and the surviving concrete evidence together [that] established a case'.[50] Using the example of the Danby family from North Yorkshire, Capern concludes that the 'surviving Chancery records and private family papers allow the trail of vicious stories to be followed from the Danby family to neighbours, to court, and back again'. In this manner, Capern is able to follow the discussion of rumour and hearsay both within and outside the court, in what she labels 'Fama-in-transit'.[51]

This is a common approach employed by scholars working on a range of early modern courts. Steve Hindle has undertaken a close analysis of several Star Chamber suits involving the Jacobean magistrate Sir John Newdigate. By cross-referencing these cases with 'sources generated in the local environment of parishes and manors', Hindle is able to illuminate 'the complex relationship between the actual experience and the public representation of magistracy in early seventeenth century England'.[52] As Tim Stretton has argued, 'Each

48   Christine Churches, 'Business at Law: Retrieving Commercial Disputes From Eighteenth-Century Chancery', *The Historical Journal*, 43 (2000), pp. 937–954, p. 939.
49   Ibid., p. 940.
50   Amanda Capern, 'Rumour and Reputation in the Early Modern English Family', in Claire Walker and Heather Kerr (eds), *'Fama' and Her Sisters: Gossip and Rumour in Early Modern Europe* (Turnhout, 2015), pp. 85–114, p. 96.
51   Ibid., p. 103.
52   Steve Hindle, 'Self-Image and Public Image in the Career of a Jacobean Magistrate: Sir John Newdigate in the Court of Star Chamber', in Michael J. Braddick and Phil Withington (eds), *Popular Culture and Political Agency in Early Modern England and Ireland: Essays in Honour of John Walter* (Woodbridge, 2017), pp. 123–144, pp. 124–125; for further research relating to Sir John Newdigate, see Steve Hindle, 'Below Stairs at Arbury Hall: Sir Richard Newdigate and his Household Staff, c.1670–1710', *Historical Research*, 85 (2012), pp. 71–88; Steve Hindle, 'Sir Richard Newdigate and the "Great Survey" of Chilvers Coton: Fiscal Seigneurialism in Late-Seventeenth-Century Warwickshire', in Christopher Dyer and

record, each archive, and each scholarly purpose requires a specific approach, depending in particular on the availability of corroborative material relating to the case within and outside legal archives'.[53] For Stretton, the survival rates of certain documents, coupled with the constraints of legal formalism, mean that corroborative material becomes essential in order to reconstruct the background details of a suit.[54] Elsewhere, I have undertaken a similar approach, combining Chancery material with private correspondence in order to recreate the wider plot, story, or script of a dispute and place it within the context of actions and words that were occurring in the local community.[55]

While supplementary material can always be of use to a historian, it does not mean that a body of Chancery records cannot be analysed in isolation. It simply means that a different narrative and representation of the past is presented. The methodological approach employed in the book does not allow for the inclusion of additional material, such as private family or business papers, petitions to parliament, and proceedings from other courts. As such, there are limitations placed on the ability to reconstruct the background details of individuals involved in suits, and the narratives occurring within the community which provide context to the wider social conflict to which a case referred. However, the methodology employed throughout does enable a greater understanding of the procedural elements of the court, and how the narrative in cases altered according to the particular stage of proceeding.

Having highlighted some methodological challenges that have arisen over the past fifty years with the use and utilisation of legal records, the next two sections provide detailed accounts of the procedure of the court and the development of the equitable jurisdiction of Chancery. Particular attention is paid to the processes, procedures, and individuals involved in the creation of a wide range of documents relating to bankruptcy litigation, and how these changed at different stages of the legal process. I argue that it is essential to have a firm understanding of the practicalities of how the court conducted its business – and how this changed as a suit progressed – in order to utilise Chancery records as evidence of financial and personal failure.

Catherine Richardson (eds), *William Dugdale, Historian, 1605-1686: His life, His Writings and His County* (Woodbridge), pp. 164–186.

53 Stretton, 'Women, Legal Records, and the Problem of the Lawyer's Hand', p. 694.

54 For a discussion of social effects of lawsuits over bonds and promises and the use of supplementary material, see Tim Stretton, 'Written Obligations, Litigation and Neighbourliness, 1580–1680', in Steve Hindle, Alexandra Shepard, and John Walter (eds), *Remaking Social History: Social Relations and Social Change in Early Modern England* (Woodbridge, 2013), pp. 189–210.

55 Collins, 'The Interconnected Nature of Family Indebtedness'.

The Procedure of the Court

The process, procedure, and decision-making in Chancery were governed by the Lord Chancellor. William Jones has suggested that during the sixteenth century, the Lord Chancellor's governmental importance continued to decline, and the Chancellor was regarded, 'first and foremost as a judge, and it is not surprising that a post once associated with ecclesiastics was to become a prize for some of the greatest common lawyers in the land'.[56] Sir Thomas More – Lord Chancellor 1529–1544 – was the first of these modern lawyer-Chancellors, but there continued to be statesmen and ecclesiastics appointed throughout the sixteenth century. Thomas Egerton – later Lord Ellesmere 1596–1617 – and Francis Bacon – 1617–1621 – were two prominent lawyers who worked towards establishing the modern procedure and jurisdiction of the court, making Chancery an equal, if not superior, authority compared to the common law courts.[57] After the tenure of Bacon, only two Chancellors – John Williams 1621–1625 and the Earl of Shaftesbury 1672–1673 – were not practising lawyers.[58] By the late seventeenth century, Chancery was a distinct institution, with a legally trained Lord Chancellor, who was appointed by the monarch, at the head of an established bureaucracy.

From the reign of Henry VIII, the Lord Chancellor was assisted in his duties by the Master of the Rolls, the chief of the Masters in Chancery, who was appointed by the monarch. As well as the Master of the Rolls, the court employed Masters in Ordinary, initially eleven in number but which had been reduced to ten by the late seventeenth century. Throughout the sixteenth century, the Master of the Rolls was delegated a particular jurisdiction by special commission, empowering him to hear general cases. This elevated his standing above that of the other Masters, essentially creating the position of general deputy to the Lord Chancellor. By the seventeenth century, it had become accepted that in the absence of the Lord Chancellor, the Master of the Rolls could hear causes and make orders and decrees under his own authority.[59] This assumption was eventually confirmed by legislation enacted by the statute of 3 George II (1729), which declared that all orders made by the Master of

---

56 W. J. Jones, *The Elizabethan Court of Chancery* (Oxford, 1967), p. 7.

57 See J. H. Baker, 'The Common Lawyers and the Chancery: 1616', *Irish Jurist*, 4 (1969), pp. 368–392.

58 While Shaftesbury was educated as a lawyer he had never practised, and Holdsworth has stated, 'it was no doubt a scandal that a non-lawyer should be made Chancellor at that date, for the rules of Equity were fast developing into a settled system', Holdsworth, *A History of English Law*, vol. 1, pp. 410–411.

59 Ibid., vol. 1, pp. 416–420.

the Rolls were valid, subject to appeal to the Chancellor.[60] However, even after the clarifying act, the authority of the Master of the Rolls was limited by the requirement that he act in conjunction with at least two of the Masters in Ordinary, or two common law judges, while the enrolment of final decisions – known as decrees – still required the signature of the Chancellor.[61] For clarity, the term 'Master' is utilised throughout to refer to the ten Masters in Ordinary, while the term 'judge' refers to the presiding authority of either the Lord Chancellor or the Master of the Rolls.

In the early history of the court, Masters' duties were various and general in their nature, meaning it was necessary for a Master to be acquainted with the common law as well as the canon and civil law.[62] Throughout the medieval period, Masters were referred to by various titles, all of which demonstrated that they were assistants to the Chancellor. One example can be seen in their comparison to the *pedanei judices* of the later Roman law, as the Chancellor could delegate the duty of hearing and reporting upon certain parts of a case.[63] However, this system of delegation seems to have been utilised to excess prior to the seventeenth century, and under a 1618 order from Francis Bacon, their role was defined and restricted. This order, coupled with the growing jurisdiction and increased business of the court, meant that their role became specialised, with their chief duty confined to reporting on specific matters referred to them.[64] As such, the ten Masters in Chancery played an increasingly important role in the court as a fact-finding agency, to whom the Lord Chancellor referred a range of matters which were pertinent to the outcome of a suit. At the beginning of the seventeenth century, the majority of the Masters of the Rolls and the eleven Masters in Ordinary were Doctors of Civil Law, having been trained at Oxford and Cambridge. However, by the late seventeenth century, civil lawyers became a declining minority amongst Masters.[65] As well as these officials, the court also had recourse to Masters Extraordinary, appointed because of the pressure of the business of the court, or to handle inquiries best pursued in the localities, although Henry Horwitz has suggested that this only occurred 'on occasion'.[66]

---

60   3 George II. C.30 (1729); The new office of Vice Chancellor was not created until 1813, see Michael Lobban, 'Preparing for Fusion: Reforming the Nineteenth-Century Court of Chancery (part 1)', *LHR*, 22 (2004), pp. 389–427, p. 393; Michael Lobban, 'Preparing for Fusion: Reforming the Nineteenth-Century Court of Chancery (part 2)', *LHR*, (2004), pp. 565–599.

61   Henry Horwitz, *A Guide to Chancery Equity Records and Proceedings 1600–1800* (Kew, 1995), p. 9.

62   For a detailed historical account of the role of the Chancery Master, see Edmund Heward, *Masters in Ordinary* (Chichester, 1990).

63   Holdsworth, *A History of English Law*, vol. 1, pp. 416–418.

64   Ibid., vol. 1, p. 418.

65   Horwitz, *A Guide to Chancery Equity Records*, p. 2.

66   Ibid., p. 80, n. 29.

Below the Masters in the hierarchy of the court were the Six Clerks. Initially, the Six Clerks were the attorneys of Chancery, with a monopoly of acting for complainants in the court. During the 1620s – having just rebuilt their offices in Chancery Lane after a fire destroyed their previous quarters – they were on the way to being sinecurists. As the business of the court grew, it made it impossible for the Six Clerks to continue to act as solicitors to the parties. Instead, parties began to employ the assistants to the Six Clerks, known as the Under Clerks – eventually converted into Sworn Clerks by order of Lord Keeper Bridgeman in 1668 – and from the beginning of the seventeenth century their own solicitors.[67] From around 1711, the Sworn Clerks began to urge a reduction of their own number – originally ninety in 1688 – by not filling the position when it was left vacant by death. This approach was officially adopted by the Master of the Rolls in 1718 and it reduced their number to sixty-five by the 1730s, before reaching its lowest number of forty-seven in 1776. Such a decline in officers obviously left fewer Sworn Clerks to deal with a similar case load, increasing the duration of suits.[68] In a pamphlet from the middle of the eighteenth century, the Sworn Clerks defined themselves as 'the only Attorneys of the Court' and their primary function was 'to file all the Pleadings ... and to do all other Acts of Attorneys'.[69] Horwitz has suggested that throughout the seventeenth century, most suitors 'employed their own solicitors to look after the management of their suits and feed counsel to advise on strategy and to argue their positions when formal hearings were held'.[70] Similarly, Mike Macnair has shown that since the mid-fifteenth century, the staffing of the court, 'shifted from career civil servants (and among the actual Chancellors senior aristocrat politicians), to qualified canonist and civilian lawyers'.[71] As such, there was a dramatic increase in privately employed legal experts to supplement the work of the court at every stage of proceeding.

During the sixteenth century, Chancery became a tribunal – in the form of a trial process – in which each stage of proceeding was recorded in writing.[72] The initiation of a suit began with the complainant – or plaintiff – filing a written bill of complaint. In principle, these bills were supposed to follow a standard tripartite format, with the plaintiff stating their name, place of abode,

---

67 Ibid., p. 14; Holdsworth, *A History of English Law*, vol. 1, pp. 422–433.

68 Henry Horwitz, 'Record-Keepers in the Court of Chancery and Their "Record" of Accomplishment in the Seventeenth and Eighteenth Centuries', *Historical Research*, 70 (1997), pp. 34–51.

69 *The Case of the Sworn Clerks, and Waiting Clerks of the Six Clerks Office* (London, 1749?) p. 1.

70 Horwitz, *A Guide to Chancery Equity Records*, p. 14.

71 Mike Macnair, 'Development of Uses and Trusts: Contract or Property, and European Influences and Images', *Studi Urbinati, A – Scienze Giuridiche, Politiche Ed Economiche*, 66 (2016), pp. 305–333.

72 Horwitz, *A Guide to Chancery Equity Records*, p. 3.

and their status and/or occupational ascription. The bill would then set out the facts and pertinent details of their complaint, before explaining that it was impossible to secure a remedy without the court's action and asking for a subpoena for the appearance of the defendant(s).[73] By the seventeenth century, a further standard allegation of confederacy between the named defendants and unnamed other parties had been added in a set phrase or convention: the defendants had 'combined and confederated' against the plaintiffs 'with persons unknown' to 'defeat or defraud' them.[74] This technical manoeuvre allowed for the inclusion of additional defendants to the bill at a later date.[75]

During the Elizabethan period, defendants had to physically appear in court to be sworn under oath.[76] However, throughout the seventeenth century, the court became more flexible in several ways. Firstly, those living outside of London could give their answer to a commission created for that purpose. The commission would be accompanied by a copy of the complainant's bill – at an additional cost to the defendant – until the requirement was abolished in 1706 after recurrent complaints of the unnecessary costs. Secondly, it became acceptable for a legal representative to appear in court in place of the defendant to provide an answer, but again, such answers would have to be taken under oath. Finally, legislation in 1732 meant that after public advertisement in the *London Gazette*, a suit might proceed *ex parte* and, if necessary, render judgment in the absence of the defendant. It appears that even after 1732, the court was reluctant to proceed without the answer of the defendant, which inevitably led to further delays.[77]

Aside from the most common response of a sworn answer, several alternatives were available to a defendant, all of which were to be presented in written form. A disclaimer took the defendant out of the suit by disavowing any interest in the matter and ceding any claim that he might be thought to have in the matter in complaint. A plea sought to raise an objection to a point in law, seeking to forestall the complaint. Often, such an objection would relate to questions of jurisdiction, whereby the defendant felt that the complaint was not a matter to be heard in equity, but rather in a court of common law or an ecclesiastical court. A demurrer sought to evade the force of the complaint

73   Ibid., pp. 3–4; see also M. R. T. Macnair, *The Law of Proof in Early Modern Equity* (Berlin, 1999).
74   Mary Clayton, 'The Wealth of Riches to be Found in the Court of Chancery: The Equity Pleadings Database', *Archives: The Journal of the British Records Association*, 28 (2003), pp. 25–31.
75   Horwitz, *A Guide to Chancery Equity Records*, p. 14; see Christine Churches, '"Equity Against a Purchaser Shall Not Be": A Seventeenth-Century Case Study in Landholding and Indebtedness', *Parergon*, 11 (1993), pp. 69–87, p. 78.
76   Jones, *The Elizabethan Court of Chancery*, p. 214.
77   Horwitz, *A Guide to Chancery Equity Records*, p. 16.

by admitting the truth of the complainant's factual allegations, but arguing that such facts did not present a cause which they might reasonably answer. Demurrers were commonly referred to a Master for recommendations for acceptance or rejection, while pleas surrounding a clear-cut point of law would be referred to common law judges. If either were rejected, then the defendant would need to submit an answer. As such, it was common for defendants to submit both simultaneously, so that if the demurrer or plea was rejected, the suit would go forward on the basis of the answer. David Yale has pointed to the decline in the importance of pleas and demurrers throughout the eighteenth century to demonstrate the court's principled desire to thoroughly investigate each complaint. As pleas and demurrers were submitted with the intent to bring the suit to an abrupt termination, Yale argues that this effect 'did not altogether accord with a procedure modelled to explore all the merits of a case'.[78] One final option was to file a cross-bill, making the complainant the defendant in a second but interrelated suit.[79] The bill and the defendant's response were known collectively as 'the pleadings'.

One of the main reasons a complainant would file a bill in Chancery was to secure an injunction, which took two forms. A 'common injunction' would prevent the defendant from continuing a case that had already been executed in another jurisdiction, most commonly a common law court; whereas a 'special injunction' would prevent the defendant from undertaking any action that would irreparably damage the plaintiff. A common example can be seen in the use of a special injunction being executed to 'bar the committing of waste on a tenement in which the plaintiff claimed an interest'.[80] Requests for injunctions were granted as a matter of course and stayed in force until the defendant answered, and in some circumstances until the cause had been heard and concluded in Chancery.[81]

There was always the possibility for additional documentation to be added to the pleadings. For example, it was common in bankruptcy suits for defendants to add schedules of account – usually simply written at the end of an answer on the same piece of parchment – to support their position.[82] Similarly, a complainant might offer exceptions to an answer, claiming it 'contained

---

78 Heneage Finch, *Manual of Chancery Practice*, pp. 56–57.

79 Ibid., pp. 14–15; Holdsworth, *A History of English Law*, vol. 9, pp. 376–408; Jones, *The Elizabethan Court of Chancery*, p. 208.

80 Horwitz, *A Guide to Chancery Equity Records*, p. 3; the cost of an injunction in the last seventeenth century was listed as £1 1s. 1d., *The Country-Mans Counsellour, Or, Every Man Made His Own Lawyer* (London, 1682), p. 7.

81 Horwitz, *A Guide to Chancery Equity Records*, p. 3.

82 In my sample, 50 out of 228 cases included at least one schedule of account, which is roughly 22 per cent of the total. For an example of both parties providing detailed accounts, see TNA, C6/381/15, 'Browne v Bamforth' (1696), Bill of Complaint; Answer of George Bamforth.

impertinent or scandalous matter', or that it simply did not admit or deny the allegations in the bill, and was therefore insufficient. The defendant was then required to submit a 'further answer'. While in theory this process could go back and forth – the plaintiff submitting a replication and the defendant replying with a rejoinder – Horwitz has concluded that before the eighteenth century, 'bill, answer, and replication constituted the normal pleadings'.[83] In certain circumstances – for example, if a party had died, there was a change in a woman's marital status, or if the deadline for further action had passed – the suit would be 'abated' and could only be reinstated by way of a bill of revivor. In these circumstances, it was common for plaintiffs to add a supplementary bill of complaint in order to broaden the scope of the pleading.[84] Ultimately, it was the parties who determined the pace at which the suit proceeded, as while the court had deadlines to abide by, it was up to those involved in the case to observe and enforce these rules. This of course gave rise to multiple possibilities to employ delay tactics which could add to the cost of a suit.[85]

Once a suitable reply had been submitted, then the case could proceed to the evidentiary stage of proceeding. Most commonly, this took the form of depositions, whereby lists of questions – known as interrogatories – were submitted by parties in the suit and their answers – called depositions – were transcribed by clerks of the court to be sealed, and if necessary, read out upon the hearing of the cause at a later date. If the parties lived within ten miles of London, then witnesses were required to attend one of the Chancery Examiners at the Rolls Office. Parties outside this jurisdiction were examined in their local communities.[86] If the suit was referred to a Chancery Master, then a second form of evidence was utilised, which broadly took two forms. The first involved individuals submitting a range of personal documentation – such as account books, inventories, schedules of account, paper instruments, etc. – to be examined by the Master. The second involved a Master personally questioning a witness via written interrogatories, which was known as an 'examination'. These two processes were not mutually exclusive and could occur within a single case. At the completion of a case, the parties usually reclaimed any evidence that had been brought before the court, known as Masters' exhibits. However, for whatever reason, it was common for parties to leave such evidence in the possession of the court, and an abundance of such documentation survives. Ultimately, the documentation found at this stage of proceeding could either

83   Horwitz, *A Guide to Chancery Equity Records*, p. 17.
84   Ibid., p. 22.
85   Ibid., p. 11.
86   For a detailed explanation of this process, see Christine Churches, '"The Most Unconvincing Testimony": The Genesis and the Historical Usefulness of the Country Depositions in Chancery', *The Seventeenth Century*, 11 (1996), pp. 209–227.

have been brought to the court as evidence or could have been created by the court to inform the decision-making process.[87]

Once both parties had submitted evidence then the case could be heard in open court. The presiding judge would render their decision, which would be recorded verbatim by a register of the court in the entry book. Any order or decree made by the judge throughout the case was also recorded in the entry book, which outlined how the case had progressed.[88] This decision, which was preceded by summaries of the suit – the contents of the pleadings, depositions of witnesses, and any Masters' reports – could then be formally written out and enrolled on parchment after the payment of the requisite fees. Until the decree was enrolled, it only had the force of an 'interlocutory order', meaning that it could be altered upon a rehearing or sometimes upon a motion.[89]

Horwitz explains the common characteristics of cases before the court of Chancery: '(1) a substantial minority never proceeded beyond the plaintiff's filing of his bill; (2) a considerable majority never proceeded beyond the pleadings; and (3) depositions were taken and/or a decree issued in only a distinct minority of instances'.[90] The observation of George Norburie, a sixteenth-century clerk – whose remarks were later reprinted in an eighteenth-century collection – summarises this point: 'it is to be observed, that of ten bills brought into this court, hardly three have any colour or shadow of just complaint. The rest are found *omni fundamento carere* [lacking any basis] and to be exhibited either of malice, or out of a turbulent humour wherewith too many are possessed, or else to shelter themselves for a while from some imminent storm'.[91] The vast majority of suits never made it to the laborious and expensive end stage of proceeding, as cases were withdrawn, compromised, or subject to an order from the Lord Chancellor after the pleadings had been entered.

The main stages of a proceeding – pleadings, depositions, exhibits, and decrees and orders – were all recorded in writing. However, there were other forms of documentation that could form part of a case. For example, affidavits were a written statement confirmed by oath, and were broadly concerned with matters of process, such as the issuing of subpoenas. Similarly, if a case was referred to a Master, then this would create supplementary documentation,

---

87   Chancery Masters' exhibits can be found in numerous series at TNA, see the description of the associated records, stable URL: https://www.nationalarchives.gov.uk/help-with-your-research/research-guides/chancery-equity-suits-after-1558/#8-chancery-masters-and-the-associated-records (accessed 25/03/2024).

88   Series C33 at TNA.

89   *The Practical Register in Chancery* (London, 1714), pp. 123–125.

90   Horwitz, *A Guide to Chancery Equity Records*, p. 26.

91   George Norburie, 'The Abuses and Remedies of Chancery', in Francis Hargrave (ed.), *A Collection of Tracts Relative to the Law of England* (London, 1787), p. 434.

such as reports, accounts, and papers, which could be filed in numerous places. Finally, it was possible for solicitors representing the parties to petition the court – either in writing or *viva voce* – for a specific action or request; for example to extend the deadline to submit an answer. These actions would have been recorded in the entry book, so even if they were submitted orally, or the petitions themselves have not survived, there is a written record of how the suit progressed. While it is not as straightforward as suggesting that every single action or manoeuvre that took place in Chancery was recorded in writing, the fundamental stages of proceeding were recorded in written form. As such, it is crucial to have an understanding of the procedure of the court, and the numerous people involved in the creation of legal records, before analysing the physical documents which have survived.

The court would not hear cases worth less than £10 in value – or for land worth less than 40s per annum – and according to the barrister Joshua Fitzsimmonds, the common cost of continuing a case to a hearing in 1751 was at least £20.[92] Amy Erickson has suggested that the cost of the initiation of a suit in Chancery was 'not especially high ... but initial costs multiplied quickly with commissions to take evidence in the country, complications in pleadings, extended by delays and bribes'.[93] Complaints about the excessive costs in Chancery, and especially in following a case to completion, were commonplace. For example, compare Fitzsimmonds' assessment to an anonymous tract from the same period, which suggested that suing for anything less than £500 was counterproductive.[94] It is extremely difficult to assess the cost involved in pursuing a case in Chancery, especially as parties would have to pay their private solicitors and legal experts to advise and undertake a range of tasks. However, it has been estimated that an income of £50 per annum was the threshold for the middle rank of society during this period.[95] Coupled with the fact that bankrupts had to have owed more than £100, the cases initiated in Chancery were for substantial sums, often amounting to several thousand or tens of thousands of pounds. While bankrupts were often comfortably part of the aspiring middling sorts, they became increasingly engaged in a market that was reliant on credit to maintain their raw materials and trading stock, often leading to their ultimate failure.

92   Horwitz, *A Guide to Chancery Equity Records*, p. 30; Joshua Fitzsimmonds, *Free and Candid Disquisitions, On the Nature and Execution of the Laws of England, Both in Civil and Criminal Affairs* (London, 1751), p. 20.
93   Amy Erickson, *Women and Property in Early Modern England* (London, 1993), p. 117; it cost an extra 1s. to swear an affidavit, an extra 9d. for fifteen lines of any copies, and a further 8d. to file documents, H. R., *The Country-Mans Counsellour*, p. 7.
94   *Animadversions Upon the Present Laws of England* (London, 1750), p. 8; for detailed costs see Samuel Turner, *Costs and Present Practice of the Court of Chancery* (London, 1795).
95   Earle, *The Making of the English Middle Class*, pp. 14–15.

During the late seventeenth century, the court of Chancery – alongside other central courts – saw a dramatic decline in its level of business.[96] However, the duration of suits in Chancery continued to lengthen, leading Horwitz and Polden to claim that Chancery's performance, 'degenerated seriously' in the period of this study.[97] The Lord Chancellor held very little authority over the conduct of his staff, who were permitted to undertake their duties as they saw fit. This led to consistent and ongoing complaints of expense, delay, inefficiency, and fraud throughout. Horwitz suggests that the way in which the court and its officials handled the cases that came before them, 'was a mixture of genuine idealism and bureaucratic self-interest, compounded by overwork and complicated by the manoeuvres of the opposing parties for whom delay and obfuscation might well be advantageous'.[98] Ultimately, Horwitz suggests that entering the seventeenth century, Chancery was an institution which was 'greatly affected by two concerns which pulled it in different directions'. The first was the commitment of the Lord Chancellor to understand the fundamental complaints brought before the court in order to render appropriate relief, while the other was the pressure to deal with the rising number of cases initiated in Chancery. Such a surge in business tended to prolong suits, especially as the court was short of judges.[99]

Chancery as a Court of Equity

Under the stewardship of Lord Chancellor Nottingham – 1673–1682 – both the formal structure of the court and the jurisdiction of bankruptcy underwent a dramatic re-evaluation. The court of Chancery's equitable jurisdiction was not an intentional creation, and the procedures associated with its jurisdiction evolved in an uncoordinated way. From around the fourteenth century, equity

96   Christopher W. Brooks, 'Interpersonal Conflict and Social Tension: Civil Litigation in England, 1640–1870', in A. L. Beier, David Cannadine and James Rosenheim (eds), *The First Modern Society: Essays in English History in Honour of Lawrence Stone* (Cambridge, 1989), pp. 357–399; Christopher W. Brooks, *Pettyfoggers and Vipers of the Commonwealth: The 'Lower Branch' of the Legal Profession in Early Modern England* (Cambridge, 1986), pp. 54–55; Christopher W. Brooks, *Law, Politics and Society in Early Modern England* (Cambridge, 2008); Brooks, *Pettyfoggers and Vipers of the Commonwealth*; Brooks, *Lawyers, Litigation and English Society Since 1450*; see also Lobban, Begiato, Green (eds), *Law, Lawyers, and Litigants in Early Modern England*.
97   Henry Horwitz and Patrick Polden, 'Continuity or Change in the Court of Chancery in the Seventeenth and Eighteenth Centuries?', *Journal of British Studies*, 35 (1996), pp. 24–57, p. 53; *Observations on the Dilatory and Expensive Proceedings in the Court of Chancery* (London, 1701), p. 6.
98   Horwitz, *A Guide to Chancery Equity Records*, pp. 9–10.
99   Ibid., p. 9.

became institutionally separated from the common law, and by the late fifteenth century, Chancery came to be recognised as a court with its own unique identity, as the Lord Chancellor made decrees in his own name.[100] William Holdsworth has stated that this new and independent development arose from three factors: hostility to the rigidity of the common law, ideas about the way in which equitable rules should be governed by conscience, and a distinct procedure that allowed each individual case to be determined in the correct, equitable manner.[101] By the sixteenth century, these three factors led to three types of suit being heard within Chancery: (1) where the common law held no juris-diction, (2) where there was a jurisdiction but 'owing to the disturbed state of the country, or to the power of the defendant', the courts could not act, (3) or where there was a jurisdiction but the law itself was at fault.[102]

F. W. Maitland has suggested that prior to the abolition of courts of equity in 1875, equity itself could be defined as a 'body of rules' which were 'admin-istered only by those Courts which are known as Courts of Equity'.[103] Equity was seen as synonymous with the jurisdiction of these courts, and several other early modern courts held an equitable jurisdiction. The court of Exchequer developed an equity side to proceedings in the sixteenth century, but the volume of its business was far outstripped by that of Chancery, leading Horwitz to refer to Exchequer as Chancery's 'younger sister'.[104] Initially, the court of Requests, and the Councils in the North and Wales held equitable jurisdictions, but both were abandoned during the Civil War, while the three independent palatinate counties of Chester, Durham, and Lancaster saw the volume of their equitable business decline rapidly over the seventeenth century.[105]

Throughout the seventeenth and eighteenth centuries Chancery was the primary court of equity, so much so that the *Oxford Dictionary of Law* defines equity as 'That part of English law originally administered by the Lord Chancellor and later by the court of Chancery, as distinct from that adminis-tered by the courts of common law'.[106] Dennis Klinck has suggested that early modern Chancery was a 'court of conscience', as the Lord Chancellor was the keeper of the sovereign's conscience and certain acts were prohibited because

---

100 Jones, *The Elizabethan Court of Chancery*, pp. 9–10.
101 Holdsworth, *A History of English Law*, vol. 2, pp. 346–347; see Timothy S. Haskett, 'The Medieval English Court of Chancery', *LHR*, 14 (1996), pp. 245–313.
102 Ibid., vol. 1, p. 405.
103 F. W. Maitland, *Equity, Also the Forms of Action at Common Law: Two Course of Lectures* (Cambridge, 1929), p. 1.
104 Henry Horwitz, 'Chancery's "Younger Sister": The Court of Exchequer and its Equity Jurisdiction, 1649–1841', *Historical Research*, 72 (1999), pp. 160–182.
105 Erickson, *Women and Property in Early Modern England*, p. 31.
106 Jonathan Law and Elizabeth A. Martin (eds), *Oxford Dictionary of Law* (Oxford, 2014); see also F. W. Maitland, *Equity, also the Forms of Action at Common Law* (Cambridge, 1929).

they were 'against conscience'.[107] Willard Barbour states that conscience was a 'juristic principle' within fifteenth-century Chancery, while A. W. B. Simpson elaborates that conscience was the 'primary principle of decision' throughout the fifteenth and sixteenth centuries.[108] Mike Macnair has stated that throughout the history of the court, the 'examination of the *conscientia* of the defendant was the absolute centre of the fact-finding procedure of Chancery and other equity courts'.[109] Finally, C. K. Allen notes that the one general principle which more than any other influenced equity as it was developed by Chancery was 'a philosophical and theological conception of conscience', demonstrating that an understanding that conscience played a central role in the development of equity was now commonplace.[110]

To modern readers, it may seem self-evident that conscience seems a private, subjective notion, while the law is, and ought to be, an objective judgement and not a matter to be decided by personal morality. This seeming contradiction was not lost on early modern legal commentators, as throughout its development equity was based upon moral, rather than legal or juristic grounds, and was therefore liable to individual interpretation.[111] Indeed, any scholar of the common law is familiar with the English jurist John Selden's oft-quoted critique, that the dimensions of the Chancellor's conscience – and therefore legal justice – might be as variable as the length of his foot.[112] An enduring challenge to equity was that the law, by its very nature, was intended to be consistent and predictable. As Francis Bacon observed, the 'Primary Dignity of Laws' is

---

107   Dennis Klinck, *Conscience, Equity and the Court of Chancery in Early Modern England* (London, 2010), p. vii.

108   Willard Barbour, 'Some Aspects of Fifteenth-Century Chancery', *Harvard Law Review*, 31 (1918), pp. 834–859, p. 838; A. W. B. Simpson, *A History of the Common Law of Contract: The Rise of the Action of Assumpsit* (Oxford, 1975), p. 397.

109   Mike Macnair, 'Equity and Conscience', *Oxford Journal of Legal Studies*, 27 (2007), pp. 659–681, p. 676.

110   C. K. Allen, *Law in the Making*, 6th edn (Oxford, 1958), p. 389; Macnair, 'Equity and Conscience', pp. 659–681; Richard Hedlund, 'The Theological Foundations of Equity's Conscience', *Oxford Journal of Law and Religion*, 4 (2015), pp. 119–140.

111   Yale, *Lord Chancellor Nottingham's Chancery Cases*, vol. 1., p. xxxix.

112   The full quote reads: 'Equity is a roguish thing. For Law we have a measure, know what to trust to; Equity is according to the conscience of him that is Chancellor, and as that is larger or narrower, so is Equity. 'Tis all one as if they should make the standard for the measure we call a "foot" a Chancellor's foot; what an uncertain measure this would be! One Chancellor has a long foot, another a short foot, a third an indifferent foot. 'Tis the same thing in the Chancellor's conscience', in Frederick Pollock (ed.), *The Table Talk of John Selden* (London, 1927), p. 43; *The Table Talk* was a compilation of Selden's private conversations transcribed by a secretary and was initially published in 1689, some forty-five years after his death; see also Dennis Klinck and Loris Mirella, 'Tracing the Imprint of the Chancellor's Foot in Contemporary Canadian Judicial Discourse', *Canadian Journal of Law and Society*, 13 (1998), pp. 63–98.

'that they be certain'.[113] Paradoxically, it was the very notion of equity's flexible application to which its advocates clung. As one anonymous tract summarised in 1682, the nature of Chancery 'is to moderate the exact rigours of Law, and therefore is called a court of Equity'.[114] This meant that on the one hand, equity was seen as offering flexibility from the strictures of the common law, while on the other, it was seen as imparting subjectivity and arbitrariness to legal decisions.[115] Entering the late seventeenth century, conscience was identified as the central principle for the decision-making process of Chancery, but was constantly attacked as being contrary to the very idea of law as comprised of determinate and knowable rules.[116] Lord Chancellor Nottingham attempted to address these issues to formalise and regulate the implementation of the equitable jurisdiction of Chancery.

Klinck describes Nottingham as a 'seminal figure in the history of English equity', as it was under his stewardship that equity began to be governed by certain rules and regulations.[117] Holdsworth states that Nottingham's success as Lord Chancellor was 'due partly to his own industry and genius, partly to the fact that the time was ripe for the beginning of such a settlement'.[118] At this point, the future administration of equity was at a critical juncture; either the court would be ruled by an increased fixity in its doctrine, or it would retain an emphasis on the moral, and therefore relatively unstable instinct, in judicial decisions.[119] Holdsworth concludes that in this manner 'the man and the opportunity happily coincided; and so, whether we look at his influence upon the principles of equity, or upon the character of equity itself, we must admit that he deserves his traditional title of the Father of Modern Equity'.[120] David Yale elaborates by stating that the whole tendency of Lord Nottingham's work was towards a 'scientific arrangement of equity', noting he was the 'father

---

113   Francis Bacon, 'Example of a Treatise on Universal Justice or the Foundations of Equity, by Aphorisms' appended to Book 8 of *De Augmentis*, in J. Spedding, R. L. Ellis and D. D. Heath (eds), *The Works of Francis Bacon* (New York, Garrett, 1968), vol. 5, p. 88.

114   H. R., *The Country-Mans Counsellour*, p. 5.

115   Dennis Klinck, 'Imagining Equity in Early Modern England', *Canadian Bar Review*, 84 (2005), pp. 217–247.

116   Klinck, *Conscience, Equity and the Court of Chancery*, p. 3; see also J. C. Campbell, 'The Development of Principles in Equity in the Seventeenth Century', in Peter R. Anstey (ed.), *The Idea of Principles in Early Modern Thought: Interdisciplinary Perspectives* (London, 2017), pp. 45–76.

117   Dennis Klinck, 'Lord Nottingham and the Conscience of Equity', *Journal of the History of Ideas*, 67 (2006), pp. 123–147, p. 123.

118   Holdsworth, *A History of English Law*, vol. 6, p. 548.

119   Yale, *Lord Chancellor Nottingham's Chancery Cases*, vol. 2, p. 7.

120   Holdsworth, *A History of English Law*, vol. 6, p. 548.

of systematic equity'.[121] Lee B. Wilson has gone as far as to state that early modern England had a 'culture of equity', which was reflected in contemporary literature, politics, religion, and the law.[122]

While equitable principles of justice did become increasingly formalised under the stewardship of Nottingham, there is a danger in overstating its 'modern' processes of decision-making. Even as late as 1759, there was concern that equity might endanger itself by excessive rigidity, as Lord Hardwicke stated: 'Fraud is infinite, and were a court of Equity once to lay down rules, how far they would go, and no farther, in extending their relief against it, or to define strictly the species of evidence of it, the jurisdiction would be cramped, and perpetually eluded by new schemes, which the fertility of man's invention would contrive'.[123] As Klinck concludes, beneath the rhetoric of fixed rules, 'there remain what might be considered significant elements of fluidity'.[124] Ultimately, while Nottingham attempted to make Chancery more 'law-like' through the regularisation of equity, he did not abandon conscience as the reference point of decision making. While Chancery was coming to rely upon established principles and rules, it still allowed a flexibility in administering justice according to the particular circumstances of the case.

The Chancellor's jurisdiction over bankruptcy also developed in an uncoordinated way. The 1571 act implicitly introduced the original jurisdiction, as debtors had to petition the Lord Chancellor to execute a commission of bankruptcy.[125] Technically speaking, several Chancellors oversaw multiple commissions of bankruptcy to ensure that commissioners did not abuse their power, but none reviewed their decisions until Nottingham. Put simply, this meant there was no appeal to Chancery until Nottingham. As Sir Samuel Romilly stated in the House of Commons in 1813, commissions were first intended to determine bankrupt causes without appeal, and consequently 'there was no appeal until the time of Lord Chancellor Nottingham'. Romilly went on to suggest that between the Chancellorship of Lord Nottingham and the beginning of Lord Hardwicke's tenure in 1737, there were only twenty reported cases of appeals.[126] It was not until the statute of 5 Geo 2 (1731) that the Chancellor was granted direct control over bankruptcy proceedings. Yet, this can simply be seen as a

121   Yale, *Lord Chancellor Nottingham's Chancery Cases*, vol. i., p. xlv.

122   Lee B. Wilson, *Bonds of Empire: The English Origins of Slave Law in South Carolina and British Plantation America, 1660–1783* (Cambridge, 2011), pp. 168–169.

123   Joseph Parkes, *A History of the Court of Chancery* (London, 1828), p. 508.

124   Dennis Klinck, 'Lord Nottingham's "Certain Measures"', *LHR*, 28 (2010), pp. 711–748, p. 714.

125   13 Elizabeth I c.7 (1571).

126   Sir Samuel Romilly, quoted in Yale, *Lord Chancellor Nottingham's Chancery Cases*, vol. i, p. cxv.

means of the law catching up with the reality of the situation in Chancery, as Nottingham had effectively established this direct control himself.[127]

In 1815, Henry Maddock succinctly outlined the Chancellor's jurisdiction in bankruptcy, which was:

> of the utmost importance, and was subject to no Appeal. It was in the first instance *ministerial*, and so far original. It was secondarily, *appellate*; but the original and appellate Jurisdiction were frequently blended in exercise. The issuing of Commissions of Bankruptcy, and all the questions arising upon the Issue, were matters of original Jurisdiction.[128]

From its statutory creation during the sixteenth century, the Lord Chancellor assigned commissioners allowing the Chancellor to execute the bankruptcy laws via a commission of bankruptcy.[129] Commissions were appointed on a case-by-case basis to examine the specificities of that particular failure, demonstrating an individuality about bankruptcy proceedings.[130] As Maddock continues, commissioners were entrusted with investigating all issues pertaining to bankruptcy, and as such, 'the whole business of a Bankruptcy might have been transacted without further application to the Chancellor'. This meant that if the process went smoothly, then the only further application to the Chancellor would have been to grant a certificate of conformity to the bankrupt to receive his discharge. However, as Maddock further outlines:

> all the proceedings of the Commissioners were liable to revision by the Chancellor, and so far his Jurisdiction in Bankruptcy was appellate. His control was also continual over the Commission itself, and over the conduct of the Commissioners in its execution, as well as over their judicial Decisions. In all cases his Jurisdiction was exercised summarily.[131]

When discussing the development of this specific jurisdiction, Maddock could not specify how or when the Chancellor's authority came into being:

> It is a matter now only of curious inquiry, in what manner the Chancellor acquired what was termed his *appellate* Jurisdiction in Bankruptcy. No Statute directly confers it. An able Writer considers the Authority exercised

---

127   5 Geo 2 c.30 (1731); Ibid., vol. 1, p. cxiv.
128   Henry Maddock, *A Treatise on the Principles and Practice of the Court of Chancery*, 3rd edn (London, 1837), vol. 2, pp. 785–786.
129   Ibid., vol. 2, pp. 785–786.
130   See Jérôme Sgard, 'Bankruptcy, Fresh Start and Debt Renegotiation in England and France (17th to 18th Century)', in Safley (ed.), *The History of Bankruptcy*, pp. 223–235.
131   Maddock, *A Treatise on the Principles and Practice of the Court of Chancery*, vol. 2, pp. 785–786.

by him, under this appellate Jurisdiction, as *recommendatory* only, and not binding on the Commissioners, but that the Chancellor by means of his power of displacing Commissioners was thus enabled to enforce his recommendations.[132]

As William Jones has stated, by the middle of the seventeenth century it came to be understood that the Lord Chancellor 'could not refuse a petition for issue of a commission'.[133] This was further clarified in 1677, as Nottingham declared that a Chancellor could not deny the granting of a commission of bankruptcy, but he could enact the power to 'supersede' a commission 'if they proceed indiscreetly'. In this instance a new commission of 'wiser men' could handle the remaining business.[134]

During the Chancellorship of Nottingham, the court of Chancery could not only oversee the commission, but for the first time was also able to hear appeals from parties in the process and overrule the assigned commissioners. This development in jurisdiction has significant ramifications for a study of bankruptcy in the court. First, all of the cases in my sample had either been initiated while a commission of bankruptcy was ongoing or had been executed after at least one individual had been declared a bankrupt by the commission. Secondly, Holdsworth has stated that prior to the Chancellorship of Nottingham, if commissioners encountered any 'legal difficulties', they usually applied to the common law courts, while Yale has suggested that when commissioners were in doubt upon a decision, they 'seem to have consulted the judges extra-judicially'.[135] Obviously, this informal approach would have left no available record to the modern historian. Holdsworth believed that no instance of a bankruptcy application to the Chancellor existed until 1676, when applications began to become more frequent.[136] While subsequent cataloguing of the records has shown that bankruptcy suits can be dated to 1674, there seem to be few, if any, applications to the Lord Chancellor before this period. To clarify the frequencies of bankruptcy during this period, Jones has estimated that the annual number of bankruptcies between 1642 and 1649 stood at twenty-five per year, rising to only thirty-one in 1653 and forty-one in 1654.[137] The establishment of Chancery as an appellate court for bankruptcy, coupled with the

132 Ibid., pp. 785–786; the 'able writer' to which Maddock refers is Edward Christian, *The Origin, Progress, and Present Practice of the Bankrupt Law, Both in England and Ireland* (London, 1818).

133 Jones, 'The Foundations of English Bankruptcy', p. 10.

134 Heneage Finch, Earl of Nottingham, *Manual of Chancery Practice, and Prolegomena of Chancery and Equity*, D. E. C. Yale (ed.) (Cambridge, 1965), pp. 161–165.

135 Holdsworth, *A History of English Law*, vol. 1, p. 470; Yale, *Lord Chancellor Nottingham's Chancery Cases*, vol. 1, cxv.

136 Holdsworth, *A History of English Law*, vol. 1, p. 470.

137 Jones, 'The Foundations of English Bankruptcy', p. 5.

formalisation of equity as a juristic principle under Lord Nottingham, has provided a chronological starting point for an investigation of bankruptcy proceedings within the court of Chancery.

Conclusion

This chapter has provided an overview of the development of the equitable jurisdiction of Chancery and the procedural elements of the court in order to establish a conceptual and methodological framework for the analysis of financial and personal failure which follows. During this period, Chancery emerged as the sole appellate jurisdiction for bankruptcy, and it is crucial to have a firm understanding of the way in which individuals involved in cases sought to construct their arguments to conform to the legal requirements of an equitable jurisdiction. Private individuals worked alongside officers of the court in a growing and established bureaucracy to create a range of written documents which have survived. In order to put forward a compelling argument relating to economic and personal failure, I argue that scholars must provide background and context to the jurisdiction under discussion, the type of document being used, and the stage of proceeding from which these sources have been taken. As each stage of proceeding required a different ordering of language, each subsequent chapter reveals a slightly different angle on the complex and multifaceted nature of bankruptcy cases as they progressed within the court. While such a methodology provides the groundwork for the analysis which follows, it also has wider ramifications for the use and classification of legal documents by historians, both within and outside Chancery.

2

Disparity Between Legal Theory and Practice

Margrit Schulte Beerbühl has suggested that due to the penalising character of the law, bankruptcy 'was something to be avoided at nearly any price ... conflict reduction and prevention for the benefit of good governance have been the guiding principles throughout the centuries'.[1] This statement is certainly oversimplifying attitudes to early modern bankruptcy, especially as after 1706 the discharge provision provided certain incentives to debtors. However, Beerbühl does promulgate the need for researchers to 'not only study the provisions of the bankruptcy laws, but look at the practice of handling failures by the parties concerned'.[2] This chapter undertakes such an approach by analysing pleadings – bills of complaint and their subsequent answers – found at the first stage of proceeding. In doing so, the chapter assesses the reasons why individuals initiated a suit in Chancery and sought the assistance of the court in the ongoing debt-recovery process. Because bills of complaint needed to show that the suit fell within the equitable jurisdiction of the court – and the defendants had somehow acted against conscience – pleadings provide a clear, chronological description of the path that the commission of bankruptcy had taken, and the specific details of how this procedure had failed. Rather than approaching pleadings as containing strategic and convincing storytelling which can inform us about norms and values of the period, this chapter will focus on the specific details provided to us in the documents that survive. Undertaking such an approach will demonstrate that there were clear disparities between the legal ideals established in the statutes and contemporary commentary and the practical realities of bankruptcy procedure.

In any legal or bureaucratic system there are bound to be disparities between the idealised procedure and the practical realities of day-to-day experience. As Lee B. Wilson has shown, early modern law was far more flexible than an emphasis on statutory law suggests. Many legal transactions occurred outside of courts of law and involved significant divergencies in

---

1 Beerbühl, 'Introduction', p. 14.
2 Ibid., p. 13.

practice and procedure.[3] In this manner, pleadings reveal specificities about the problems and issues which arose as this process was underway. Analysing pleadings in isolation not only allows a greater quantity of cases to be utilised, but also enables a fuller discussion of how failure reveals itself at this stage of a proceeding.

The chapter is divided into three sections. The first section pays close attention to the composition of bills of complaint and how these documents were created and utilised by individuals seeking redress from the court. Specific attention is paid to how a range of scholars have approached and used these sources in their research. The second section analyses cases where individuals were involved in international trade and had dealings 'beyond the sea'. While cases involving international trade are fairly extreme examples – as the goods, estate, and very often the bankrupt were overseas – they demonstrate the frustration and inability of those involved in a commission of bankruptcy to bring the process to a conclusion. By analysing these suits in comparison to legal ideals, we can begin to extract the 'fault lines' of bankruptcy procedure and establish how and why individuals sought the overarching authority of the court of Chancery.

The final section analyses three disparities between legal ideals and day-to-day experience in greater detail. First, while the discharge provision formally entered the statute books in 1706, forgiving a portion of debt and returning some of the estate to the bankrupt was happening in an informal manner prior to this date. As such, the 1706 statute will be examined in two ways: as a means of the law catching up with the realities of the bankruptcy process, and as the law altering the practicality of procedure. Secondly, despite bankruptcy procedure placing all creditors on an equal footing and providing greater authority and certainty, creditors still exhibited a genuine concern that they would receive less than another party in the process. Numerous individuals were accused of manipulating the legal process for their own benefit and to the detriment of others. Finally, from the total of 228 cases utilised in this chapter, there are twelve examples where a bankrupt appears as a plaintiff, and in four of these cases the bankrupt took direct aim at the work of the commission itself. These suits are illuminating, as they demonstrate ongoing debates between the work of the commissioners and the assignees on the one hand, and the individual most directly affected by the process on the other. Such debates problematise the notion of delegated conscience and failure within the court. If the plaintiff is a bankrupt – who had failed in an economic and moral sense – then what right did they have to demand an appraisal of other actors within this process?

3   Wilson, *Bonds of Empire*, pp. 1–8.

Analysing these complex cases will provide new insights into the role of equity, conscience, and failure in wider society.

The Creation of Bills of Complaint

The procedural rules of common law – through the purchase of a writ in Latin – ensured that the case was confined to a single issue, narrowly defined, in order to initiate a particular type of action. In Chancery, a complainant did not have to specify their form of action, instead submitting a bill of complaint in non-technical language, outlining their situation and asking for relief in general terms.[4] Chancery cases were often interconnected in terms of subject matter, which has led to difficulties in the modern cataloguing of these documents.[5] Cases involving bankruptcy can be placed within a crude spectrum concerning the level of involvement of bankruptcy in each individual suit. At one end of the spectrum are cases such as *Browne v Bamforth* (1696), whereby bankruptcy was the central issue to be litigated, as the entirety of the suit concerned the size of the bankrupt's estate that had come into the defendant's possession. At the other end of the spectrum are cases such as *Charitable Corporation v Chase* (1735), which named at least twenty-five defendants, only four of whom were assignees of two bankrupts.[6]

Charitable Corporation v Chase was initiated in Chancery in 1735 as part of several ongoing and extended legal battles, after a massive fraud within the company had been discovered. Through an ongoing scheme of embezzlement by their previous management, the plaintiffs estimated their losses to be over £400,000. A commission of bankruptcy was taken out against two former employees, George Robinson and John Thomson, and while they absconded abroad and did not appear as defendants in the suit, four of their surviving assignees were named as defendants.[7] The central issue of a case involving such a large corporation and such a monumental fraud was clearly related to issues outside of the bankruptcy process. Only two of the nineteen answers were from the assignees. Yet, even within these circumstances, we can still begin to see how bankruptcy intersects with such issues. William Wilkinson, the surviving assignee of Thomson, promised to satisfy the claims of all creditors who 'come in and seek relief under the said Commission'. Wilkinson stated

4 Henry Horwitz, *Exchequer Equity Records and Proceedings, 1649–1841* (Kew, 2001), p. 10.
5 For a discussion surrounding the issues of cataloguing cases according to type of suit, see Clayton, 'The Wealth of Riches to be Found in the Court of Chancery', p.27.
6 TNA, C11/521/10, 'Charitable Corporation v Chase' (1735).
7 Ibid., Bill of Complaint.

that once the plaintiffs had proven their debts within the commission, he would be ready and willing to 'satisfy the same out of the said Thomsons Estate ... in proportion with his other Debts in such manner as this Honourable Court shall Direct'.[8] The assignees of Robinson similarly agreed to satisfy the debts of the complainants, contingent on them paying their contribution money and entering the commission. From supplementary material, Peter Brealey has suggested that out of a potential estate of several tens of thousands of pounds, the assignees were only expecting to recoup a few hundred.[9] The case demonstrates how the plaintiffs would have had to seek their debts in accordance with the correct procedure outlined within a commission of bankruptcy. Even with cases whereby bankruptcy only appears to be part of a wider dispute, we can still see how bankruptcy procedure intersects with issues surrounding early modern society and the economy.

Many Chancery bills asked for relief from the consequences of the technicalities of common law procedure. As William Jones states, this 'tradition of flexibility' held a real basis in fact and was not to fade even after the Chancellorship of Nottingham.[10] In *Ray v Thornbury* (1725), the plaintiffs – Walter Ray a grocer and William Scott a saddler – were assignees of Nathaniel Carpenter, all of whom resided in London. The plaintiffs claimed that the bankrupt had debts of over £10,000 and 'haveing had Great Losses and misfortunes in the world the said Nathaniel Carpenter failed and became a Bankrupt'. Having several dealings in the West Indies and other 'foreign parts', the bill meticulously worked through numerous debts due to Carpenter, as the assignees sought to identify and recoup the money and goods owed to the bankrupt. The bill stated that Carpenter represented himself to his creditors in a positive light, and that he had been 'looked upon and Esteemed as haveing very Great Effects in the West Indies and very great sumes of mony due to him'. As such, the plaintiffs, 'were induced by Reason thereof to give the said Nathaniel Carpenter very large Credit in the way of Trade and to advance and lend to the said Nathaniel Carpenter such Credit'. Several debtors were 'takeing advantage that they Resideing in foreign parts and that your Orators cannot bring any actions at Common law against them for recovery thereof'.[11] While the issues surrounding international trade are discussed in greater detail below, this case demonstrates that the plaintiffs initiated a suit in Chancery because they could not seek a resolution through the common law courts. Henry Horwitz has suggested that the development of Chancery procedure can be seen as 'ample testimony to the Court's commitment to investigate thoroughly each complaint brought before

8   Ibid., Answer of William Wilkinson.
9   Brealey, 'The Charitable Corporation for the Relief of Industrious Poor', pp. 708–729.
10   W. J. Jones, *The Elizabethan Court of Chancery* (Oxford, 1967), p. 195.
11   TNA, C11/1451/21 Ray v Thornbury (1725), Bill of Complaint.

it'.[12] However, in contrast to depositions – discussed in detail in chapter four – very little scholarship has focused on the process of composing and creating bills of complaint in Chancery.

One notable exception is the work of Timothy Haskett, who argues that despite the less formal procedure in Chancery in comparison to the purchase of a common law writ, the court 'did not offer an opportunity for success upon slipshod or uniformed petitions: bills could and did fail'. Just as a common law suit would be unsuccessful if the incorrect writ was purchased, so too would a Chancery case fail if the bill submitted was faulty in substance or form.[13] Medieval Chancery bills displayed a distinct canon of form – which Haskett divides into eleven sections – and 'composers, scribes and assessors worked hard to ensure correctness', in order to increase their chances of success.[14] John Fisher has suggested a good hand and proper use of legal language was still the 'monopoly of a small body of professionals' during the fifteenth century, likely to have been educated in Chancery tradition.[15] However, in order to account for the sheer scale of Chancery bills being presented to the court, Haskett argues that the knowledge of this 'core group' had to have been disseminated – through training and by example – to a larger number of individuals outside of Westminster.

Such a transfer of knowledge was conducted at an increasing pace over the course of the fourteenth and fifteenth centuries. This change is indicated by the maintenance in the bill of a 'canon of form, though with variable style, and in their partial use of elements of the emerging Chancery English'.[16] Rather than constricting the composers of Chancery bills, Haskett claims that the increasing formalisation actually enabled a greater scope of expression, as 'once the requirements of the form are realised the writer can exploit fully the opportunities that come into existence through the act of formalisation'.[17] Ultimately, medieval Chancery bills allowed a wide range of expression, clearly explaining

---

12   Henry Horwitz, *A Guide to Chancery Equity Records and Proceedings 1600–1800* (Kew, 1995), p. 3.

13   Timothy S. Haskett, 'The Judicial Role of the English Chancery in Late-Medieval Law and Literacy', in Kouky Fianu and DeLloyd J. Guth (eds), *Écrit et Pouvoir dans les Chancelleries Médiévales: Espace Français, Espace Anglais* (Louvain-La-Neuve, 1997), pp. 313–332.

14   Ibid., p. 323; see also Haskett, 'The Presentation of Cases in Medieval Chancery Bills', pp. 11–28.

15   John F. Fisher, 'Chancery and the Emergence of Standard Written English in the Fifteenth Century', *Speculum: A Journal of Medieval Studies*, 52 (1977), pp. 870–899, p. 896.

16   Timothy S. Haskett, 'Country Lawyers? The Composers of English Chancery Bills', in Peter Birks (ed.), *The Life of the Law: Proceedings of the Tenth British Legal History Conference, Oxford 1991* (London, 1993), p. 19.

17   Haskett, 'The Judicial Role of the English Chancery in Late-Medieval Law and Literacy', p. 329.

how an individual, or set of individuals, had become involved in a particular situation, as well as the specific redress they sought from the court. It is crucial to understand the construction, formulation, and rules by which bills needed to be written and presented to court in order to analyse the written words and phrases in the documents that survive. Without this background knowledge, it is easy to take such formulations and stock phrases out of context.

While no similar in-depth analysis of Chancery bills exists for the early modern period, it is commonplace that the court saw a dramatic increase in lawyers at every stage of proceeding. Pleadings were drafted with the aid and advice of a legal expert and as far as the court was concerned, these advisers were nearly as responsible for the content of bills of complaint as the litigants. Bills were not valid unless signed by counsel or an attorney, a requirement which Jones has dated to the Chancellorship of Thomas More, demonstrating a 'long established indication of responsibility' on the part of legal experts. This insistence can be seen as an attempt to eliminate frivolous and impermissible pleadings. Not only were bills frequently dismissed for lack of signatures, but it was also not uncommon for a legal adviser to refuse to sign a bill for fear of punishment from the court. According to Jones, this led to some plaintiffs forging the signature of counsel or simply putting their own signature, in the hope that the court would not notice and allow the suit to continue.[18] Such an increase in the use of legal experts led almost naturally to an increased complexity of the correct manner of submitting bills of complaint. As the solicitor Samuel Turner warned in 1795:

> The Bill may be drawn by the Solicitor; but, as great care and attention is generally required in the framing of a Bill, it is adviseable for the Solicitor to lay proper instructions before his Counsel, who will draw and sign a Draught of it. This saves a great deal of trouble; for, although the Solicitor may have an extensive knowledge of the theory as well as the practice of his profession, yet, if the Bill which he has drawn should be planned improperly, the Counsel will experience equal difficulty in altering and settling, as in drawing the Bill from the beginning.[19]

Witnesses could only be questioned on a matter already specified in either the bill or answer, so careful thought went into their creation. As *The Country-Man's Counsellour* (1682) outlined:

> The proceedings are here by English bill, wherein the complainant setteth forth his grievance making use of what suggestions his counsel thinks fit to

---

18   Jones, *The Elizabethan Court of Chancery*, pp. 192–193.
19   Samuel Turner, *Costs and Present Practice of the Court of Chancery* (London, 1795), p. 48.

pump and winnow out the truth from his Adversary; who is bound to answer thereunto strictly in all points upon his Oath, and if he boggle or refuse so to do, must pay cost for insufficient answers.[20]

From the outset of a suit, the parties had to consider what answers they hoped to elicit or suppress, meaning bills and answers took an elaborate form.[21] Indeed, there is ample evidence of the court's disdain for over-lengthy pleadings.[22] To use but one example, in 1621 the prominent Jacobean barrister and Member of Parliament, Sir John Moore, advised the incoming Lord Chancellor, Bishop John Williams, that 'if men do put in answers or bills of extraordinary length above XV sheets the bill and XX sheets the answer, his Lordship mindeth to punish the parties with good costs'.[23] However, J. H. Baker has categorised the documents created in most suits as 'elephantine', as by the eighteenth century Chancery pleadings had become 'verbose and complex'.[24] It is certainly true that several Chancery bills seem unnecessarily long-winded and repetitive. In one suit taken from my sample, the defendants submitted a demurrer as the plaintiff's original bill included over sixty defendants, running 'above ninety sheets of paper' in length, in which the charges had 'no manner of Relation' to one another.[25]

While the increased activity of legal experts in the composition of bills is unquestioned during this period, there was still an emphasis placed on the importance of the plaintiff being directly involved in the process. Penelope Tucker has demonstrated how as early as the late fourteenth century, Chancery was accepting bills 'which were sometimes composed and perhaps even written by the plaintiff himself'.[26] Christine Churches has shown how Sir James Lowther – a prominent landowner, industrialist, and Whig politician – was personally involved in the most specific aspects of the legal process and out-of-court tactics relating to Chancery suits. Churches notes that it was Lowther himself 'who revised the attorney's drafts, and supplied his own notes on the

20   H. R., *The Country-Mans Counsellour*, p. 6.
21   Christine Churches, 'Business at Law: Retrieving Commercial Disputes From Eighteenth-Century Chancery', *The Historical Journal*, 43 (2000), p. 952.
22   Yale has claimed that 'vexatious and prolix pleading was a perennial difficulty to the Chancellors', Heneage Finch, *Manual of Chancery Practice*, p. 51.
23   Ibid., p. 80.
24   Jones, *The Elizabethan Court of Chancery*, p. 194; J. H. Baker, *An Introduction to English Legal History* (Oxford, 2019), p. 121.
25   TNA, C11/1194/33, 'Nicholls v Gardiner' (1720), Answer of Edward Nicholls and 67 others.
26   Penelope Tucker, 'The Early History of the Court of Chancery: A Comparative Study', *The English Historical Review*, 115 (2000), pp. 791–811, p. 791.

case for them to consider'.[27] Further down the social scale, Amy Erickson suggests that the prevalence of conveyancing manuals during the sixteenth century meant that 'even ordinary people in rural areas' managed to secure their own property transactions in Chancery with legal evidences, demonstrating the striking popular awareness of legal issues throughout England during the period.[28] Bills of complaint still exhibited a remarkable individuality of expression, which was relatively unconstrained by the procedure and jurisdiction of Chancery.

In terms of the narrative presented in pleadings, Churches states that Chancery, 'allowed (and even by its form of procedure, encouraged) a much more expansive story-telling to relate how the complainant had become embroiled in the particular dilemma'.[29] Undertaking a case study of two prominent merchants, Churches turns her attention towards dissecting a specific bill of complaint in Chancery, as within this bill:

> a series of three separate tales describe how the various defendants severally owed Thomas Lutwidge large sums of money, which more than cancelled out the amount they were suing him for at common law. Such storytelling tended to rely on a great elaboration of circumstantial detail to provide 'colour' to the plea, and could of course be used to insinuate all sorts of other misdemeanours committed by the other side, and against other parties besides the complainant.[30]

While Churches has incorporated supplementary evidence to give a fuller understanding of the business and legal dealings of the Lutwidge family, what is interesting in this account is the way in which she describes the narrative constructed within a single written document. Churches claims that while the deeper context is invisible in the bill of complaint, she uses the terms 'stories', 'tales', and 'prevarication' in order to illustrate the fictional nature of the legal claims – or facts – made by parties in a suit. However, referring to legal documents as 'stories' is not uncommon. Laura Gowing has suggested that narrative in the legal process, and justice in the church courts, depended on 'story-telling', a phrase she uses throughout her 1998 publication *Domestic Dangers: Women, Words and Sex in Early Modern London*.[31] Similarly, in a

---

27   Churches, 'Business at Law', p. 951, see also Wilfred Prest, 'Lay Legal Knowledge in Early Modern England', in Jonathan A. Bush and Alain Alexandre Wijffels (eds), *Learning the Law: Teaching and the Transmission of Law in England, 1150–1900* (London, 1999), pp. 303–313.
28   Amy Erickson, *Women and Property in Early Modern England* (London, 1993), p. 23.
29   Churches, 'Business at Law', p. 944.
30   Ibid., p. 944.
31   Laura Gowing, *Domestic Dangers: Women, Words and Sex in Early Modern London* (Oxford, 1998), esp. ch.2.

section of a chapter examining the individual agency of married women within the court of Exchequer, entitled 'Tales of the Exchequer', Margaret Hunt suggests that despite the high proportion of cases that were dropped after the initiation of a suit, 'these cases are still recognizable stories'. In this manner, the adversarial character of the court led to individuals presenting moral absolutes, meaning pleadings were 'manifestly full of lies, omissions, temporal transpositions and eccentric interpretation of events'.[32] Hunt explains that as pleadings were carefully crafted, they present a clear chronological timeline of disputed events, which were organised into a 'compelling narrative', displaying a chronologically arranged, and 'clearly recognizable beginning, middle and end'.[33] However, referring to pleadings as 'stories' seems to undermine the factual details provided, presenting the documents as simply fictitious or fanciful accounts. While other scholars are not so explicit in their descriptions, there is still a danger in treating all pleadings as simply constructed to conform to the legal process and composed to achieve a desirable outcome.

When discussing marital disputes in the late medieval court of Chancery, Sara Butler makes the obvious claim that it is difficult to know whether the victim truly experienced the level of alleged abuse, and it is 'all too possible that these bills represent a degree of fiction intended to gain a sympathetic ear'. However, Butler goes on to suggest that by telling the Chancellor about these events, the petitioner 'strongly believed' they would improve their chances of securing a judgment in their favour.[34] Pleadings can therefore take the shape of 'fictional' narratives constructed not only to reflect cultural norms and values, but also to inform historians of instances that their authors hoped would be convincing, or at least believable, to the authority of the court.[35] In relation to marriage disputes, they offer abundant insights into a world the Chancellor – and therefore wider society – was intended to find condemnable, demonstrating the accepted norms of early modern marriage.[36] Parallels can be drawn to bankruptcy proceedings, as complaints inform us of the correct path the commission was expected to take, before the practicality of its failure is revealed in greater detail. Such a breakdown can inform us of the way in which certain individuals had failed to act according to expected norms and values of the period.

---

32 Hunt, 'Wives and Marital "Rights"', pp. 112–113.

33 Ibid., p. 113.

34 Butler, 'The Law as a Weapon in Marital Disputes', pp. 291–316.

35 Natalie Zemon Davis, *Fiction in the Archives: Pardon Tales and Their Tellers in Sixteenth-Century France* (Stanford, 1987); Steve Hindle, '"Bleedinge Afreshe"? The Affray and Murder at Nantwich, 19 December 1572', in Angela McShane and Garthine Walker (eds), *The Extraordinary and the Everyday in Early Modern England: Essays in Celebration of the Work of Bernard Capp* (Basingstoke, 2010), pp. 224–245.

36 Butler, 'The Law as a Weapon in Marital Disputes', pp. 291–316.

Merridee Bailey has suggested that the mobilisation and use of narrative in Chancery bills can inform us of social, cultural, legal, political, and emotional norms of the period, and how they were used as 'a strategy of persuasiveness'.[37] Similarly, Amanda Capern has utilised Chancery pleadings to discuss the emotions that litigants brought to, experienced, and expressed about Chancery during the sixteenth and seventeenth centuries. Capern states that the link between neighbourly relations and kinship with Chancery was 'dialectical and complex'. As the court made decisions based upon the concept of fairness, it was 'embedded in collective, local consciousness as a space for the articulation of emotions in exchange for redress'.[38] Suggesting that the twinned concepts of trust and honour were invoked to encapsulate a sense of being ill-treated, Capern believes that these concepts became 'legal trope' which were 'placed centrally (in terms of persuasive location) within Chancery pleadings'.[39] In another article, Capern undertakes a case study of female litigants acting in the capacity of mothers in Chancery, analysing the way in which 'gendered tropes' – such as 'poor mother' – were utilised as maternal narratives in pleadings. As Capern states, her intention is to 'demonstrate how social and legal maternal identities were used to produce strategic storytelling by mothers and their lawyers in rhetoric that they hoped would advantage their cases'.[40] Capern utilises a range of legal formulations – 'legal trope', 'persuasive location', 'strategic storytelling', and 'linguistic construction' – to show that the statements and formulations of the parties within suits were being transformed into legal evidence.

The point to make here is that by describing pleadings as 'stories' or other such fictional formulations, it moves the focus away from the document under consideration and towards the particular historical discourse under discussion. It is not necessary to comment on the truthfulness or factual reliability of the details provided in Chancery pleadings, as we can never ascertain what really happened. But simply suggesting that pleadings can tell us about norms, values, and persuasiveness makes us too far removed from the specific details provided to us in the documents which survive. In relation to the bankruptcy process, pleadings can inform us of particular instances, and specific examples, of how a commission of bankruptcy broke down.

A few brief examples from my sample are sufficient to illustrate these points. *Bythell v Keeble* (1699) involved money owed to the bankrupt, John Grosvenor,

37　Bailey, 'Most Hevynesse and Sorowe', p. 28.
38　Amanda Capern, 'Emotions, Gender Expectations, and the Social Role of Chancery, 1550–1650', in Susan Broomhall (ed.), *Authority, Gender and Emotions in Late Medieval and Early Modern England* (Basingstoke, 2015), pp. 187–209, p. 188.
39　Ibid., p. 191.
40　Amanda Capern, 'Maternity and Justice in the Early Modern English Court of Chancery', *Journal of British Studies*, 58 (2019), pp. 701–716.

as well as an intricate network of family indebtedness. The plaintiff, William Bythell of London, suggested that at the time of becoming a bankrupt, several people were indebted to John Grosvenor, a haberdasher of hats, for money he had lent to them. For example, on 6 June 1696, Grosvenor lent £100 to Edward Keeble, who in turn assigned a bond to Grosvenor in the penal sum of £200. When the bond came due, and in fear of not receiving payment, Grosvenor had Keeble arrested to force repayment. Upon hearing this news, Richard Keeble, the father of Edward, himself became bound for his son's original debt, which allowed more time for its repayment. According to the plaintiff, John Grosvenor was unable to carry on trading or keep his shop open and was forced to abscond and conceal himself from his creditors. Fearing the ensuing commission of bankruptcy, Grosvenor directed Richard Keeble to put the bond in the name of John Jenner, who was in 'some way related to the said John Grosvenor', before finally being drawn by Robert Jenner, 'he being the said Grosvenors wifes father'.[41] The change of recipient of the bond was clear evidence to the complainant that Grosvenor was attempting to defraud his creditors and keep the debt away from the commission of bankruptcy. However, in his answer, Richard Keeble gave a dramatically different interpretation of events.

Keeble stated that on 1 December 1696, his son and Johanna Grosvenor – the wife of the bankrupt and Richard's wife's niece – came to him to ask for a loan. Having traded his stock very quickly, Edward Keeble claimed he 'had sold most part of his Goods on Trust to several good and substantial Customers', and needed to borrow £100 over the course of six months in order to 'keep up his Credit and go on with his Trade'. Johanna Grosvenor claimed that her husband would have lent Edward the money if he could get what was due to him, but failed to mention to Richard that Edward was indebted to her husband. Not having the £100 at hand, Richard suggested that if they could find someone to put out £100 at interest, he would take up the offer and give it to his son. John Jenner offered to lend £100, and so Richard therefore explained that he was legitimately bound to Jenner, and not to Grosvenor. Reflecting upon the course of events, Richard concluded that the signing of the bond was, 'a Trick to get mony of this Defendant without any design of ever paying him again'.[42]

On the surface, this seems an extremely complex case. In reality, the facts of this suit are relatively straightforward: John Jenner was in possession of a bond, which had been assigned by Richard Keeble. In common law, this would be a routine case, as the physical bond would stand as evidence of a debt due from one individual to another. In Chancery, we see the detailed descriptive narrative giving background and context to a simple dispute over a single bond. We could describe either account as 'stories' as we can never

41 TNA, C6/378/62, 'Bythell v Keeble' (1699), Bill of Complaint.
42 Ibid., Answer of Richard Keeble.

be certain as to the motivations behind the execution of the bond. There are several other formulations that may be used more appropriately – legal rhetoric, argument, or formulation – but what is clear is that both the individuality of the bankruptcy process, coupled with Chancery procedure, enabled parties within a suit to provide detailed and intricate backgrounds, presenting a chronological timeline of events to explain – albeit from opposing points of view – how they had become embroiled in such a dispute. It seems clear in *Bythell v Keeble* that the bill of complaint was submitted with the intention to discover the reason and motivation behind the issuing of the bond in an attempt to claim it as a legitimate debt within John Grosvenor's commission of bankruptcy. By focusing on the specific document, and the details contained within it, it is possible to understand how individuals within a suit dealt with particular issues and attempted to circumnavigate problems that had arisen in the process.

This approach can be directly applied to illustrate the way in which a commission of bankruptcy had broken down. Numerous examples can be used to illustrate how the ideal, linear path to debt-recovery had failed. To choose one from 1698 – *Hamersley v Vanheythuson* – the plaintiffs Thomas Hamersley and Henry Caldecott – two linen drapers from London – set out how Gerrard Lodowick – a linen draper from the parish of St Gyles in the fields, Middlesex – became indebted to them, as well as the path the commission of bankruptcy had taken. Lodowick, by 'buying and selling' in the trade of a linen draper, became indebted to the complainants and several other creditors for 'great summes of money', although the amount is not specified. Unable to pay his creditors, Lodowick absconded from his 'usual place of abode' on 26 June 1697, and thereby 'became a Bankrupt within the meaning of the several statutes made against Bankrupts'. The complainants, on behalf of themselves and the other creditors of Lodowick, petitioned the Lord Chancellor on 12 January 1697 to execute a commission of bankruptcy. The bill stated that the commissioners found Lodowick a bankrupt 'to all intents and purposes within the meaning of the severall Statutes made concerning Bankrupts', and by an indenture dated 2 February 1697 did 'bargaine sell assigne and sett over' to the complainants all the 'goods and chattels' of Lodowick. The bill then specified several household goods that had been legally assigned to the plaintiffs as assignees, but remained in the hands of the named defendant, Gerard Vanheythuson, a merchant from London.[43] The plaintiffs claimed to have informed the defendant of the ongoing commission of bankruptcy, but the defendant either denied having possession of the goods, or refused to assign them over. Ultimately, the plaintiffs were seeking a discovery of any part of the bankrupt's estate that had come into the defendant's possession, and desired the court to assign over any goods for the satisfaction of their debts.

43   TNA, C6/313/16, 'Hamersley v Vanheythuson' (1698), Bill of Complaint.

In this bill we can establish the specific timeline the commission of bankruptcy was *expected* to follow. The creditors had established a definitive debt with Lodowick through buying and selling in the linen trade, and Lodowick had unreasonably and illegally avoided and denied payment by absconding from his usual place of abode. As such, the plaintiffs took it upon themselves to petition the Lord Chancellor to execute a commission of bankruptcy to examine the circumstances surrounding Lodowick's failure. After examination, the commissioners found Lodowick to have been a bankrupt in the true intent and meaning of the statutes, and so assigned his estate over to the plaintiffs as named assignees. It is at this point that the linear timeline breaks, as the assignees accused the defendant of denying them access to Lodowick's estate. However, in his answer, the defendant suggested that the bankrupt owed his uncle, also Gerard Vanheythuson, £150 17s 11d. His uncle had since died and, upon proving his will, the defendant, as executor of the will and for further personal debts due from the bankrupt to himself, had received a warrant of attorney from the court of King's Bench. With the aid of the local sheriff, the defendant secured the bankrupt's goods on 28 June 1697.[44] Within this case, we can clearly see that there are several overlapping and competing claims on a single estate. The defendant had successfully used an alternative path – the common law court of King's Bench – to satisfy the debts due to his family's estate. Having achieved this two days after the initial act of bankruptcy, we could surmise that those within the bankrupt's trading circle were well aware of his financial situation and sought to recover their debts via alternative means.

The bankruptcy process appears to have gone smoothly until the assignees sought to gain access to the bankrupt's estate in order to make sufficient dividends. The complainants had initiated the suit solely for the purpose of identifying and discovering which goods belonging to the bankrupt were in the possession of the defendant. They were seeking a judgment from the Lord Chancellor to force the defendant to hand over such goods and repair the bankruptcy procedure. Such an order from the court would complete the linear recovery process, and the plaintiffs, along with other creditors of the bankrupt, would receive a proportional satisfaction of their just debts. However, when the defendant answered the bill with what appeared to be a legitimate alternative claim on the goods, we begin to see how larger issues surrounding credit, debt recovery, and the wider economy intersect with bankruptcy. These interconnected issues complicate our understanding of failure, which itself becomes a multifaceted concept.

Discussing early modern marriage disputes, Margaret Hunt has suggested that the cases which came before the court were not representative of 'normal' marriage during eighteenth-century England. However, through their careful

44 Ibid., Answer of Gerard Vanheythuson.

examination, the modern historian can reveal the 'fault lines' which were central to many more marriages than the ones that ended up in court, demonstrating the manner in which marriage 'should' operate, and the ways in which women defended such ideals in court.[45] Writing in 1941, the legal anthropologists Karl N. Llewetjtren and E. Adamson Hoebel suggested that situations in which a system breaks down often yield the most interesting information about the nature of that system.[46] A similar approach can be taken to Chancery pleadings. As we have already seen, these suits are not representative of bankruptcy procedure, as the vast majority would have been concluded outside of the scope of the court. As such, these suits are exceptional as the very initiation of a bill of complaint demonstrates that at some point within the process an individual engaged in a commission of bankruptcy had sought redress from the court. However, by analysing these suits in comparison to legal ideals, we can begin to extract the 'fault lines' of the bankruptcy process and establish the specific disparities between these ideals and day-to-day experience.

Bankrupts 'Beyond the Sea'

There is an established scholarship on international networks of trade within the early modern British Atlantic.[47] Lee B. Wilson has shown how English custom relating to merchants and trade set the foundations for the establishment of a law of slavery in British Plantation America.[48] Similarly, a burgeoning literature is now providing a more nuanced understanding of cross-cultural trade and the ways in which merchants navigated geopolitical, linguistic, and religious boundaries in an attempt to decrease risk and encourage economic cooperation.[49] For example, the importance of the family – and in particular the role of women – has been reintegrated into the history of Atlantic business

45 Hunt, 'Wives and Marital "Rights"', pp. 107–129.
46 Karl N. Llewetjtren and E. Adamson Hoebel, *The Cheyenne Way: Conflict and Case Law in Primitive Jurisprudence* (Norman, 1941).
47 John J. McCusker and Kenneth Morgan (eds), *The Early Modern Atlantic Economy* (Cambridge, 2000); Trivellato, *The Familiarity of Strangers*; Jones and Talbott, 'Sole Traders?', pp. 1–30; Hamilton, 'Local Connections, Global Ambitions', pp. 283–300; Haggerty, '"You Promise Well and Perform as Badly"', pp. 267–282.
48 Lee B. Wilson, *Bonds of Empire: The English Origins of Slave Law in South Carolina and British Plantation America, 1660–1783* (Cambridge, 2011), pp. 1–8.
49 Marsha Hamilton, 'Commerce around the Edges: Atlantic Trade Networks among Boston's Scottish Merchants', *International Journal of Maritime History*, 23 (2011), pp. 301–326; Albane Forestier, 'Risk, Kinship and Personal Relationships in Late Eighteenth-Century West Indian Trade: The Commercial Network of Tobin & Pinney', *Business History*, 52 (2010), pp. 912–931; Haggerty, 'You Promise Well', pp. 267–282; Hancock, 'The Trouble with Networks', pp. 467–491.

networks.[50] Here, I use cases involving international trade to demonstrate the numerous ways in which a commission of bankruptcy broke down and came to be litigated in Chancery. With goods, estate, finance, and people crossing national boundaries, assignees, creditors, and those involved in a commission found it exceptionally difficult to identify and recoup credit and debts relating to a single bankruptcy.

Knowledge of individuals amassing goods on credit and absconding overseas was well known during the period. In 1705, two cloth merchants from London, Thomas Brerewood and Thomas Pitkin, enacted a spectacular fraud, whereby Pitkin absconded with £50,000 worth of goods before being apprehended in Holland. Known as 'the Pitkin Affair', the fraud engulfed several prominent members of English high society and led to acts of parliament being passed in an attempt to prevent it from happening in the future.[51] Similar accusations of outright fraud can be found in my sample. In *Coleman v Burridge* (1730), the three plaintiffs – William Coleman a merchant, Henry Marshall a grocer, and Thomas Corbett a sugar refiner – were the assignees of George Cressenger, a grocer, all of whom resided in London. The bill of complaint was submitted on 26 March 1730 and named the bankrupt and his wife alongside seven other defendants. The bill claimed that for several years before his bankruptcy, Cressenger 'carried on and Experienced the Trade or Business of a Wholesale grocer within the City of London … and was reputed to be in very Wealthy and Affluent Circumstances'. As such, George Cressenger 'did take upon Credit and buy of your Orators and divers other Persons divers Large Quantities of Goods Wares and Merchandizes to a very great value which he promise faithfully to pay for in a Short time'. In September 1727, Cressenger owed over £55,000, and:

> intending to make a very unfair use of the monys he had got into his hands and had raised by and out of the Produce of the Goods and Merchandizes which your orators and others had furnished and sold to him upon Credit and designing to convert the same to his own use without making due satisfaction to your Orators and his other Creditors for the same … with the assistance of the said Mary his wife before he quitted this Kingdom privately sent away and remit divers large sums part of the said monys to some persons unknown to your Orators in Trust for him in Foreign parts.

50   W. R. Lee and Pat Hudson (eds), *Women's Work and the Family Economy in Historical Perspective* (Manchester, 1990); Amy Erickson, 'Married Women's Occupations in Eighteenth-Century London', *Continuity and Change*, 23 (2008), pp. 267–307; Amanda Capern, Briony McDonagh and Jennifer Aston (eds), *Women and the Land 1500–1900* (Woodbridge, 2019); Jones and Talbott, 'Sole Traders?', pp. 1–30; Collins, 'The Interconnected Nature of Family Indebtedness', pp. 1–27.
51   Kadens, 'The Pitkin Affair', pp. 483–570.

On 13 September 1727, Cressenger did:

> secretly and Clandestinely … withdraw himself from the usual Place of his Habitation and carry away divers other large sums … and several very considerable Quantities of his most Valuable Effects along with him into France or Italy or some other Foreign Parts out of his Majesties Dominions and has continued there with the same in Fraud and prejudice of your Orators and other his just Creditors and has never since returned to the Place of his said Former Habitation.[52]

This case aligns with the notorious example of Thomas Pitkin. Notably, that Cressenger presented himself as a wealthy and prosperous individual, amassed substantial goods on credit, and then absconded overseas and out of reach of his creditors.

Similarly, in *Lawton v Hesketh* (1740), the plaintiff-creditors stated that on 18 September 1738, the bankrupt Francis Bissart, a merchant from London, 'failed and absconded from his Creditors and withdrew himselfe with his said wife and Family out of England into parts beyond the seas unknown to your orators where he and his said wife still remain'. The creditors took out a commission of bankruptcy the next day and received an indenture of the bankrupt's goods on 11 October 1738. Somewhat unsurprisingly, they were still seeking to identify and recover the bankrupt's estate in 1740.[53] In these cases, we see examples of the bankrupt and his family absconding and moving out of the reach of the commission, who found it extremely difficult to identify and reclaim the estate. The location of the bankrupt is a complete mystery, and the narrative is presented as a straightforward accusation of fraud. However, in other cases, we see the narrative of fraud presented in a more complex way.

On 4 July 1720, three assignees of John Smith, a saddler from London, submitted their bill of complaint and named the bankrupt alongside Joseph Chamberlain, George Walker – alias George Vaughan – and Edward Blakeway. They accused Walker of 'pretending to be arrested in an action of debt for twenty pounds or some such sume … at the suite of one Edward Blakeway'. Chamberlain explained that he had some 'extraordinary business' with Walker and took Smith to a public house in Fenchurch Street, whereby Walker 'very earnestly and pressingly persuaded the said Smith to be bayl' for him. The plaintiffs explained that Smith was an 'ignorant man and wholly unacquainted with those things and not knowing the dangerous consequences of being bayl'. After Smith and Chamberlain stood bail, Walker 'absconded and had left his place and fled from his bayl', leaving his job as a coachman in London. Walker 'went into Wales or Ireland and could never afterwards be heard of or spoke

---

52 TNA, C11/1318/33, 'Coleman v Burridge' (1730), Bill of Complaint.
53 TNA, C11/1829/16, 'Lawton v Hesketh' (1740), Bill of Complaint.

with'. The plaintiffs claimed that Chamberlain, Blakeway, and Walker had all confederated against Smith in order to recover the penalty of £40. The bill concluded that in March 1720 Smith was 'ruined and undone and failed in the world' and a commission of bankruptcy was taken out against him.[54] Here, the bankrupt appears as a gullible pawn, having stood bail for an untrustworthy individual. Indeed, it is not the bankrupt who absconded but Walker who had fled his bail, further highlighting the complex and interconnected nature of bankruptcy procedure. Rather than attempting to identify the whereabouts of Walker, the plaintiffs simply wanted Chamberlain to pay his share of the defaulted bail for the benefit of the commission of bankruptcy.

In contrast, other cases highlight a much broader range of issues relating to debt recovery. The surviving assignees of William Meddon submitted two bills of complaint in 1715. They explained that Meddon had been declared a bankrupt three years earlier and was a master or commander of a ship called the 'William and Sarah', in Bideford, Devon. Meddon had travelled from Newfoundland to Waterford, and the plaintiffs sought the recovery of £215 2s 5d worth of goods that had been shipped to Ireland. While the assignees sought the return of the goods so that they could sell them for the benefit of the creditors, they complained that the goods had already been sold after Meddon had been declared a bankrupt. Because of the movement of the ship and the international nature of trade, the plaintiffs stated that they were not informed of the sale, and named four defendants who had combined and confederated to keep the money hidden from the commission.[55] In response, two of the four defendants, Thomas Knowles and William Pawley, stated that they were examined by commissioners on 9 May 1713, who were satisfied by their responses and declared that they had acted legally.[56]

In 1735, William Wilkinson, the surviving assignee of John Thomson, submitted a bill whereby he stated that between 1726 and 1727, he 'dealt very considerably in several sorts and kinds of Merchandize to several places beyond the sea'. This included sending 'several kinds of Goods of a considerable value to St Petersburgh to John Napier'. The bill specified that in 1729 the assignment of goods totalled £2210 9s 6d, and Wilkinson accused one defendant, George Cruikshank, of taking several jewels to St Petersburg to be sold 'to the Risque of the said John Thomson'. Wilkinson listed numerous 'Goods and effects [which] arrived safe at St Petersburgh' and were sold for the benefit of Cruikshank and Thomson. On 18 October 1731, Thomson was declared a bankrupt. Since that time, Wilkinson was unable to establish a definitive account and only had rough estimates for the quantity of trade between the two individuals. He questioned

---

54 TNA, C11/36/30, 'Olds v Chamberlin' (1720), Bill of Complaint.
55 TNA, C11/1166/26, 'Darracott v Knowles' (1715), Bill of Complaint.
56 Ibid., Answer of Thomas Knowles and William Pawley.

the legitimacy of several bills of exchange and demanded that Cruikshank submit an answer detailing his dealings with Thomson before his bankruptcy.[57]

A similar case can be seen in *Robles v Wilkinson* (1740). The two plaintiffs – Isaac Robles, a jeweller of Aldgate, London and John Le Roux, a watchmaker of Covent Garden – were assignees of Joseph Dubois, a jeweller from Middlesex. The plaintiffs named the bankrupt, Pinckney Wilkinson, and a Master Southern as defendants. The plaintiffs suggested that they sent goods to be sold in Lisbon, but the three defendants had not paid for the goods upon receipt of them. The assignees demanded their payment or the return of the goods.[58] In *Clarke v Savage* (1720), the surviving assignee of John Kelly, a merchant from London, named the bankrupt and Charles Savage as defendants. The bill stated that Kelly, 'being a Merchant by Trade and having for severall years in Good Credit and Reputation Operating in the Kingdom of Portugal did during his Continuance there' communicate with several other merchants in London. Savage sent numerous orders throughout 1719 for 'great Quantities of red Wines and White Wines'. The bill accused Savage of sending orders from Portsmouth docks for the bankrupt to buy 100 pipes of wine in Portugal. The plaintiffs claimed that these were extravagantly expensive, and they asked for their return from Portugal for the benefit of the commission.[59] In his answer, Savage simply said that while he did order the wine, the bankrupt had not paid for it and he was a legitimate creditor of Kelly.[60]

In *Metcalfe v Letchmere* (1720), the assignees of Francis Collins, a merchant from London, submitted their bill in Michaelmas term 1720, and named Thomas Lechmere and John Mico as defendants. The bill claimed that Collins traded frequently to New England, 'buying divers masts for ships Oares Pipe Staves and other Goods and Comodities' from the two defendants and co-partners, who lived in Boston. The assignees valued these transactions at over £4000 and demanded 'an Account and Satisfaction from the said John Mico and Thomas Lechmere of and for the Estate and Effects of the said Francis Collins that at the time of his becomeing a Bankrupt were remaining in their Hands'. A commission of bankruptcy was taken out on 13 August 1711, and Collins was declared a bankrupt on 5 November 1711. The plaintiffs claimed that the defendants were debtors to Collins and had £3785 3s 8d, and four farthings worth of his goods in their possession. However, being 'strangers in these Parts' they could not secure possession of the goods for them to be sold for the

57 TNA, C11/2445/40, 'Wilkinson v Cruckshank' (1735), Bill of Complaint. While this appears to be the same William Wilkinson and John Thomson who are named in Charitable Corporation v Chase (1735), this is a separate suit and highlights how individuals could be involved in numerous cases in Chancery. The same individuals are discussed in chapter five.

58 TNA, C11/2293/24, 'Robles v Wilkinson' (1740), Bill of Complaint.

59 TNA, C11/1710/1, 'Clarke v Savage' (1720), Bill of Complaint.

60 Ibid., Answer of Charles Savage.

benefit of the commission. As such, they proposed to give Richard Lechmere, a merchant from London, 'some abatement in the Price' of the goods and, 'take less then the same were valued' if he could get the goods to London. However, the assignees never got custody of the goods and submitted a bill in Chancery for the discovery of their whereabouts.[61]

While scholars such as Sheryllynne Haggerty, Siobhan Talbott, Albane Forestier, and Douglas Hamilton have undertaken a qualitative analysis of private papers – such as account books, letter books, and correspondence – to gain a greater understanding of the motivations and actions of individuals involved in international trade, official court records reveal a different narrative.[62] The failure of these networks led to an inability to effectively calculate credit, debt, and even the quantity and price of specified goods. Assignees were very often simply the largest creditors, working on behalf of all creditors who came in and paid contribution money. As such, they only had a part of the picture and limited access to books, paper writing, and witnesses, leading to a lack of information regarding the overall trading activities of those involved in a single failure. The inability to access pertinent information led to numerous suits being initiated in Chancery, with the hope of encouraging or forcing named defendants to come to a more accurate account of their business dealings.

In *Lacy v Hyam* (1740), Mary Lacy – the widow of the bankrupt Joseph Lacy – sought payment of a £2600 marriage portion that was still due from her brothers-in-law. Mary stated that at the time of their marriage Joseph was 'a Considerable merchant and an Extensive Trader so as to employ thirty sail of ships in a year [and] some hundreds of people in a manufactory of Tobacco'. In October 1725, Joseph, 'in order to carry on such Correspondence and not with any Sinister or unfair view or Intent went to France'. While abroad, a commission of bankruptcy was taken out against Joseph, and on 17 November he was arrested and 'confined in the Bastill in Paris in France where he continued a long time deprived of Pen Ink and Paper or Free Liberty to Converse with your Oratrix'. On 25 November 1725, Mary applied to the assignees in 'her lay and the best of her knowledge fully discovered and disclosed' all of her husband's estate, including the bonds relating to her

---

61   TNA, C11/1418/24, 'Metcalfe v Letchmere' (1720), Bill of Complaint.

62   Sheryllynne Haggerty, *The British-Atlantic Trading Community 1760-1810: Men, Women, and the Distribution of Goods* (Leiden, 2006); Sheryllynne Haggerty, *Merely for Money'? Business Culture in the British Atlantic 1750–1815* (Liverpool, 2012); Siobhan Talbott, *Conflict, Commerce and Franco-Scottish Relations, 1560–1713* (London, 2014); Sophie H. Jones and Siobhan Talbott, 'Sole Traders? The Role of the Extended Family in Eighteenth-Century Atlantic Business Networks', *Enterprise and Society*, 23 (2021), pp. 1–30; Forestier, 'Risk, Kinship and Personal Relationships in Late Eighteenth-Century West Indian Trade', pp. 912–931; Hamilton, 'Local Connections, Global Ambitions', pp. 283–300.

marriage. She sought to prove that the commission was 'irregullarly sued out and consequently would be superseded'.[63]

The assignees 'solemnly assured and most Religiously promised' that she would be 'secure in her demands by virtue of the aforesaid Bond if she could by any means prevail on him to come into such Terms as they should propose and not take advantage of the Irregularity of suing out the Commission of Bankruptcy against him'. The creditors sought a deal for ten shillings in the pound, but assured Mary that she did not need to come in as a creditor under the commission. Mary was further reassured that her bond would be paid and there would be 'sufficient to answer her said demand'. With such assurances, Mary agreed not to enter the commission – which she claimed had paid out £8000 to creditors – but now accused the defendants of keeping her marriage portion. All of which, 'they well know the same was by very undue means gotten from your Oratrix'.[64] While the complexities of the marriage contract, the irregularity of the commission, and the failure of Mary to join with the other creditors are clear to the reader, we also see an implicit mention of the intention of Mary's husband in going abroad. Indeed, intent was of crucial significance in bankruptcy proceedings, and the reason for going abroad was either seen to be done with the intention to commit fraud and to conceal goods from creditors, or for genuine reasons of trade.

In Thomas Davies' advice manual, *The Laws Relating to Bankrupts* (1744), the author uses the case of William Gulston to demonstrate how the act of going abroad must have been done with the purpose or intent to defraud the debtor's creditors.[65] Gulston was a trader in wine, but also had dealings in several plantations in Barbados, making multiple trips abroad between 1725 and 1737. On 19 March 1737, he made one such trip with his wife and children, informing his creditors he would return within eighteen months. Instead of returning, he stayed in Barbados until 1742, making remittances to some creditors in England at the expense of others. A commission of bankruptcy was executed against Gulston on 16 February 1742 by George Dale, to whom he owed over £4000. Gulston initiated a suit in Chancery, questioning the validity of the commission, as he claimed never to have committed an act of bankruptcy.[66] Furthermore, Gulston claimed that his intention was:

> well known to all persons with whom the petitioner had any dealings, and was concealed from none of them, and particularly was well known to George Dale, who had several dealings with the petitioner, and was with him almost every day, and sometimes oftener, for six weeks, or two months before the

63   TNA, C11/1884/8, 'Lacy v Hyam' (1740), Bill of Complaint.
64   Ibid.
65   Thomas Davies, *The Laws Relating to Bankrupts* (London, 1744), pp. 30–40.
66   Ibid., pp. 30–40.

time of the petitioner's so going abroad, and who had several goods packed up at the house of the petitioner, to be sent abroad with him.[67]

The evidence presented to the commissioners to prove him a bankrupt came from a porter, who stated that Gulston ordered him to deny him to two creditors. However, one of these creditors, a Master Shipston, stated that he 'saw him several times, and that Gulston never refused to see him when he asked for him'.[68] On 13 December 1743, the Lord Chancellor referred the case to a trial in King's Bench, and the question posed to the jury was whether travelling to Barbados was an act of bankruptcy. Gulston claimed that he had left England with the 'Consent of his Creditors' and had traded since he left to the amount of 'several Thousand Pounds'.[69] Lord Chief Justice Lee summarised to the jury that the matter to be decided on was whether Gulston's 'going abroad, was with an Intention to defraud his Creditors? Or, whether it was publickly known and consented to though he staid longer than the Time' he had agreed. The issue to be decided related solely to the 'Length of Time' Gulston was abroad, with the jury eventually finding that no act of bankruptcy had been committed.[70]

More explicit debates surrounding intention arise in other cases. In *Langton v Flindell* (1730), the three plaintiffs – David Langton, Richard Archer, and William Codd – were assignees of Thomas Edwards, a leather cutter from London. The bill claimed that the bankrupt owed Langton £146, Archer £117 4s, and Codd £113 16s, all for goods sold and delivered to the bankrupt. On 22 January 1719, Edwards left his house and 'went into Holland and carried with him a considerable part of his Estate and effects in order to defraud his Creditors of the same'. The bankrupt had 'absconded and left his house ... for fear of being arrested by his Creditors and [they] had received Information that the said Thomas Edwards was gott to Rotterdam'. The plaintiffs named John Flindell, a carrier from Ipswich, Suffolk, as the only defendant. They accused Flindell of employing Allan Roycroft as his attorney or agent in Rotterdam to prosecute Edwards in an attempt to recoup £80 on an individual payment and outside of the commission of bankruptcy. The bankrupt paid Roycroft 880 gilders, 'being the value of Eighty pounds Sterling', which they demanded he refunded to the commission so the creditors may have 'an equall share and dividend of the Estate and effects as in Justice and equity they ought and your orators well hoped that he the said John Flindell would so have done'. Ultimately, the assignees claimed that Edwards was declared a bankrupt on 29

---

67   LX, 'In the Matter of William Gulston a Bankrupt; upon the Petition of William Gulston, and a cross Petition of George Dale and Others' (1743), Court of Chancery, 26 ER 125.
68   Ibid.
69   Davies, *The Laws Relating to Bankrupts*, pp. 30–40, p. 31.
70   Ibid., p. 39.

January 1730, and the money was paid on 16 February 1730, which made the payment legally part of the commission of bankruptcy. As all witnesses were 'either dead or gone into parts remote and beyond the seas unknown to your orators so that your orators cant have the benefit of their testimony', they required the authority of the court to force Flindell to repay the money to the commission.[71]

Despite agreeing that a commission of bankruptcy was taken out on 29 January 1730, the defendant did 'not admit nor believe that the said Thomas Edwards did then become a Bankrupt', and was a 'stranger' to the proceedings and 'knows nothing thereof'. In terms of the motivation behind going to Holland, Flindell claimed that he could not say:

> whether such his going into Holland was in order or with view Intent or Designe to defraud his just Creditors of the said goods But this Defendant hath been informed and believes it to be true that the said Thomas Edwards some time before he left his House and went to Holland as aforesaid He had made some Agreement with the Complaints and others his Creditors for the payment of his Debts.[72]

Flindell believed that Edwards left England with the knowledge and consent of the complainants and was advised not to pay the money to the plaintiffs as he did not believe Edwards was ever declared to be a bankrupt. These examples demonstrate that the intention of the debtor was of crucial importance in determining whether or not they had committed a criminal act of bankruptcy. While touched upon here to demonstrate the way in which a commission of bankruptcy had broken down, a fuller analysis of the acts and actions of bankrupts in relation to an act of bankruptcy will be undertaken in the following chapter.

The Practical Implementation of Bankruptcy Procedure

Garrett v Blackerby (1692), is a case which highlights several discrepancies between legal ideals and day-to-day legality in practice. The plaintiff, Nicholas Garrett, a weaver from Middlesex, was a creditor of the bankrupt John Barrington, a mercer from London. Garrett named Barrington alongside five other defendants and complained that dividends from the commission of bankruptcy had been distributed unfairly, with other creditors receiving more than him. Garrett goes on to accuse the defendants of threatening him,

---

71 TNA, C11/1272/35, 'Langton v Flindell' (1730), Bill of Complaint.
72 Ibid., Answer of John Flindell.

by claiming he would not receive a 'groat of my debts' if he pursued a suit at law.[73] While in theory official bankruptcy procedure provided greater authority and certainty by placing all creditors on an equal footing, this is clearly not the case in this suit. Garrett shows his perceived fear of receiving less than the other creditors, taking direct aim at the distributions made under the ongoing commission of bankruptcy. We also see the insinuation that he was coerced into acting in accordance with the other creditors' wishes. While three defendants vehemently denied threatening the plaintiff, they established that a form of discharge was being employed prior to 1706, and demonstrated an inventive way of enabling a portion of the bankrupt's estate back to his family for subsistence. It was agreed by 'most' of the above one hundred creditors that if Barrington appeared before the commissioners to be examined, and delivered up his whole estate, then some person would be admitted 'as a creditor for six hundred pounds in trust for the Wife and children of the said Barrington'. Having met all the creditors' demands – and even sending his wife and servants to be examined – the creditors allowed Nicholas Martin to come in as a creditor for £600, further agreeing not to sue or prosecute Barrington for debt for the term of sixty years.[74]

No further information is provided about Nicholas Martin and he is not named as a party in the suit. However, it can be assumed that he was not an original creditor of the bankrupt, as he was not involved in the original commission of bankruptcy. It seems that Martin was simply an acquaintance of the creditors – and possibly the bankrupt – who was used as a tool to provide a significant level of subsistence back to the bankrupt and his family. While the overall debt of Barrington is not disclosed, it must have been a substantial amount to allow a subsistence of £600, a sum that was three times the statutory limit prescribed in 1706. Without a specific legal stipulation in place to allow the commission to return a subsistence directly to the bankrupt himself, the creditors manipulated the law to provide for the bankrupt's family.

With limited information, it is difficult to comment on the motivation behind this seeming act of charity. If the plaintiff is to be believed, then it appears that the creditors had acted fraudulently by returning a disproportionate amount to the bankrupt, at the expense of Garrett. If, on the other hand, the defendants are to be believed, then the return of the £600 could be seen as an act of charity and kindness, by ensuring that the bankrupt's family were cared for. Perhaps the most realistic option is that this act could be seen as an attempt to incentivise cooperation, by insisting that if the bankrupt acted honestly then his reward would be an informal form of discharge, the return of a proportion of his estate, and a promise not to prosecute him for a term of sixty years. Returning

73 TNA, C6/416/14, 'Garrett v Blackerby' (1692), Bill of Complaint.
74 Ibid., Answer of Samuel Bayley, Edmund Bayley, and Nicholas Baker.

to the argument of Emily Kadens that the 1706 act was the first time such incentivisation was made explicit in the statutes, it appears that creditors were undertaking this tactic in an informal manner prior to this date.[75] If this case were to have happened after 1706, then the statutory limit of £200 would have been placed on the subsistence level, and 'most' of the creditors would need to be clarified as at least four fifths in number and value. As well as seeing the statute as catching up to the realities of the existing system, the law would have significantly altered the outcome in this instance.

Further cases can be used to illustrate these issues. *Mill v Sedgwick* (1693) is one example of a declared bankrupt, Adiel Mill, appearing as a plaintiff. In the bill of complaint, Mill explained that his creditors caused his 'goods, Stock, Bookes, Paper and other estate to bee seized and sold by the said Commissioners and disposed off as they pleased'. However, Mill claimed that 'in Compassion' for himself, his wife, and seven children, his household goods were appraised, and £1000 was assigned to Mill, 'the better to Enable your Orator to provide a maintenance for himselfe and family'.[76] The answer of William and Susan Sedgwick, creditors of Mill, corroborates Mill's version of events. However, the couple stated that they refused their portion of the payment, as Mill had not acted honestly and provided a true account of his debts.[77] Despite not receiving the full amount, it appears that the creditors and the bankrupt had, in principle at least, agreed to a substantial maintenance for Mill's family, at least part of which had been paid. This suit can again be seen as an attempt at incentivised cooperation, as the bankrupt and his family were given the opportunity to receive a substantial financial settlement if Mill truthfully revealed his total assets. However, there is also evidence of coercion and a form of informal punishment for failure to comply, as the defendants claimed to have refused Mill their share of his subsistence as he was said to have acted dishonestly.

In *Barton v Parsons* (1699) the bill of complaint accused Michael Scrimshire, a bankrupt goldsmith, of accumulating over £50,000 worth of debts and then absconding. Scrimshire had proposed a deal whereby if his creditors signed a letter of licence, with which 'he might gaine his Liberty and be freed from all arrests and suits', he would pay them five shillings in the pound. Upon accepting this deal, he would then pay 'five shillings in the pound more of each and every of their said debts att the end of three months … or ten shillings in the pound att the end of twelve months … or as soon as he could gett in recover and retrieve' several debts due to him. In this case, it is the bankrupt who had attempted to entice creditors into an agreement by promising a greater return on their debt if they granted him a longer period to repay. However, because of delay and the sheer number of creditors, a commission of bankruptcy was

---

75   Kadens, 'The Last Bankrupt Hanged', pp. 1228–1229.
76   TNA, C6/327/24, 'Mill v Sedgwick' (1693), Bill of Complaint.
77   Ibid., Answer of William Sedgwick and Susan Sedgwick.

eventually taken out against Scrimshire. While the creditors hoped to receive a dividend of fifteen shillings in the pound, at the time of the bill of complaint only three dividends of four shillings in the pound had been paid.[78]

Perhaps the most obvious example of incentivised cooperation can be seen in a complex case from 1698, in which Mary Herbert, a widow and sole heir to her father's estate, was the only plaintiff. After a disagreement between Mary's father, Roland Hunt, and her husband, Edward Herbert, her father had left three bonds totalling £3000 in the hands of his brother, Thomas Hunt, to be invested for the benefit of Mary and her two children. However, Thomas became bankrupt and there arose several competing claims on the bonds in his possession. From Thomas's answer, we again see that an agreement had been reached between him and his creditors regarding his liberty and subsistence. As the bankrupt's estate was worth more than his debts, and being thankful for his candour, his creditors were willing to grant the bankrupt his liberty for ninety-nine years. To support his family, the creditors were willing to pay the sum of £5 out of every £100 received, raising to £7 10s out of every £100 received once £10,000 had been distributed amongst his creditors. This incremental rise in payment to the bankrupt can only be viewed as a means to encourage truthful cooperation from Thomas Hunt.

When discussing the legal validity of his agreement, the bankrupt Thomas Hunt stated that he 'Humbly presumes he hath a legall right to his Liberty and the allowance given him by the said Creditors'.[79] This statement suggests that such a practice was commonplace and a familiar occurrence in bankruptcy procedure. While there are several issues surrounding the bankruptcy process in these three suits which needed to be resolved, at no point are these informal agreements – to provide a subsistence and to discharge a bankrupt from future liabilities – debated as a matter of fact. All parties questioned on these issues acknowledged that such agreements had been reached, demonstrating an implied understanding that they were legally valid. Returning to John C. McCoid II's work on discharge, the author concludes that unlike legal historians, early modern practitioners did not see the provision as momentous, as it continued quite naturally from steps already taken. As a rule of law, discharge had existed 'as early as the middle of the seventeenth century'.[80] It seems that not only were legal provisions in the 1706 act previously present as a rule of law, but there were instances of this being the case within the bankruptcy process itself. These suits provide a glimpse into ongoing negotiations between debtors and creditors, as it seems that creditors were willing to treat debtors amicably, allowing them the chance to provide for their family while simultaneously encouraging truthful

---

78 TNA, C6/318/30, 'Barton v Parsons' (1699), Bill of Complaint.

79 TNA, C6/361/42, 'Herbert v Herbert' (1698), Answer of Thomas Hunt.

80 McCoid II, 'Discharge: The Most Important Development in Bankruptcy History', p. 182.

cooperation, and punishing fraudulent activity. While we could interpret these statements as persuasive arguments demonstrating acceptable norms and values of the period, these cases inform us of practical issues and procedures occurring in the debt-recovery process.

Within these suits, we see explicit references to the 'maintenance' and 'trust' of the bankrupt's family, which creditors did through 'compassion' and consideration. At the same time, we also see various forms of informal coercion and punishment levelled against individuals who acted in a seemingly inappropriate manner. We see a pragmatic approach to debt recovery, as the creditors had clearly come to the realisation that rather than punishing the debtor for non-payment, it was in the majority's best interest to gain full cooperation from parties within the process. While it could be argued that such creditors were simply acting in a compassionate, kind, and thoughtful manner towards their fellow traders, these suits demonstrate that pragmatism was the reason behind these approaches. Indeed, in *Fox v Grantham* (1710), the assignees claimed that in November 1708 the bankrupt absconded from his house as he was fearful of being arrested. In response, the assignees, 'being sensible of the Dangers they were in of looseing their said debts' took out a commission of bankruptcy on 29 November 1708 for a debt of £200. Here, we see a rational and pragmatic approach to a debtor committing an act of bankruptcy. Yet, despite acting in a reasonable manner, the plaintiffs were still seeking the repayment of £62 19s 8d from the defendant in June 1710.[81] More broadly, refusing a portion of subsistence for non-compliance with the creditors' stipulations, and offering an incremental return dependent on the amount the creditors received, illustrates that it was an early form of incentivised cooperation being implemented, rather than a compassionate payment.

Even after 1706, we see examples of creditors raising issues with the discharge provision. In *Harkness v Stanyforth* (1725), Thomas Halsey, a merchant from London, was declared a bankrupt in January 1720 and received his certificate of conformity some time thereafter. However, two assignees, John Harkness and Thomas Briscoe, submitted a bill of complaint on 10 April 1725, and suggested that they were unaware of several dealings between the bankrupt and the named defendant, Disney Stanyforth, dating back to 1717. As these dealings were before the execution of the commission of bankruptcy – and were still ongoing – the plaintiffs argued that they should have been incorporated within the commission. In this manner, the assignees had granted the bankrupt his certificate under false pretences and without the relevant information. The bill demanded that Stanyforth come to an account for the credits and debts between him and Halsey.[82] It appears that the assignees regretted discharging

81   TNA, C6/410/41, 'Fox v Grantham' (1710), Bill of Complaint.
82   TNA, C11/858/49, 'Harkness v Stanyforth' (1725), Bill of Complaint.

the bankrupt and were attempting to recover debts even after the commission had been officially closed and Halsey was no longer a bankrupt.

As well as issues surrounding the provisions entered in the 1706 statute, several cases demonstrate further disparities between the ideal pathway of bankruptcy procedure and the realities of its implementation. In a suit from 1715, John Riley, an assignee of Daniel Browne, an apothecary from Worcester, sought to revive a bill he entered three years previously. Riley claimed that the bankrupt had accumulated debts in excess of £600, but he had been unable to regain anywhere near that amount. As such, Riley was seeking a discovery of any goods or estate that had come into the hands of the eleven named defendants.[83] In two of the three answers that survive, the defendants explained that the reason Riley was unable to identify and recover such a large amount was because the bankrupt did not owe more than £200 to his various creditors. Henry Blake claimed he was not aware of the commission as he was never summoned to a meeting of the creditors, despite being the largest creditor for a total debt of £138 12s, Blake estimated the debts owing to the creditors within the commission to be £136, and therefore, Browne should never have been declared a bankrupt, as he had not reached the £200 threshold.[84] In this instance, the defendants questioned the decision made by the commissioners, and suggested that Browne had not satisfied the statutory legal criteria. While commissioners held jurisdiction over the commission of bankruptcy, this was one of several examples whereby suits were initiated which took direct aim at the commission, intent on altering its trajectory.

Further cases survive whereby the bankrupt submitted a bill complaining about an open and ongoing commission to which he was engaged. In *Ellis v Winnock* (1690), the only document that survives is the demurrer of two defendants, Samuel Winnock and John Lewis. From this response, it appears that the bankrupt had submitted a bill demanding the creditors prove the veracity of their claims. The defendants concluded that the only reason the bill was exhibited was to put them to 'wrongfull vexation and Charge and Cost and Expences in law', as the bill contained 'nothing but what relates to and falls under the power of the Commissions of Bankrupt'.[85] In a similar case from 1700, the five named defendants did submit an answer, but it was short and to the point. They explained that as the commission of bankruptcy was still in force and had not been superseded, 'the Complainant is not entitled to exhibit or proceed upon his Bill in this High and Honourable Court nor to have any

83   TNA, C11/1790/18, 'Riley v Browne', (1715), Bill of Complaint and Bill of Revivor.
84   Ibid., Answer of John Yarnold and Elizabeth Yarnold; Answer of Henry Blake.
85   TNA, C6/407/28, 'Ellis v Winnock' (1690), Demurrer of Samuel Winnock and John Lewis.

further or other Answere thereto'.[86] These suits are extreme examples, as the audacity of the actions of the bankrupts is apparent to the modern reader. It appears that the motivation behind these suits is an attempt to delay, disrupt, or increase the costs to the defendants. What is clear, is that the defendants demonstrated a clear legal understanding of the correct route and jurisdiction of bankruptcy procedure and utilised this to strengthen their argument. Furthermore, the short and direct answers tend to show that having previously failed themselves, bankrupts were in no moral or ethical position to take aim at others, who were in theory of a firmer social standing in the wider community.

In *Paradice v Peach* (1745), the plaintiffs were creditors of the bankrupt, while the two assignees were named defendants. In his answer, Thomas Carpenter from Gloucester suggested he was 'much Surprized' at the plaintiffs in submitting a bill to discover the estate and effects of the bankrupt that had come into his possession. Put simply, the defendant felt that all creditors should have taken the 'ordinary Course prescribed by the Laws of Bankruptcy', namely a commission of bankruptcy. Indeed, from the time he had been made assignee, he had always been 'ready and willing' to account with the commissioners, 'as the Laws of Bankrupcy Direct'. Carpenter claimed that he took great pride in his work, all of which had been done 'within the Time prescribed by Law for that Purpose and always was and is desirous to do in all Things according to the Duty of his said Trust'. Carpenter concluded that he was not aware of any mismanagement, confederacy or concealment amongst the individuals operating the commission of bankruptcy, and that the plaintiffs were premature in submitting their bill, as all time and expense could have been spared.[87] The success of these commissions was largely dependent on the work and cooperation of all those involved in the procedure. As such, it is not surprising that several suits took direct aim at the individuals granted authority to pursue such actions.

In *Furly v Buckley* (1709–1710), the bankrupt Benjamin Furly appeared as a plaintiff and named six defendants. While all that survives is the answer of three defendants, it appears that Furly and his deceased brother, Jonathan Furly, became bankrupt in July 1705 and agreed a composition with their creditors to pay nine shillings in the pound, as long as they offered 'reasonable security for payment'. The bankrupts mortgaged several premises near Colchester, Essex for five hundred years 'with a provision to be void on payment of the said nine shillings in the pound'. As the plaintiff had only paid four shillings in the pound, the defendants were seeking the 'sale of the said mortgaged premises for payment of the remainder of the said composition money'. The defendants were previously plaintiffs in a case against the bankrupts in Chancery, and on 21 July 1709, a Master of the Court ordered the sale of the lands for the benefit

86   TNA, C6/365/48, 'Airey v Forster' (1700), Answer of Rebecca Richardson, John Foster, George Usher, William Wilkinson, and Susannah Punshoon.
87   TNA, C11/1609/14, 'Paradice v Peach' (1745), Answer of Thomas Carpenter.

of the creditors.[88] However, the defendants had yet to find a suitable buyer and were seeking a speedy sale of the lands and estate to recoup the five shillings in the pound they were still due. It appears that the bankrupt had submitted a bill in Chancery to prevent the sale of the property and to attempt a different resolution to settle his debts.

Another example of a bankrupt taking direct aim at the actions of the commissioners can be seen in *Bowlby v Fitzhertbert* (1705). The two answers that survive are both from commissioners who, residing in Nottingham, would have been assigned the role by the Lord Chancellor. Richard Burbidge suggested that the creditors of the bankrupt employed an attorney named Nathaniel Bate from Mansfield to sue forth the commission. Burbidge was displeased with Bate for assigning him the role without asking in advance, as Burbidge saw himself as 'not very well skilled in affairs of that nature'.[89] The other commissioner, John Fitzhertbert, provided a similar account, whereby he was 'very uneasey and much displeased with the said Bate' for executing the commission, and not 'informeinge this Defendant or takeinge his consent' beforehand. Fitzhertbert stated he was in 'A greate measure unacquainted with the methods of proceedinge', and as such refused the role several times. He finally yielded and accepted the position, seeing it as his 'neighbourly duty' to help the plaintiff. However, since being drawn into this 'Unreasonable and Vexatious Suite', both defendants demanded the sum of 20s per day, for their 'paines and trouble in attending the execucion of the said Commission Ten days', which was seen to be 'the Usuall and accustomed Fee Gratuity in Cases of the like nature'.[90] In contrast to the cases above, which demonstrate an intricate awareness of bankruptcy legislation and procedure, in this suit the two commissioners were reluctant to take on the responsibility, being wholly ignorant of the correct method by which to execute their roles. Through a combination of coercion and civic duty they undertook the position, but both concluded they were due financial recompense for their time and effort.

In further examples, while we do not gain as much detail, we still see members of the public rejecting the position, or being removed or replaced once in power. In *Sole v Arnold* (1735), the plaintiffs were two assignees of William Tappenden, a chapman from Kent. The bill suggested that after a commission of bankruptcy had been initiated on 2 May 1734, two original assignees were chosen but rejected the position. Pursuant to an order from the Lord Chancellor, dated 17 September 1734, the creditors were forced to meet again and named the current plaintiffs assignees.[91] In a strange case from 1730,

---

88   TNA, C6/411/44, 'Furly v Buckley' (1709–1710), Answer of Joseph Buckley, Abel Wilkinson and Thomas Hide.
89   TNA, C6/378/47, 'Bowlby v Fitzhertbert' (1705), Answer of Richard Burbidge.
90   Ibid., Answer of John Fitzhertbert.
91   TNA, C11/1523/19, 'Sole V Arnold' (1735), Bill of Complaint.

William Jones was named an assignee after a commission of bankruptcy had been executed on 22 August 1722. When Jones subsequently died, his daughter and executrix Mary became an assignee in December 1723. However, by an order of the Lord Chancellor dated 16 March 1724, Mary Jones was 'discharged from acting as assignee', and in October 1730 a new commission of bankruptcy was executed. After a meeting at Guildhall the following November, the plaintiff was finally chosen as an assignee and the commission was allowed to continue.[92] In this final case we get a clear example of the Lord Chancellor's jurisdiction over bankruptcy, as the original commission was superseded, Mary Jones was relieved of her duty, and a new commission executed. While a clear under-standing of legal jurisdiction and procedure had been utilised to add weight to the arguments of parties within a suit, in these instances we also see ignorance fulfilling a similar role. In this manner, it becomes clear that parties were manip-ulating the legal process by demonstrating an astute awareness of the law when it suited them, while claiming ignorance of the law in other circumstances.

In *Browne v Bamforth* (1696), the plaintiffs filed a cross-bill against George Bamforth, an assignee of Thomas Eyre. Being executors of another assignee of the bankrupt Cuthbert Browne, the plaintiffs claimed to have been unable to come to an account with Bamforth, despite him receiving over £5000 of the bankrupt's goods and estate over the course of seven years.[93] In his answer, George Bamforth explained that during this period he had paid £1401 8s 6d, to creditors, and had no estate left in his possession. Bamforth claimed that Eyre owed over twenty-two people above £6000, and in a long and protracted affair the creditors were 'very well satisfied with this Defendants proceedings as he verily believes and that he shall be ready to account with them when he hath recovered what is due to them from the Complainants'.[94] It is clear that in Bamforth's original bill he was seeking repayment for any estate that had come into the hands of Cuthbert Browne. While there are competing views and interpretations of the accounts of the assignees, Bamforth cites the creditors' satisfaction with his work as evidence of his claim. *Jacobs v Sheppard* (1720) is a rare example of the plaintiffs and defendants coming to an agreement. The plaintiffs exhibited their bill in February 1719, hoping to revive a bill from 1711 in order to seek a discovery of the bankrupt's estate, which had still not been identified. In response, the defendants suggested that the estate under question was more than sufficient to satisfy the complainants' demands, and so the original suit should be revived.[95]

92   TNA, C11/2426/38, 'Smith v Platt' (1730), Bill of Complaint.
93   TNA, C6/381/15, 'Browne v Bamforth' (1696), Bill of Complaint.
94   TNA, C11/1790/18, 'Riley v Browne', (1715), Answer of George Bamforth.
95   TNA, C11/2370/46, 'Jacobs v Sheppard' (1720), Bill of Complaint, Answer of Mary Sheppard, Francis Sheppard, and Samuel Sheppard.

Similarly, in *Evance v Micklethwaite* (1700–1701), the bankrupt-plaintiff – Matthew Evance, a haberdasher of small wares from London – named a widow called Joanna Micklethwaite as the only defendant. In the bill, Evance explained that he 'met with very many greate losses and disappoyntments in the way of his trade and having a greate family of Children and having contracted greate debts', he and his brother Thomas Evance were declared bankrupt in 1697. A composition of ten shillings in the pound was agreed amongst the creditors to be satisfied from their joint estate, which was worth £695 11s 3d, and one farthing. Despite accepting the composition, Micklethwaite continued to prosecute Evance for a £400 penalty on a bond in the court of King's Bench. As such, Evance sought an injunction to halt the proceedings.[96]

In her answer, dated 2 May 1701, Micklethwaite claimed that she had employed John Thurlby, a scrivener from London, to lend out money at interest, and while she had heard that the brothers had failed in 1697, and a commission of bankruptcy was issued against them, 'she never concerned herselfe in nor was privy to the suing out of the said Commission ... and doth not know anything of her owne knowledge of the same or any proposall whatsoever that was at anytime made'. As she was now seventy-two years old, her 'memory is very much impaired and decayed by such her great Age and therefore she cannot Answer more certainly particularly or positively'. She concluded that, 'haveing waited butt in vaine' for her payment, she 'did then cause the Complainant to be arrested as in the said bill setforth butt this Defendant saith she is ready and willing and never refused to accept of the said composition of tenn shillings in the pound of her said Debt'.[97] Despite having knowledge of the commission, Micklethwaite became impatient and arrested Evance to force repayment. While bankrupts were legally protected from arrest, and with an ongoing and clear path to debt-recovery established, the practical realities of experience were not as straightforward. On this occasion, it seems the two parties came to an agreement regarding the composition and the repayment of the debt. Ultimately, these two cases are rare examples of the plaintiffs and defendants both agreeing – not only that the bankruptcy process had failed, but also on the manner in which all parties should proceed.

In other cases, the bankrupt appeared as a plaintiff alongside the assignees. In *Mount v Ceney* (1730), the bankrupt John Basket, a printer from London, joined his three assignees in submitting a bill against John Ceney. The bill claimed that the defendant had agreed to lease a property in Fulham to anyone who could 'repair the same and make such alterations and Conveniencies therein as were necessary for a Family'. After several meetings between the defendant and the bankrupt, it was agreed that 'your Orator John Baskett should at his own Costs

---

96 TNA, C6/407/80, 'Evance v Micklethwaite' (1700-1701), Bill of Complaint.
97 Ibid., Answer of Joanna Micklethwaite.

and Charges erect and build some new Lodging Rooms and other Rooms and one or more Coach Houses and repair the stables together with the washhouse and other Conveniencies and apartments as an addition to the said House'. However, after the work was completed, there was 'some dispute' between the two about the specific terms of the lease. Under the pretence of collecting some of his personal belongings, John Ceney entered the property and 'locked up the said House and refused to return the Key … but kept the possession thereof for several weeks' and denied the bankrupt entry. Basket subsequently gained access to the property and put a padlock on the door, but the defendant 'soon afterwards Caused the said Padlock to be knocked off and Entered upon the said premises so lett to your Orator John Baskett in a forcible manner and hath ever since kept the possession thereof'.[98] The defendant submitted a Plea and refused to answer the bill, stating that he never made a lease, and no such agreement was to be found in any writing or document.[99]

In *Chowne v Baxter* (1740), the bankrupt John White, a silversmith from Middlesex, appeared alongside two assignees who were both goldsmiths from London, and named William Baxter as the only defendant. The bill was submitted on 4 February 1741, and claimed that White had previously submitted a bill on 26 June 1739 in an attempt to compel a performance of two agreements against William Baxter. He also sought an injunction against any proceedings at common law for a judgment of £104 5s, and costs. On 24 April 1740, a commission of bankruptcy was taken out and an assignment was made of the bankrupt's goods on 8 May 1740. As such, 'all the Estate and Effects of the said John White as also the Benefit of the aforesaid agreements in the Original Bill mentioned became vested in your Orators the said assignees In Trust aforesaid and they are thereby well Entitled to have the Full benefit thereof against the said William Baxter which they hoped he would have agreed to'. Because the agreements and common law judgment had occurred before the commission of bankruptcy was taken out, then they were to be encompassed within the commission for the benefit of all the creditors of the bankrupt. However, Baxter refused to engage with the commission, 'Threatening and giving out in speeches that he will Endeavour to get the said Injunction dissolved … and will thereupon take out Execution for the said one hundred and Four pounds and Five shillings and costs'.[100]

Finally, in *Cockburn v Monck* (1750), the bankrupt Eustace Peacock appeared alongside two assignees and three other plaintiffs and named William Monck as the sole defendant. Alongside John Cockburn, the bankrupt had previously submitted a bill against the defendant, whereby the Lord Chancellor ordered

98   TNA, C11/1823/26, 'Mount v Ceney' (1730), Bill of Complaint.
99   Ibid., Plea and Answer of John Ceney.
100 TNA, C11/541/15, 'Chowne v Baxter' (1740), Bill of Complaint.

Monck to pay £1000 to each individual, as he was an executor of a deceased Admiral Lestock. Similarly, another plaintiff, Margaret Knowles, was owed an annuity of £100 per year from Monck and the bill sought the enforcement of these awards.[101] In these three cases, we see the bankrupt working alongside the assignees, and the commission appears as one coherent unit litigating a single defendant. The bankrupt's right to litigate in Chancery, and the elements of his conscience and equitable jurisdiction, are seen to be part of the ongoing commission of bankruptcy. The bankrupt had appeared as one member of a larger group engaged in a debt-recovery process. The justification for the bankrupt appearing as a plaintiff can be seen in the named defendants acting against conscience and preventing the completion of a commission of bankruptcy. While the bankrupt had economically failed, and the commission had legally failed, the defendants had – allegedly – morally failed in their conscionable duty. All of which had to be understood, and untangled, via the processes and procedures in Chancery.

Conclusion

The methodological approach employed in this chapter means that it is not possible to know how many of these suits progressed beyond the initial stage of proceeding, and if they did, the form this took within the court. It is likely that the vast majority were withdrawn or compromised at this early stage. However, analysing pleadings in isolation allows a fuller discussion of how bankruptcy reveals itself at this stage of a proceeding. The picture we get is not one of a sole trader collapsing, or even of a single issue to be decided by the court, but rather of larger interconnected and overlapping principles of debt recovery intersecting with the bankruptcy process. In most instances, it is not possible to ascertain how and why an individual bankrupt failed, except for vague references to misfortune and overtrading. However, we can gain direct access to how the commission of bankruptcy broke down and the specific elements which needed the overarching authority of the court in an attempt to complete the process.

When discussing the *ratio decidendi*, or the rule of law on which a judicial decision is based, Eileen O'Sullivan has shown how such processes are rarely straightforward and linear. For O'Sullivan, the non-linearity of the decision-making process, 'is evident when decisions produced by courts come to different conclusions, or when they come to the same conclusions but for different

---

101   TNA, C11/2508/6, 'Cockburn v Monck' (1750), Bill of Complaint.

reasons'.[102] A similar point can be made about bankruptcy pleadings, as these suits are not about straightforward and linear debt recovery. Emily Kadens has shown how default itself was not a binary concept, and there arose a spectrum of repayment from outright failure to repayment in full.[103] As an ideal, bankruptcy procedure had many advantages over alternative routes available to creditors. In reality, the process encountered various problems and obstacles which needed assistance from the court in order to be completed. Multiple external pressures were placed on commissions of bankruptcy and pleadings demonstrate individual breaks in the ideal, linear timeline of debt recovery established in the legal statutes and contemporary commentary.

Taken in isolation, the types of documents found in pleadings grant us insights into the way individuals dealt with specific issues and managed to circumnavigate problems within a commission of bankruptcy. Collectively, they demonstrate that the ideals established in the statutes did not always conform neatly to the practical realities of procedure. It appears that both creditors and debtors held a keen understanding of established legal principles and knew how to manipulate the process for their own benefit. This manipulation took a variety of forms, ranging from individuals demonstrating an acute awareness and understanding of precise legal principles to others demonstrating complete ignorance of the most basic concepts of trade. Undoubtedly, the cases utilised in this chapter can inform us of many aspects of early modern society. They could, for example, shed light on issues surrounding attitudes towards destitution, Christian and community standards of charity, support networks for families, the poor laws, and several other interrelated topics. But in relation to the bankruptcy process, one aspect of change has been overlooked by scholars. The 1706 act continues to hold historical and academic interest, as it is viewed as a monumental change in the laws of England which had a long-lasting effect on insolvency and bankruptcy laws in many Western states. While the motivations and reasons for the introduction of this statute continue to be debated, the two central provisions of 1706 – providing a discharge from future liabilities and allowing a subsistence back to the bankrupt – were clearly being practised prior to this date. In many respects, the introduction of the 1706 act can be seen as a means for the law to catch up with the practical realities of debt recovery. Furthermore, while the 1706 act formalised incentivised cooperation, as well as legal coercion and punishment for failure to comply, these concepts can be seen as the key motivations behind the informal practice outlined above. These changes can be viewed as the law altering the

---

102 Eileen M. O'Sullivan, 'Law and Chaos: Legal Argument as a Non-Linear Process', in Andrew Lewis and Michael Lobban (eds), *Law and History* (Oxford, 2004), pp. 433–452, p. 433.
103 Emily Kadens, 'Pre-Modern Credit Networks and the Limits of Reputation', *Iowa Law Review*, 100 (2015), pp. 2429–2507.

practicality of procedure, as it regulated informal processes, placing statutory defined limits upon their implementation.

The diversity and individuality of cases are shown through colourful and distinctive narratives, allowing access to the specificities of the details of these disparities. As such, we can analyse the ongoing complaints towards, and attempted repair of, this form of debt recovery, illuminating nuanced and specific sub-themes relating to financial and personal failure. Notably, several creditors undertook a pragmatic approach to bankruptcy, attempting to incentivise cooperation for the benefit of all parties within the process. The specificities of such discrepancies have been overlooked in the historiography of bankruptcy and bankruptcy procedure and add another layer of complexity to the reasons why the legislature acted to regulate the debt-recovery process.

3

Knowledge and Circulating Judgements
of Failure in Bankruptcy Pleadings

Discussing trust and credibility in the early modern economy, both Alexandra Shepard and Craig Muldrew begin sections of their work by referencing Thomas Hobbes. Shepard begins her 2015 publication, *Accounting For Oneself*, with the following epigraph: 'For let a man (as most men do,) rate themselves at the highest Value they can; yet their true Value is no more than it is esteemed by others.'[1] Similarly, Muldrew begins a chapter in *The Economy of Obligation* (1998) with a similar extract: 'The Value, or WORTH of a man, is as of all other things, his Price; that is to say, so much as would be given for the use of his Power: and therefore is not absolute; but a thing dependent on the need and judgement of another.'[2] Both scholars utilise Hobbes to demonstrate how social estimation was dependent upon the observations of wider society. While Muldrew focuses on the degree of trust in communities which formed a 'culture of credit', Shepard explores the language of self-description in relation to the 'worth' of an individual, which led to a 'culture of appraisal'.[3] Similarly, Toby Ditz has shown how private correspondence between merchants in eighteenth-century Philadelphia was tactically constructed to preserve or earn 'the trust of other men … what mattered most in safeguarding reputation was the judgment of other men'.[4] In contrast, this chapter analyses the narrative in pleadings surrounding a dynamic series of events which led to an individual failure. In this manner, it is possible to see how those involved in the bankruptcy process began to judge the demise of an individual which led to a commission of bankruptcy.

Shepard has suggested that entering the late seventeenth century, interpersonal credit was becoming less stable and increasingly difficult to quantify

---

1 Alexandra Shepard, *Accounting For Oneself: Worth, Status, and the Social Order in Early Modern England* (Oxford, 2015), p. 1.
2 Craig Muldrew, *The Economy of Obligation: The Culture of Credit and Social Relations in Early Modern England* (Basingstoke, 1998), p. 148.
3 Ibid., pp. 148–150; Shepard, *Accounting For Oneself*, p. 28.
4 Toby Ditz, 'Shipwrecked; or, Masculinity Imperiled: Mercantile Representations of Failure and the Gendered Self in Eighteenth-Century Philadelphia', *The Journal of American History*, 81 (1994), p. 53.

and judge. One aspect of this assessment is that Shepard analyses witness statements in the present tense, as it was 'the goods and chattels *in people's possession*', which determined status and social position within the community.[5] While Carl Wennerlind suggested that 'honesty and punctuality' were behavioural ideals through which creditworthiness could be identified and defended, Emily Kadens has argued that reputation was becoming increasingly difficult to evaluate because of a general allowance of late payments.[6] When failure struck and a commission was executed, we see the inability to effectively judge trustworthiness and credibility become heightened in Chancery. Indeed, the types of credit networks litigated in Chancery differed dramatically from those explored by Muldrew and Shepard, as they involved vast amounts of debt, were multifaceted in nature, and were restricted to merchants and traders. However, the complex nature of bankruptcy suits is further highlighted when we analyse the way in which individuals sought to clarify the failure of an individual involved in the process.

This chapter analyses the flow of information, and the transfer of knowledge, throughout the trading community in terms of circulating judgements about individual bankrupts. While pleadings were submitted in the present tense in an attempt to secure an immediate judgment from the court, those involved in the bankruptcy process sought to look back and quantify the timing of certain actions as they related to a commission of bankruptcy. Similarly, a central feature of the narrative presented in pleadings was the degree of risk, investment, and potential return involved in future dealings. As such, bankruptcy can inform us of multiple aspects of the temporality of trade, as well as certain social features of failure, as individuals sought to assess the actions – both in the past, and opportunities in the future – of those involved in debt recovery. The complexities of bankruptcy procedure unsettled the ability to formulate clear judgements about individual failures.

The chapter is divided into two broad sections. The first section explores how the law and legal advice manuals sought to clarify the timing of bankruptcy procedure, and in particular, the exact moment a debtor could be declared a bankrupt. As discussed in the previous chapter, there were often disparities between legal ideals and the practical realities of experience, and the timing of bankruptcy was no different. The second, and much larger section, pays closer attention to the cases themselves, and is itself further broken down into four

---

5 Shepard, *Accounting For Oneself*, p. 1, my italics.
6 Carl Wennerlind, *Casualties of Credit: The English Financial Revolution, 1620–1720* (Cambridge, 2011), p. 97; Emily Kadens, 'Pre-Modern Credit Networks and the Limits of Reputation', *Iowa Law Review*, 100 (2015), pp. 2444–2451; see also Muldrew, *The Economy of Obligation*, p. 174; Keith Wrightson, *Earthly Necessities: Economic Lives in Early Modern Britain, 1470–1750* (London, 2002), p. 127; Laurence Fontaine, *The Moral Economy: Poverty, Credit, And Trust In Early Modern Europe* (Cambridge, 2014), pp. 275–276.

manageable parts. Part one explores the specific details of these disparities by analysing certain ambiguities that arose regarding the timing of failure. Particular attention is paid to the public nature of a commission of bankruptcy and the degree to which this information was widely and commonly disseminated. The second part builds upon this notion of public knowledge and circulating judgements by analysing how particular decisions within the bankruptcy process could impact future outcomes, such as the level of dividends to be paid. The future, as well as the past, is analysed in terms of certain social aspects of trade. The chapter then moves on to assess how individuals interpreted the specific acts or actions of both creditors and debtors. Part three discusses the distinctions made between acts and actors, as well as between genuine and fraudulent debts. These distinctions are then built upon in the final part of the chapter, as we see how acting in a public manner, and trading within certain times, was seen to be acting honourably and in a trustworthy manner, while undertaking tasks in a secret and clandestine way was seen to be fraudulent and dishonest. The combination of these sub-themes provides new insights into the multifaceted nature of failure – from an individual and wider social perspective.

The Law and the Timing of Bankruptcy

One important aspect of the operation of bankruptcy was the exact moment in which a debtor committed an act of bankruptcy. It was the bankruptcy commissioners who were tasked with looking back and trying to ascertain if, and when, a debtor committed such an act. It was from this point of committing the illegal act that the debtor was considered a bankrupt, and as a legal principle, any credit, debts, or estate of the bankrupt were to be encompassed within the commission from that moment onwards. However, bankruptcy statutes and advice manuals were particularly vague on the specificities of these issues, leaving the exact moment of bankruptcy open to interpretation. In Thomas Goodinge's view, the precise timing of bankruptcy seemed unimportant:

> If the Petition (which is to set forth the Time when he became a Bankrupt) do shew, that he was a Bankrupt the *1st* of *June* … and the Commissioners find that he became a Bankrupt the *1st* of *November* following, yet it's well enough, for it sufficeth that he is a Bankrupt, and the Time is not material, so it be before the Date and suing forth the Commission.[7]

Goodinge explains that 'the Time is not material', as long as it occurred *before* a commission of bankruptcy was executed. As the author of a practical

---

7   Thomas Goodinge, *The Law Against Bankrupts*, 5th edn (London, 1726), p. 4.

advice manual, Goodinge was simply explaining to creditors that the act of bankruptcy had to have occurred prior to their petition to the Lord Chancellor to begin bankruptcy proceedings. If this was the case, then the commission was legally valid. However, when discussing the decisions of the commissioners themselves, Goodinge explained that they were generally cautious in declaring the bankruptcy from a specific time or date, 'but leave it to a Trial at Law, in Case there be any Question or Doubt of it; and this for their own Security against Actions that may be brought against them'.[8] Any question of fact was to be tried before a jury in the common law courts, and this was especially true regarding the timing of the act of bankruptcy.[9] Yet, Goodinge further suggested that commissioners were intentionally vague in order to protect themselves against suits being taken out against them personally. This led to a situation whereby the legal advice, and the work of the commissioners, resulted in uncertainty surrounding the date of an act of bankruptcy, and therefore when the bankruptcy had first begun. While the specific time of the act of bankruptcy was unimportant in the eyes of the law, it was of crucial importance to creditors and the bankrupt, as it determined which debts and individual actions were legally valid. For example, discussing the conveyance of goods in relation to the timing of bankruptcy, Goodinge stated that anything executed 'after the Time of Bankrupcy, is totally void'.[10] Put simply, after an act of bankruptcy, the debtor had no control over their actions, as every credit and debt, as well as the entirety of their estate, was to be encompassed within the authority of the commission. Until discharged, a bankrupt had no profession or means of earning a living, and simply held a legal status as a bankrupt.[11]

As well as the exact timing of failure, several other issues arose surrounding an act of bankruptcy. One such example concerned the public nature – and whether traders took 'notice' – of the act of bankruptcy and the subsequent commission. In his advice manual, Thomas Davies grappled with the public nature of commissions in relation to acts of bankruptcy: 'for a *Commission is a publick Act, of which all are bound to take Notice*; but an Act of Bankruptcy may be so secret as to be impossible to be known'.[12] An act of bankruptcy could consist of a trader concealing themselves in their house for as little as an hour, in order to delay or defraud their creditors. Even if their other correspondents were not aware of such action, Davies established 'that in Law, as well as Philosophy, *De non entibus & non apparentibus eadem est ratio*' [concerning things which

---

8   Ibid., p. 48.
9   See James Oldham, *English Common Law in the Age of Mansfield* (Chapel Hill, 2004), p. 107.
10   Ibid., pp. 28–29.
11   Robert Nantes, 'English Bankrupts 1732–1831: A Social Account' (unpublished PhD dissertation, University of Exeter, 2020), p. 36.
12   Thomas Davies, *The Laws Relating to Bankrupts* (London, 1744), p. 420.

are not apparent, the rule is the same].[13] This legal position created obvious problems for tradesmen dealing with debtors who were subsequently declared bankrupt by commissioners. Davies references a case litigated in King's Bench entitled '*Hill and others* against *Shish*' (1728–1729), to give a more nuanced understanding of the debates surrounding this legal principle.

In this suit, the eminent lawyer Sir Bartholomew Shower argued that if a man be arrested for a just debt of £100, and shall not pay or compound with his creditors for six months, then he should be considered a bankrupt from the time of the first arrest. In setting out possible objections to this position, Shower suggested that if such a construction was allowed then the inconvenience to other traders would be great:

> Because, if a trading Person be arrested, and bailed, and a third person knowing nothing of it intrusts him, or deals with him, that if such Person should be a Bankrupt from the first Arrest, that then every Person so dealing with him, would be forced to return the Goods, and yet lose the Money he paid for them; which they say would be so great a Mischief, that it would discourage Trade.[14]

Answering his own objections, Shower believed that no debtor would be endangered for a payment to the bankrupt before such time as he shall 'know that he is become a Bankrupt'. While an arrest in itself could not cause a man to be bankrupt – as it was not an offence to be in debt – in this suit, Lord Chief Justice Wright stated that the debtor could be considered a bankrupt at the point of rendering himself in discharge of his bail.[15] More broadly, a debtor could be considered a bankrupt if he failed to pay, or attempted to compound for, a debt of £100 or more six months after it was due, or six months after a writ to recover debt had been executed. While Bartholomew Shower believed that the laws were favourably created – and should therefore be favourably interpreted – for the benefit of the creditors, this position is paradoxical in nature, as an act of bankruptcy was a private act, but the bankruptcy must have been publicly known to the trading community.[16]

It is worth pausing on this analysis for a moment, as while this was a summary of a case litigated in a common law court, it sets out the seeming absurdity of a point of law relating to bankruptcy. This meant that there were situations whereby a debtor could have carried on his trade openly and in public, while all

13 Ibid., p. 118.
14 Ibid., pp. 116–118.
15 Ibid., pp. 116–117.
16 Ibid., pp. 116-117; W. J. Jones, 'The Foundations of English Bankruptcy: Statutes and Commissions in the Early Modern Period', *Transactions of the American Philosophical Society*, 69 (1979), p. 25.

the time being technically declared a bankrupt. During this period, it became established that a commission had to be executed within five years of a debtor committing an act of bankruptcy. Although, as the statutes were intended to be interpreted for the benefit of the creditors, there were examples where this had been extended.[17] But as Goodinge suggested, 'it's without Doubt the sooner the better for the Creditors'.[18] The flexibility afforded to creditors allowed for a remarkably large window between the initial act and the petition of the creditors. If the act occurred before the petition to the Lord Chancellor, then it had met the requirements of the law. However, as the range of circumstances that the law specified could include extremely private acts, conducted in front of a limited number of individuals, then the question arose regarding how the remainder of the bankrupt's trading partners were expected to know about such a failure. Lord Chancellor Nottingham sought to clarify this absurdity in 1681, decreeing that '*the Law was hard against Tradesmen that dealt with Bankrupts before Notice*; and the Assignees ought not to be assisted in Equity in any such case'.[19] Despite attempting to clarify such an ambiguity, this led to a theoretical position, and a moment in time after the act of bankruptcy, whereby a debtor was simultaneously a bankrupt, and not a bankrupt, depending on whether a commission of bankruptcy was ever taken out.

Crucially, the law had established that a simple act of bankruptcy could make a trader a bankrupt, while simultaneously acknowledging that tradesmen must have had 'notice' of such an act. As Goodinge concluded, any transaction completed by a debtor before he became a bankrupt 'is Without Question good; and so are all the Acts he doth before he comes *to appear to be a Bankrupt*'.[20] But this legal positioning raised serious questions about how those within the trading community resolved such a paradox and judged an insolvent debtor to be a bankrupt prior to a declaration by commissioners. Broadly speaking, the creation of new laws is reactionary, and governed by instances and scenarios that have arisen previously. While this positioning may seem absurd and paradoxical to modern readers, it needs to be placed in the context of the aims and motivations of the original bankruptcy acts. Notably, that the legislation was enacted to increase the recovery power and to extend the scope available to creditors over fraudulent and criminal debtors. In many ways, the law can be seen to be working exactly as it should be for that class of creditors who sought to impose the harshness of the law.

A similar point can be made about commissions themselves, as a commission of bankruptcy was seen as a 'matter of record', meaning it was the responsibility

17   Ibid., pp. 35–38; Jones claims that five years was seen as the 'yardstick', 'The Foundations of English Bankruptcy', pp. 31–32.
18   Goodinge, *The Law Against Bankrupts*, p. 35.
19   Davies, *The Laws Relating to Bankrupts*, p. 410.
20   Goodinge, *The Law Against Bankrupts*, pp. 94–95, my italics.

of the trading community to take notice of the proceedings. Further to placing a notice in the *London Gazette* when a commission had been executed, it was not uncommon for notices to be placed at Guildhall, the Exchange, or other 'such publick Places'.[21] A creditor who did not join in the commission was seen to have voluntarily declined to do so – as they had not taken notice – and subsequently forfeited their claim to the bankrupt's estate.[22] However, the extent to which commissions were known to the public is unclear. As one anonymous tract stated, an advertisement in the *Gazette* was an insufficient notice to creditors, who may have 'no Suspicion of a Commission ... for the Man has been really broke perhaps so long, as to be forgot'.[23] The prospect of executing a commission against debtors who had been insolvent for an extended period was uncommon, and it was unrealistic for creditors to continually take notice of public advertisements and declarations.

Contemporary advice manuals highlighted a number of ambiguities, and even absurdities, in the practical implementation of the law, but they did not provide information on how to overcome such issues. With the law and subsequent legal guidance being open to interpretation, several suits were initiated in Chancery whereby the public nature of the act of bankruptcy, the ongoing commission of bankruptcy, and the timing between these two events were vehemently debated. Similarly, several individuals exhibited a genuine concern that their financial transactions would be considered void by commissioners, as the exact date of failure had not been clarified.

Some caution should be exercised when relying solely on legal records to comment on the actions and reputation of individuals between the act of bankruptcy and the execution of the commission. The intention of bankruptcy proceedings was to look back and appraise the moment in which a debtor failed and committed an illegal act. In this manner, timing was calculated and debated for legal purposes of debt-recovery. However, we have limited information regarding the actions of debtors between these two periods. Debtors could have been acting in numerous ways, including but not limited to, comprising with creditors, hiding assets, absconding, asking for more time for repayment, acting in a respectful and public manner, trading within a family unit or in another individual's name, or simply committing outright fraud. However, what we do see in these cases are the ways in which individuals described what they perceived to be the tell-tale signs of dishonesty, respectability, and credit-worthiness around the time of the debated failure. As such, we can analyse the appraisal of the actions and words of those involved in trade networks to illuminate the ways in which individuals were seen to have failed.

---

21   Ibid., p. 44.
22   Jones, 'The Foundations of English Bankruptcy', p. 34.
23   *Considerations Upon Commissions of Bankrupts* (London, 1727), p. 15.

The Temporality of Trade in Bankruptcy Suits

Timing and the Public Nature of Bankruptcy

Questions relating to the timing of specific acts are commonplace across legal disputes, for example, party 'x' should have done 'y' at a certain time and failed to do it.[24] Similarly, in certain circumstances, the law holds individuals responsible for a failure to act in instances whereby they held a legal responsibility to do so.[25] But in relation to early modern bankruptcy, the ambiguities discussed above became amplified in Chancery, as parties involved in suits vehemently debated the exact timing of failure. We have seen in the previous chapter the correct, linear path bankruptcy procedure was expected to follow, as well as several reasons why this process failed. However, opposing parties attempted to establish their own timeline of failure, which led to the exact timing of certain events – an act of bankruptcy, the assignment of a security, the sale of goods, etc. – becoming contested.

In *Ambrose v Brookes* (1681), the plaintiff William Ambrose submitted a bill of complaint naming the bankrupt William Skinner, two commissioners, and two further creditors as defendants. All that survives from this suit is the joint answer of four defendants – not including the bankrupt – which provides a clear example of debates surrounding the timing of failure. What is interesting is that the defendants accept the majority of claims made in the bill of complaint. It is accepted that Ambrose arrested the bankrupt for the failure to repay a debt of over £90, and that Ambrose received a judgment from the court of King's Bench which assigned Skinner's house to the plaintiff to satisfy the debt. Indeed, the main objection of the defendants concerned the timing of this arrest and assignment. Quite simply, the defendants claimed that the arrest took place, 'after the said Skinner was become a Bankrupt or had done Acts whereby hee was afterwards adjudged or declared a Bankrupt before the time of the arrest'. As such, Skinner had 'committed Acts of Bankrupcy before the time of the last Assignment or Securetie was entered into'. As creditors themselves, the defendants had taken out a commission of bankruptcy, and as such, the plaintiff's only recourse was to come into the commission as a creditor,

---

24 This is particularly true in contract law, whereby those engaged in a contract either adhere to the promises made, or breach the contract, see Ian R. Macneil, 'Contracts: Adjustment of Long-Term Economic Relations Under Classical, Neo-Classical, and Relational Contract Law', *Northwestern University Law Review*, 72 (1978), pp. 854–905; Alexander J. Triantis and George G. Triantis, 'Timing Problems in Contract Breach Decisions', *The Journal of Law and Economics*, 41 (1998), pp. 163–208; Eric A. Posner, 'A Theory of Contract Law Under Conditions of Radical Judicial Error', *Northwestern University Law Review*, 94 (2000), pp. 749–774.

25 See John Kleinig, 'Criminal Liability for Failures to Act', *Law and Contemporary Problems*, 49 (1986), pp. 161–180.

pay his contribution money, produce his securities as proof of the outstanding debt, and receive a dividend.[26]

Similarly, in *Price v Gough* (1730), the assignees of James Gough, a broker from London, appeared as defendants. In their answer, they established that a commission of bankruptcy was taken out on 7 February 1727, and James Gough was declared 'to have been a Bankrupt before the date and suing forth of the said Commission'. The defendants were attempting to establish that the commission was legally executed, and the commissioners had declared Gough a bankrupt. However, the defendants claimed to not be aware of when the bankrupt committed any acts of bankruptcy, concluding, 'But when or upon what day particularly the said James Gough did first become a Bankrupt these Defendants do not know and Cannot set forth.'[27] In relation to a specific assignment of South Sea stock, the assignees suggested that if Gough was a bankrupt before the first execution of the stock, 'which these Defendants have not yet discovered', they would demand that they, 'shall be well intitled to the Dividends and Produce of the said stock and Annuitys during the lifetime of the said James Gough'.[28] In this example, even the assignees were uncertain of the exact date of bankruptcy and could not definitively establish whether the South Sea stock should fall within the scope of the commission or not. By suggesting that they had yet to 'discover' whether the act of bankruptcy occurred before the assignment, they leave the timing of bankruptcy to the decision of the court.

In *Glover v Evans* (1697), the plaintiffs, John Glover a merchant and John Allen a glass seller, were assignees of James Briggs. The plaintiffs requested that the defendant, John Evans, come to an account for a consignment of cloth that he had sold in Constantinople for the benefit of the bankrupt.[29] In his answer, Evans stated that he traded with Briggs 'above three months before the said Briggs failed'. At this time, he was in 'good credit … and had therefore full power and authority to dispose of the said cloth'. At the time of their dealings, Briggs was trading in his own name and since his bankruptcy he had not received any goods.[30] In the above cases, the central issue concerns the exact timing of a specific and debated event. However, the concept of time led to more complicated suits.

In *Nickalls v Mawson* (1735), the plaintiffs were assignees of Moses West, a joiner and chapman of St Mary Le Strand, London, and named Thomas Mawson and Moses West as defendants. The bill claimed that in April 1734, Mawson had contracted West 'to pull down two Messuages or Tenements

26   TNA, C6/369/77, 'Ambrose v Brookes' (1681), Answer of William Brookes, John Johnson, Francis Scott, and Daniel Duthais.
27   TNA, C11/2034/33, 'Price v Gough' (1730), Answer of Edmund Crull and Phillip Hale.
28   Ibid.
29   TNA, C6/415/77, 'Glover v Evans' (1697), Bill of Complaint.
30   Ibid., Answer of John Evans.

situate at the bottom of Swan Yard in the Strand and in the place and stead thereof to erect and build for him the said Thomas Mawson two new brick messuages or tenements and also to find materials for the same and to repair several other brick houses'. The bankrupt was to find and provide materials, and when the work was done, it was to be 'measured and valued' with West being reimbursed from Mawson. While the work was completed, West was declared a bankrupt before any payment was made. A commission was taken out on 26 April 1734 and an indenture of the bankrupt's estate was made to the assignees on 15 May 1734. Since that time, the plaintiffs stated that they had not been given access to the building to conduct their own valuation and accused the defendant and the bankrupt of combining and confederating to keep the money out of the hands of the commission. Ultimately, the original valuation for the work done was £713 16s 10d, which was still due to the assignees.[31]

In his answer, Mawson stated that he had employed the bankrupt as a carpenter and joiner for several years and he had paid him for the work he had done, providing five schedules of account as evidence. As such, the defendant meticulously worked through the dealings he had with the bankrupt and the work he had paid for. All of which happened before he became a bankrupt in 1734.[32] This is a rare example of a bankrupt gaining credit for services rather than for the buying and selling of products, and we can see how the bankruptcy process upset the timeline of the payment for manual labour. Bankruptcy procedure was intended to be limited to merchants or traders who made their living through 'buying and selling'. However, this case adds further evidence to the fact that by this period the statutes were being liberally interpreted and a wider range of traders were becoming incorporated into the meaning and definition of a trader.[33]

Finally, in *Camfield v Warren* (1699–1700), the plaintiff Francis Camfield was an assignee of Thomas Field, and submitted a bill whereby he accused the bankrupt of 'fraudulently and with Evil intent' assigning a large portion of his estate to the other six defendants. Much of the suit centred around the timing of specific paper instruments.[34] In his answer, Jeremiah Cole stated, 'he beleiveth it to be true' that a commission of bankruptcy was issued against Field, but did not know 'whether the said Thomas Field Committed any act of Bankrupcy before the Issueing forth of the said Commission'. Cole concluded that 'if the said thomas Field did Comitt any Act of Bankrupcy and became a Bankrupt the same was done as this defendant verily believes after the said Assignment and Judgment and not before'. A number of securities 'were given to this Defendant

---

31   TNA, C11/520/51, 'Nickalls v Mawson' (1735), Bill of Complaint.
32   TNA, C11/520/51, 'Nickalls v Mawson' (1735), Answer of Thomas Mawson.
33   Aidan Collins, 'Bankrupt Traders in the Court of Chancery, 1674–1750', *Eighteenth-Century Studies*, 55 (2021), pp. 65–82.
34   TNA, C6/391/16, 'Camfield v Warren' (1699–1700), Bill of Complaint.

before any Commission of Bankruptcy issued against the said Thomas Field and before any act of Bankrupcy was committed by the said Thomas Field to the knowledge or beliefe of this Defendant'.[35] In his answer, Thomas Warren stated that he was unaware of Field committing an act of bankruptcy, but was willing to have the goods in his possession appraised, 'in case upon a Tryall at Law … it should be found that the said Thomas Fields did become a bankrupt before his Executing the said Bond'.[36] These cases demonstrate the inability of creditors, assignees, and commissioners to establish a specific date for failure.

This inability created practical difficulties in the bankruptcy process as competing parties debated the goods, transactions, and estate to which they held a legal right. However, what these suits also show is the inability to effectively judge the social and economic standing of the bankrupt around the time of their failure. References in individual statements to their 'belief' or 'knowledge' of the declarations of the commission, or the actions of the bankrupt, demonstrate that circulating judgements regarding individual traders were difficult to quantify. In a bill submitted in 1745, Sir Thomas Webster accused two co-bankrupts of owing him over £900 and committing 'divers flagrant and notorious Acts of Bankruptcy', seemingly in an attempt to prove that the failure of the bankrupts was well known.[37] More broadly, the complexities of bankruptcy, and the ambiguities present in its procedure, upset the manner in which circulating judgements were communicated and known within the wider community.

These complexities are clearly illustrated in a case of extended indebtedness from 1689, in which the facts of the case are undisputed, and presented as follows. John Todd borrowed £50 from James Robinson, in which the plaintiff Joshua Guest stood security. Todd subsequently furnished the Earl of Westmorland with several parcels of wine to the value of £50, and the Earl directed his assistant John Arney to satisfy the bill of sale by paying Todd for the goods. Todd then assigned the bill of sale over to Guest, which would have completed the intricate circle of transactions and settled all outstanding debts. Indeed, upon seeking guarantees from all parties concerned, Guest paid the initial loan of £50 back to Robinson, and awaited payment from Arney. However, Guest claimed that unbeknown to him, a commission of bankruptcy had already been issued against Todd, and as such, Arney refused to honour the bill of sale.[38] In his answer, Arney agreed with the plaintiff's version of events, but suggested that he was 'afraid to pay the Complainant the said Fifty pounds for feare he may be lyable to pay the same over againe', by order of the

35   Ibid., Answer of Jeremiah Cole.
36   Ibid., Answer of Thomas Warren.
37   TNA, C11/2103/30, 'Webster v Sawbridge' (1745), Bill of Complaint.
38   TNA, C6/416/12, 'Guest v Arney' (1689), Bill of Complaint.

commissioners.[39] While the veracity of this claim is impossible to establish, the response seems credible, as if Todd was declared a bankrupt, then the commission of bankruptcy would have held legal rights over all of Todd's credits, debts and estate, including the bill of sale. Therefore, if Arney had paid the bill of sale after Todd was known to be a bankrupt, then this transaction would be considered void, and it is possible that the commissioners could demand that Arney satisfy the bill of sale a second time. This is a good example of the way in which knowledge – or a lack of knowledge – of the bankruptcy process had unsettled established credit networks. There is an inherent fear presented in this suit, whereby the uncertainty surrounding the outcome of bankruptcy had directly influenced the actions of certain individuals.

In *Bosville v Denne* (1704–1706), the defendant Robert Sandford was indebted to William Nehoffe for timber sold to him, amounting to £74 18s. Sandford issued a note, dated 6 December 1704, which was to be satisfied before 26 January. Shortly after receiving the note, and having 'occasion for money', Nehoffe applied himself to the plaintiff, John Bosville, in an attempt to get the note discounted. Having asked Sandford about the legitimacy of the note, and being assured that it would be paid on time, the plaintiff paid £74 for the note on 13 December 1704, leaving a potential future profit of 18s. Yet, sometime between the discounting of the note and its due date, a commission of bankruptcy was awarded against Nehoffe, and his goods were assigned to a second named defendant, Cornelius Denne. Bosville claimed very confidently that the commissioners could not touch his note, as it was discounted long before any commission of bankruptcy was executed. However, the plaintiff also stated that Sandford had refused to satisfy the note, as he 'feared that in case he payd the said money to your Orator he might be in danger of paying the same over again'. Ultimately, Bosville alleged that the bankrupt and these two defendants had confederated to defraud him of his just debts, as they claimed that the note was not discounted until after Nehoffe had been declared a bankrupt.[40]

In the only answer that survives, Cornelius Denne admitted that no act of bankruptcy was committed until 19 January 1705, but denied that any money was ever due to the plaintiff.[41] If we take Denne's response at face value, then it can be concluded that the note was definitively discounted prior to any acts of bankruptcy being committed. However, we can see in this example how the complexity of financial arrangements, involving several parties, could lead to various interpretations of the chronological timeline of events. Here, we see how the disputed act is the discounting of the note – rather than the issuing of the note itself – interacting with the complexities of bankruptcy. Throughout these

39   Ibid., Answer of John Arney.
40   TNA, C6/379/39, 'Bosville v Denne' (1704–1706), Bill of Complaint.
41   Ibid., Answer of Cornelius Denne.

cases, the difficulty in attempting to establish exactly when a debtor became a bankrupt, both legally, and in the eyes of the wider community, is clearly illustrated. Largely, this is because of the uncertainty of the flow of information and the circulation of public knowledge regarding the timing of bankruptcy.

Several suits in Chancery directly and more explicitly commented on the public nature of proceedings. As the first meeting of creditors had to take place within two weeks of the declaration of bankruptcy by commissioners, many creditors remained ignorant of the very existence of a commission, and others would have been unable to attend a meeting in London at short notice. This led to the possibility of assignees being chosen from an unrepresentative selection of creditors, and accusations of fraud were commonplace. In *Fotheringham v Fell* (1720), the defendants complained that the commission of bankruptcy was 'kept private or not proceeded upon for a long time'.[42] As such, the creditors suggested that they were unable to enter the commission in due time and had been purposefully excluded. In one case from 1750, the only defendant, Richard Corcott, claimed to be an 'entire stranger' to the initiation of a commission of bankruptcy which occurred eight years previously. Corcott 'refused to inform the Complainant what right he had or claimed to the said Houses Stables and Premises and this Defendant is advised and humbly insists that he is not obliged' to disclose the same unless the plaintiff showed him some title to the property.[43] With no knowledge of the commission, Corcott asked for proof of the plaintiff's right to the property in question before he complied with the wishes of the assignees.

In *Croxton v Moffatt* (1730), the plaintiff George Croxton was a merchant from Manchester and the assignee of John Hornblower, a trader from Abergavenny, Monmouthshire. In his bill of complaint, dated 16 April 1730, Croxton accused the bankrupt and several defendants of fraudulently executing a commission of bankruptcy in 1729, with the intent of 'Excluding your Orator and other his Creditors in the Country from their proportionable Shares thereof'. Croxton claimed that knowledge of the commission had not reached any creditors outside London, which was done in order to allow the bankrupt to return home and enter into 'fresh credit' in the country. By doing this, it was hoped that the bankrupt could raise extra money in his local community in order to pay his creditors in London their full demands.[44] Croxton had managed to get the initial commission superseded and a new one executed by claiming that the creditors in London had kept the commission, 'in their pockets and Concealed from the knowledge of your Orator'.[45] In contrast, the

42   TNA, C11/38/15, 'Fotheringham v Fell' (1720), Answer of John Frost and Thomas Dunckley.
43   TNA, C11/1643/27, 'Hazard v Corcott' (1750), Answer of Richard Corcott.
44   TNA, C11/250/14, 'Croxton v Moffatt' (1730), Bill of Complaint.
45   Ibid.

three defendants denied that the bankrupt had any prior knowledge of the commission, suggesting he was 'much Surprized and Solemnely protested to these defendants that he had not committed any act of Bankruptcy'.[46] Within this suit, we clearly see debates surrounding the ability to circulate information about a commission throughout the country.

In *Kellaway v Smith* (1730), the plaintiff William Kellaway suggested that the two assignees and defendants, Thomas Barton and William Dicks, both wine coopers from London, executed a commission of bankruptcy against William Smith, a vintner from London, in order to nominate themselves assignees. As these individuals were all experts in the same trade, Kellaway alleged that the commission was fraudulently devised so that Barton could buy the bankrupt's goods at a much lower value than their true worth.[47] This was a common accusation levelled against bankrupts, whereby they were accused of quickly, and fraudulently, filling initial meetings with friendly or fictitious creditors in order to nominate compliant assignees.[48] In their answer, both Smith and Barton explained that a bankrupt cannot choose an assignee, and both assignees were chosen from amongst the creditors who entered the commission. Yet, what is damning for the plaintiff, is that both defendants claimed that Kellaway was first offered the role of assignee but turned it down. Furthermore, Barton stated that the meeting of the creditors was advertised in the *Gazette*, and was open to the public for all to see and attend if they so wished.[49] Barton focused on the public nature of proceedings to counter accusations of fraud, as acting openly and in public during the time of proceeding quashed the notion that they had acted in a clandestine manner. By suggesting that the plaintiff had knowledge of the commission, and had refused the role of assignee, Barton refutes any accusation of executing the commission with the intention of benefitting the bankrupt.

In *Collins v Ongley* (1694–1695), the plaintiff, Thomas Collins, a linen draper from London, was an assignee of a linen draper named John Shergold. Collins stated that in July 1693, Shergold had debts of over £1000 and 'being either not able or not willing to pay the same he ... privately conveyed away the greatest parte of his goods into the Mint or White Fryers and ... left his said shop and trade and went into the White Fryers to hide and protect himselfe from his creditors where he still continued'. The bill claimed that the eight defendants took out individual cases against the bankrupt in the common law courts, and took possession of some of his linen cloth as security. They undertook these actions despite being 'Creditors to a small value and being

---

46 Ibid., Answer of James Moffatt, Francis Risden, and Lancelot Andrews.
47 TNA, C11/2426/18, 'Kellaway v Smith' (1730), Bill of Complaint.
48 Nantes, 'English Bankrupts 1732–1831', pp. 58–59.
49 TNA, C11/2426/18, 'Kellaway v Smith' (1730), Answer of William Smith; Answer of Thomas Barton.

well assured That a Comission of Bankrupts would be taken out by the rest of the Creditors'. A commission was eventually taken out on 2 December 1693.[50] In their answer, four defendants accepted that they took goods worth £49 4s 8d, but insisted they were still owed £79 9s 4d. Ultimately, they 'hope they shall not be compelled to pay the same or any part thereof to the plaintiff' and they 'Ought as they are advised to be admitted to have the benifitt of the Comission of Bankruptcy if any such there be for what is still due to them'.[51] Here, the defendants seemed to jump the gun and take out individual actions prior to the execution of the commission. However, now the commission was underway, they wanted to be admitted as creditors in the ongoing process.

Risk, Reward, and Future Returns

Discussing the various options available to businessmen, Julian Hoppit has suggested that 'Debt collection was indeed akin to an investment', as creditors had to weigh up the cost of repayment against estimated returns.[52] More recently, Siobhan Talbott has used merchant correspondence to show how individuals made judgements about risk and reward in legal proceedings.[53] *Pollard v Launder* (1725) is a case worth analysing in detail, as while it speaks to several issues discussed above, it also demonstrates how the bankruptcy process could affect future decisions.

The two plaintiffs were assignees of three co-partners, Henry, Mary, and Elizabeth Brunsell, all mercers from Middlesex. In their bill of complaint, dated 13 April 1725, the plaintiffs claimed that the three bankrupts had fraudulently assigned various securities to several defendants, including bonds for a 'considerable penalty', a warrant of attorney, and a mortgage for a property in Nottinghamshire. The plaintiffs stated that the bankrupts were never truly indebted to these defendants, and all securities were entered into, 'under some Secret promise Trust or engagement in order to secrete and conceal the said Bankrupts Estate from other their reall Creditors'. At the time of executing these transactions, and to add legitimacy to their actions, the defendants pretended that the co-partners were in 'declining circumstances', but really the securities were transacted for 'a farr greater summe than was really due'. Any securities were given after the co-partners became bankrupts, which the defendants 'well knew in their consciences to be true'.[54] In contrast, all three defendants insisted that any financial transactions were entered into as genuine securities for money lent. One defendant, Benjamin Wilcox, stated that while a commission

50   TNA, C6/394/37, 'Collins v Ongley' (1694-1695), Bill of Complaint.
51   Ibid., Answer of Samuel Ongley the elder, Samuel Ongley the younger, Oliver Andrews, and John Page.
52   Julian Hoppit, *Risk and Failure in English Business 1700–1800* (Cambridge, 1987), p. 41.
53   Siobhan Talbott, *Knowledge, Information and Business Education in the British Atlantic World, 1620–1760* (Oxford University Press, forthcoming 2024).
54   TNA, C11/291/33, 'Pollard v Launder' (1725), Bill of Complaint.

of bankruptcy had been executed against the three co-partners, he believed that 'the said Brunsells never Comitted any act of Bankrupcy previous to the suing out of the said Comission' and as such, the plaintiffs would be unable to 'prove any act of Bankrupcy in the said Brunsells In Case the said Question should ever Come to be Disputed in a Legall and proper manner'.[55] However, this suit centred around the perceived credibility of the three co-partners at the time of executing various securities, and the defendants provided detailed accounts of their interpretations of the three bankrupts during their personal trade with them.

William Launder stated that he had dealt individually with Henry Brunsell for over two years, but was not aware that the three were mercers, or co-partners, 'untill after the time when he saw notice in the Gazette that a Commission of Bankrupt was taken out against them as partners'. Launder asserted that he did not believe Henry Brunsell 'was in bad and low Circumstances both before and at the time when he gave the said Warrant of attorney to this Defendant But this Defendant saith he believed when the same was given that he was of ability to pay all his debts'.[56] Again, we see questions relating to the public knowledge of an individual's trading activities being raised, as Launder claimed ignorance of the business partnership. However, he also claimed that the bankrupt was able to satisfy his debts at the time of executing the warrant of attorney, demonstrating that his assessment of credibility was based on his physical ability to repay.

In his answer, Charles Turner stated that he was 'intimately acquainted' with the bankrupts' late father, the Reverend Henry Brunsell, a Rector from Bingham, Nottinghamshire. Turner claimed that having a 'great value and Esteem' for the Reverend's memory, which extended to his three children, he agreed to lend the sum of £100 to carry on their trade. During this time, he believed they were in 'good circumstances', as they had inherited a property which was to be sold to repay the loan. However, in June or July 1724, Turner learned that rather than selling the property, the three had 'mortgaged the same twice over' to other creditors, and so decided to take goods as a further security, all of which occurred before the son Henry Brunsell was declared a bankrupt.[57] This is an interesting answer, as while we again see an assessment made on the three bankrupts' ability to repay, it also appears that the extension of credit was founded on the respect Turner held for the Brunsell family. Individuals engaged in the debt-recovery process struggled to look back and clarify the legal and moral standing of debtors at certain points in the past. This had ramifications for specific future events, as such uncertainty meant that financial transactions

55   Ibid., Answer of Benjamin Wilcox.
56   Ibid., Answer of William Launder.
57   Ibid., Answer of Charles Turner.

were delayed until clarification could be ascertained, either through official bankruptcy procedure or by recourse to Chancery.

As a relatively expensive process, creditors would need to try to calculate the cost of entering a commission of bankruptcy against the potential future dividends, which at certain stages could only be quantified in rough estimates. One anonymous tract suggested that even if creditors did have notice of a commission, 'the Contribution is so high, that it is not worth their while to come in; and it is probably raised so high on Purpose to keep them out'.[58] In a similar manner, assignees often found themselves in a difficult and uncomfortable position, being placed between attempting to collect and distribute the bankrupt's estate, while at the same time collecting contribution money from the remaining creditors. Examples of assignees encountering difficulties in Chancery are manifold. William Barloe of London stated that in the five years since the execution of the commission, he had only recovered £100 from the bankrupt's estate, despite being owed more than £6000.[59] The situation had become bleak for the assignees of John Prowse of Bristol, as despite owing more than £1000, the bankrupt only had a small estate, while his debtors had themselves become insolvent. Without raising substantial contribution money from further creditors, the assignees did not have 'sufficient to answer or Satisfy one Quarter part of the Charges of Executing and Carrying on the said Commission'.[60] It could be beneficial for creditors to gain a greater understanding of the size and substance of the bankrupt's estate in an attempt to assess the possibility of future returns before paying their contribution money.

The attempt to ascertain more knowledge relating to an individual failure is perhaps best illustrated by dissecting *Cotton v Hussey* (1698–1699), a complex case consisting of competing and contradictory interpretations of the role of the assignee. The plaintiffs were creditors of Simon Fydell, a chapman from Lincolnshire who was declared a bankrupt in October 1694 for debts amounting to £2000. The bill of complaint alleged that an acting assignee named John Hussey had mismanaged funds that had come into his possession. Having initially charged 2s 6d in the pound contribution money, raising a total of £1024 9s 10½ d, Hussey sought to contrive and 'deprive your Orator from all benefit and advantage by the said distribution'. Hussey was said to have acted frivolously and 'with intent only to keep the said money' to benefit himself.[61] Hussey countered the accusation by suggesting that the commission of bankruptcy was fraudulently executed by the bankrupt's brother, Joseph Fydell, 'more for the said Bankrupts benefitt' than for the benefit of the other creditors. As such,

58   *Considerations Upon Commissions of Bankrupts*, p. 15.
59   TNA, C11/587/2, 'Barlow v Boehm' (1750), Bill of Complaint.
60   TNA, C11/664/30, 'Freeke v Franklin' (1715), Bill of Complaint.
61   TNA, C6/393/8, 'Cotton v Hussey' (1698–1699), Bill of Complaint.

Hussey and several other creditors petitioned the Lord Chancellor to assign at least one additional commissioner who, once appointed, made Hussey the new assignee.

In his answer, Hussey admitted charging 2s 6d in the pound contribution money, and even accepted that one plaintiff, Cawdron Blow, did pay such a sum to the defendant. However, Blow refused to come in at the earliest point of asking and was therefore excluded by the commissioners from receiving any distribution from the first dividend, dated 18 April 1696. It was not until Blow discovered that the second dividend of 24 December 1697 was to be of a considerable amount that he became eager to enter the commission. Yet, Hussey felt this was a 'hardshipp' to the other creditors who had expended great sums in order to discover and recover the estate, 'before they knew whether they should be reimbursed any thing or not'. As such, Hussey was willing to reimburse the complainants their latest contribution money but left the decision up to 'the consideration of this honourable Court', whether they should be allowed in to receive a portion of the second dividend.[62] It appears that all parties within this suit demonstrated a fear of receiving less than they felt they were due to. However, we also become aware of the costly nature of bankruptcy procedure and the need to weigh up the potential benefits of entering this official path is seen in action. The plaintiffs were unable to effectively value the estate of the bankrupt at the time of the commission first being executed. Ultimately, this failure can be seen as an inability to quantify future payments from the bankrupt's estate.

Broadly speaking, an inability to satisfy debts resulted in ongoing conflict, not just between debtors and creditors, but also amongst creditors themselves. In *Barnes v Baldwin* (1698), a creditor was concerned with the ongoing commission of bankruptcy and so initiated a suit against every active member of the commission, consisting of four commissioners, two assignees, and the bankrupt himself. In response, the assignees and commissioners answered together, stating they were 'meer Strangers to and ignorant of all and every the thing and things matters Charges and transactions in the said bill of Complaint'. The commissioners explained that they held 'power and authority to execute the said Commission upon the examination of several witnesses upon oath'. If the plaintiff paid his contribution money and proved his debts to the commissioners, 'he shall have liberty to see all the Examinations and other proceedings upon the Commission and have an Account of what has been received'.[63] In this case, the commissioners clearly established their authority over the plaintiff and explained their role in executing the commission of

---

62   Ibid., Answer of John Hussey.
63   TNA, C6/387/74, 'Barnes v Baldwin' (1698), Answer of Samuel Baldwin, Richard Chauncy, John Cole, Thomas Reeve, John Cooper, and Renier Lampe.

bankruptcy. Similarly, in *Barnes v Baldwin* (1698), the plaintiff submitted a bill taking aim at the ongoing direction of the commission of bankruptcy. In response, six defendants claimed that Barnes would be able to view the examination and other documentation created by the commission once he had paid his contribution money, which the other creditors had already done.[64] In these cases, it appears that the plaintiffs were seeking a discovery of the ongoing investigation without having paid their contribution money.

Those creditors who had managed to take notice of the commission, and paid their contribution money, sought to extract as much as possible from the process, feeling aggrieved when they ran into stumbling blocks. Individuals within the process were well aware of the ways in which large portions of a bankrupt's estate could be channelled towards some creditors and away from others. Such a fear is highlighted by the assignees in *Marsh v Cadwell* (1720). In a bill of complaint submitted on 17 February 1721, the complainants claimed that John Clever committed an act of bankruptcy on 2 December 1720 before being declared a bankrupt by the commissioners five days later. With such a short period between these events, the plaintiffs suggested that Clever clandestinely assigned stock in the South Sea Company to several named defendants after 2 December, and as such, all stock 'ought to be restored to your Orators for the use of the said Bankrupts Creditors in general'. The plaintiffs were fearful that they would not be able to get full access to Clever's estate, and concluded that the defendants 'ought not on any pretence whatsoever to retaine' the stock for their use. Ultimately, all of the bankrupt's creditors should be 'on an equal foot, and not one preferred before or paid more than another'.[65] In this case the creditors of the bankrupt acted swiftly by executing a commission of bankruptcy five days after the initial act of bankruptcy, and subsequently initiating a suit in Chancery two months later.

In *Cady v Hunt* (1730), the plaintiffs were assignees of Gibson Moody, after a commission of bankruptcy was executed on 7 February 1727. The complainants sought a discovery of the bankrupt's estate which had come into the hands of six defendants. The bill suggested that two of these defendants, John Eley and William Baker, had illegally seized over £200 of the bankrupt's shop goods, insisting that 'the said Bill of Sale (if any such there is) was executed after such time as the said Gibson Moody had become a Bankrupt', which occurred on 30 January.[66] The bill went on to suggest that the defendants continued to insist 'that they had purchased the same from the Bankrupt before his Bankruptcy for a just and valuable consideration'.[67] To further complicate matters, another defendant named Charles Hunt claimed to be an assignee of John Eley, and

64   Ibid.
65   TNA, C11/1420/31, 'Marsh v Cadwell' (1720), Bill of Complaint.
66   TNA, C11/500/8, 'Cady v Hunt' (1730), Bill of Complaint.
67   Ibid.

suggested that William Baker had also been declared a bankrupt a short time after Moody.[68] Ultimately, there were three distinct and separate commissions of bankruptcy all claiming a legal right to Gibson Moody's estate. In their joint answer, Eley and Baker stated that the bill of sale was executed on 29 January 1727, and that Moody did not commit any acts of bankruptcy until after that date.[69] What is interesting in this case is that the timeline for failure was very concise. The plaintiffs alleged that the bill of sale was executed on 30 January, while the defendants claimed it was a day earlier, both of which dates were prior to the commission being executed. Once the date on which the bill of sale was executed had been agreed, disagreements centred on when any acts of bankruptcy were committed. Parties in this suit presented their arguments and appeared as frustrated creditors or debtors in a complex and interconnected web of indebtedness and failure.

These cases illuminate a number of interesting aspects of debt recovery. First, we again see another level added to the complexity of bankruptcy procedure, as creditors needed to try to weigh up the potential risk and reward dynamic of a commission. This became intensified when there were numerous commissions, and several claims, upon an estate. Secondly, the assignees were very often the largest creditors of the bankrupt. As such, we can clearly see the difficulties they encountered while trying to raise enough funds – through the discovery and seizure of the bankrupt's estate, as well as through contribution money from other creditors – to continue the process. However, accusations of fraud were commonly aimed at assignees for not distributing an estate evenly, or for acting on the bankrupt's behalf. We see several creditors complain, and demonstrate a substantial fear, that they would receive less than they felt they deserved, or even less than another creditor in the process. In this manner, creditors had not only lost their initial capital, but the bankruptcy process held the potential to increase such losses. Ultimately, bankruptcy suits in Chancery can grant us unique access to specific aspects of the temporality of trade regarding the way in which individuals judged the credibility of an individual in the past, as well as how creditors sought to look to the future and analyse their potential returns. With this in mind, the next section analyses how individuals within this process judged the actions and motivations of others, as well as how they assessed genuine and fraudulent debts.

The Actions and Motivations of Debtors
Within the scope of circulating judgements about failure, individuals began to question the motivation behind certain actions undertaken by parties within the bankruptcy process. Contrasting interpretations of a range of financial

---

68   Ibid., Answer of Charles Hunt.
69   Ibid., Answer of John Eley and William Baker.

transactions were largely seen as fraudulent – and done with an intent to defraud creditors – or seen as completed for a genuine and valuable consideration. As such, we can begin to analyse the language utilised around fraud and sincerity, and the manner in which such narratives were constructed within pleadings. Examples of these opposing descriptions and interpretations are numerous, but can be clearly seen in *Vognell v Mann* (1725). In this suit, the creditor-plaintiffs accused two bankrupt co-partners, Christian and Frederick Gulcher, of fraudulently assigning to the defendant Edward Mann several quantities of 'Plate Linen Jewells money … in order to Secret and Conceal the Same from their said Creditors'. When the complainants sought to come to an account with Mann for the goods he had received, Mann simply explained that the goods were assigned as part of money lent to the two bankrupts, prior to any acts of bankruptcy.[70]

In a more complex case from 1725, the assignees of Richard Wooley accused the bankrupt of a fraudulent transfer of York Building stock. One of the plaintiffs, Alexander Burn, initiated a suit against Wooley in the court of King's Bench for a debt of £120 due on bond. Wooley was arrested in October 1723, for which the two defendants, Robert Fotherby and William Lilly, stood bail. In order to indemnify the defendants against any future damage, Wooley transferred £1000 York Building stock, which was agreed to be assigned to Wooley's creditors once the suit was dropped. However, upon his release, Wooley committed several acts of bankruptcy and a commission was executed on 24 February 1724. Having appeared before the commissioners and truthfully revealed his assets, Wooley was granted a discharge, and a certificate of conformity was issued on 19 December 1724. According to the bill of complaint dated 21 April 1725, the defendants now claimed that the transfer of stock was not to indemnify them against damage for standing bail, but was assigned in consideration of a genuine debt due from Wooley, prior to the commission of bankruptcy.[71] As such, the complainants sought the appearance of the defendants and the bankrupt under oath, to clarify the reason why the stock had initially been transferred.

Similarly, in August 1730, Charles Bowler, a vintner of Bishopsgate Street, London, was arrested and imprisoned in Newgate for several outstanding debts. Three years later, a commission of bankruptcy was taken out and John Davis was named an assignee. However, while in prison, a creditor named Simeon Hayward visited Bowler and encouraged him to sign a bill of sale for several goods he had received from Bowler's wife, Susanna, for the satisfaction of his debts. Davis claimed that the bill of sale was fraudulent and that the goods assigned were worth £200 in value, and he could not gain access to them as

70   TNA, C11/2731/55, 'Vognell v Mann' (1725), Bill of Complaint.
71   TNA, C11/2730/158, 'Story v Wooley' (1725), Bill of Complaint.

assignee of the commission. In his answer, Hayward suggested that the bill of sale was genuine, and the goods that he took were only worth £21 11s 6d, as security for a debt of £53.[72]

These are fairly common accusations of fraudulent conveyance and fairly typical responses. All conveyances assigned before the act of bankruptcy were to be made void, unless it could be shown that they had been made for a genuine value and consideration. As such, the burden of proof was firmly placed upon the bankrupt, and the person involved in the conveyance, to prove the legitimacy of their financial transactions. To complicate matters further, a fraudulent conveyance could itself be judged as an act of bankruptcy, as it could be interpreted as denying creditors a due satisfaction of their claims.[73] This can be seen in *Streare v Hume* (1750), whereby the plaintiffs were assignees of Catherine Hume, a grocer and mercer from Devon. In their bill of complaint dated 6 April 1750, the plaintiffs claimed that on 26 April 1748 the bankrupt did 'Execute a pretended Bill of Sale of all her Household and shop goods and all Debts due and owing to her and of all her Books of account' to her daughter, also Catherine Hume. Any valuable consideration claimed by the bankrupt was 'false and ficticious'. Furthermore, the plaintiffs suggested that any goods assigned over in the bill of sale stayed in the hands of the bankrupt, enabling her to carry on her trade. Ultimately, this fraudulent bill of sale 'was of itself an act of Bankruptcy', which eventually led to a commission being issued on 25 November 1748. In this suit, we again see creditors looking back and surmising that because of her 'bad and desperate Circumstances', the bankrupt decided to fraudulently execute a bill of sale to her family member.[74] More broadly, suspicions were raised if a debtor had assigned much of their estate to relatives or close friends prior to failing. A common accusation made in Chancery was that debtors could foresee their own failure and so attempted to conceal portions of their estate.

In *Long v Good* (1720), the plaintiffs and assignees of John Coombe suggested that Coombe became indebted to several individuals above and beyond what he was able to pay, and had 'an unjust Intention to distribute his whole substance that remained amongst his Relations and particular Friends in or towards satisfaction of their severall Demands exclusive of his other Creditors'. According to the complainants, Coombe had warned these individuals of the 'badness of his Circumstances' and assigned several goods for satisfaction of exaggerated debts.[75] Similarly, in *Stoner v Crowe* (1720), the plaintiffs and assignees of Walter Compton suggested that the bankrupt secreted himself and his effects, while simultaneously paying his friends and

72 TNA, C11/520/13, 'Davis v Hayward' (1734), Bill of Complaint.
73 Jones, 'The Foundations of English Bankruptcy', p. 31.
74 TNA, C11/1637/23, 'Streare v Hume' (1750), Bill of Complaint.
75 TNA, C11/2284/114, 'Long v Good' (1720), Bill of Complaint.

relatives their full debts.[76] In response, three defendants stated that the goods assigned were in relation to a payment of genuine debts owed, and therefore submitted a demurrer, as they felt they should not be required to submit an answer.[77] Ultimately, certain creditors felt aggrieved at seeing others repaid in full while they had to endure the costly and time-consuming process of entering a commission of bankruptcy, only hoping to receive a portion of their debts. However, there is a clear contradiction to the modern reader throughout these arguments, as often one side was suggesting that all transactions had been enacted fraudulently, and no debt was really due; while on the other hand, the opposing side maintained that all conveyances were genuinely transferred for outstanding debts. While we can never uncover the truth behind these cases, what is interesting is the idea that despite the alternative routes available to debt recovery, a commission was somehow inevitable, and that debtors sought to evade the power of the commission in any way possible.

In *Handley v Walton* (1735), the plaintiffs were the assignees of John Chapman, a linen draper from Berkshire. In their bill of complaint, submitted on 26 February 1735, the plaintiffs claimed that 'with intent to defraud and Hinder' his creditors, Chapman assigned a bill of sale for all of his goods to the named defendants, James Walton and Petley Price. While this 'might appear to be fairly made' for the security of £150, it was in fact 'Clandestinely and fraudulently made and without any Valuable Consideration whatsoever'.[78] At the time of his absconding, all goods were still in the bankrupt's house, meaning Chapman maintained 'the peaceable and Quiet possession and Enjoyment of his said Goods Effects and Stock in Trade in the free Exercise of his said Trade in Selling and Disposing of his said Effects Goods and Stock'. Again, we see a joint accusation, as not only was the bill of sale made for a fictitious debt, but the bankrupt managed to keep hold of his goods and continued to sell them for his own benefit. The plaintiffs stated that rather than give up his goods to the commission, Chapman's servants sold them for one quarter of the price in order to quickly raise funds.[79] In response, only the answer of James Walton survives. Walton claimed to have sent his servant to Chapman's house with a writ for his arrest, after being put off by 'diverse frivolous and trifling Excuses' for non-payment of £130. However, in exchange for his liberty, Walton had accepted a bill of sale from Chapman on 5 July 1735, for security for his just debt.[80]

In *Buckle v Hendy* (1719–1720), the bill of complaint stated that Samuel Hendy, being aware that the bankrupt James Johnstone was in 'badd

76   TNA, C11/34/37, 'Stoner v Crowe' (1720), Bill of Complaint.
77   Ibid., Demurrer and Answer of Stephen Crowe, Letitia Crowe, and Charles Crowe.
78   TNA, C11/1044/14, 'Handley v Walton' (1735), Bill of Complaint.
79   Ibid.
80   Ibid., Answer of James Walton.

Circumstances and in danger of faileing', went to his premises in Cheltenham on 11 June 1719. At twelve o'clock at night, Hendy used 'many threats and menaces and other undue meanes' against Johnstone and his family, and forced Johnstone to deliver goods 'to the value of his pretended Debt' of £100. The complainants claimed that Hendy knew Johnstone had committed certain acts of bankruptcy, as Hendy threatened Johnstone at the property of William French, where he was absconding.[81] In his answer, Hendy stated that his first trip from London to Cheltenham to visit the bankrupt occurred on 11 June 1719, where he found Johnstone in 'declining circumstances'. While he admitted to meeting Johnstone at French's house, he believed that the bankrupt simply offered him goods as a security for his debt. Although he was 'displeased' with Johnstone for not satisfying his debt, he denied threatening him and claimed that any act of bankruptcy was committed after this genuine transaction.[82] In this case, the central issue was whether the goods were fraudulently assigned to benefit the defendant at the expense of the other creditors. However, the plaintiffs used this allegation as an opportunity to personally attack the defendant, simultaneously strengthening their argument relating to fraud, as well as forcing the defendant to account for his supposedly threatening behaviour.

In *Sole v Stephens*, the plaintiffs, as assignees of William Tappenden, wished to establish whether the bankrupt was in possession of an estate in Sittingbourne at the time of his bankruptcy. In particular, the complainants claimed that John Stephens had pretended to have 'lent to the said William Tappenden' the sum of £1400. On 19 April 1729, Tappenden executed a mortgage of part of his estate, worth £100 per annum rent, which would commence from Lady Day 1734, if the loan was not repaid. The bill suggested that Stephens had previously brought a bill in Chancery against the plaintiffs, for what was due on the principal and interest of the estate, but the assignees held that any mortgage was either not made at all, or 'Colourable only and made without any Valuable Consideration really paid'. The plaintiffs claimed that Tappenden had 'failed in the world and absconded' in August 1733, and a commission of bankruptcy was executed on 2 May 1734, both of which Stephens had notice of.[83]

Unsurprisingly, Stephens denied he knew of any acts of bankruptcy and stated that the mortgage was taken out for security against the money lent. At the time of Tappenden becoming a bankrupt, the property was legally in his possession.[84] Again, we see an example of a disputed event – the commencement of the mortgaged property – beginning in between the act of bankruptcy and the commission of bankruptcy. In this case, we see two dramatically different

---

81   TNA, C11/31/29, 'Buckle v Hendy' (1719–1720), Bill of Complaint.
82   Ibid., Answer of Samuel Hendy.
83   TNA, C11/1525/26, 'Sole v Stephens' (1735), Bill of Complaint.
84   Ibid., Answer of John Stephens.

interpretations of a single act, which demonstrates how individuals could use court proceedings for their own benefit. The plaintiffs were manipulating the timeline of bankruptcy to suggest that Tappenden knew he was going to fail, and as such, assigned part of his estate to Stephens to prevent his creditors gaining access to it. Despite the fact that the mortgage was assigned some five years prior to the commission of bankruptcy being taken out, the plaintiffs simply stated that this was fraudulently backdated or never executed.

When analysing the arguments presented in these suits in greater detail, several points arise. We see debates surrounding the motivation behind a single act; most notably, whether the act itself was fraudulently devised to deceive creditors, or whether it was undertaken for a valuable consideration. This led almost naturally to discussions surrounding the nature of debt, and whether the debt itself was genuine or fraudulent, with words such as 'pretended', 'fictitious', and 'fairly made' used to describe such transactions. However, in order to justify such claims, parties needed to provide background on why certain individuals would have acted in such a manner. The narrative had been altered to directly discuss the individual, rather than the act, as again, those involved in the process sought to look back and clarify the circumstances of the debtor. References to the 'bad and desperate', or 'declining', circumstances of individuals, who were 'in danger' of failing were frequently made. This led to debtors acting with an 'unjust intention' and 'with intent to defraud and hinder'. Yet, these contrasting interpretations demonstrate that the ability to judge a person's circumstances and trustworthiness was a difficult and complex task. Indeed, discussing the duality of honest and fraudulent traders, one tract – entitled *Observations on the State of Bankrupts: Under the Present Laws* (1760) – stated that a bankrupt 'stands in different lights to different people'.[85] Bankruptcy unsettled circulating judgements and the information flow regarding failure as its complexities made solidifying such assessments challenging. One way to try to overcome these obstacles – which is seen in passing above and analysed in detail below – was to discuss the secret and clandestine nature of actors and their actions. Ultimately, if an individual was trustworthy and acting in a reputable manner, then they would be undertaking such tasks in public in order to allow for, and even promote, circulating judgements about themselves.

The Public Actions of Individuals

The examination of the public nature of proceedings, as well as the actions of individuals, was used as an accusation or defence against fraud within Chancery. Largely, such a focus centred on the duration in which trading activities were seen to be occurring within the public sphere. Paul Glennie and Nigel Thrift

---

85 Nomius Antinomus, *Observations on the State of Bankrupts: Under the Present Laws. In a letter to a Member of Parliament* (London, 1760), p. 2.

have shown how traders were expected to operate during specified hours on certain days to maintain the regulation of markets.[86] There was an expectation that trustworthy and credible individuals would fulfil certain duties at specified times, and as traders looked back at the point of bankruptcy, they began to analyse how a debtor had failed in these conceptions.

The bankruptcy of Nicholas Waddington was spread across two suits in 1697, both of which concerned the ownership of several estates in Yorkshire between 1688 and 1690.[87] While only a concise copy bill and three answers survive, these documents illustrate issues surrounding the public nature and the perceived fraudulent execution of a commission. In Thomas Braddyll's answer, the defendant claimed that the plaintiff's brother 'or some neare Relation' married a sister of Waddington, and being aware of the impending commission of bankruptcy, concocted a fraudulent debt between the bankrupt and the plaintiff. These individuals then used this fictitious debt to execute a lease of some of the bankrupt's land in order to conceal it from his creditors and keep it within the family.[88] Braddyll further stated that the plaintiff must have had notice of the commission of bankruptcy, as 'the Said Commissioners proceeded openly and publickly with all fareness and justice and did sitt att some tyme or Times neare to the said Waddingtons house and att other Towns and places not farr distant'.[89] Similarly, in the joint answer of Waddington and John Burton, the two defendants claimed that Waddington could not be considered a bankrupt during this period, as he traded openly, in public, and for over £5000 between 1688 and 1690.[90] All three defendants use the public nature of actions and activities to refute accusations of fraud and failure. Waddington and Burton use this notion to argue that Waddington could not have been untrustworthy at the alleged point of failure, as he was acting in his normal manner, publicly trading for vast sums of money. As such, Waddington was available to trade within normal working hours.

Barrett v Stephens (1702–1706) not only includes several previously discussed issues relating to circulating knowledge about failure but also contains insightful information regarding the public nature of trade. In a bill of complaint submitted on 6 February 1701, Benajah Barret stated that the defendant Joshua Stephens had agreed to pay £705 for £500 East India Stock in May 1700. However, Stephens failed to complete the deal in time and the stock fell in price. It was agreed that the plaintiff would sell the stock for £646

---

86 Paul Glennie and Nigel Thrift, 'Reworking E. P. Thompson's "Time, Work-Discipline and Industrial Capitalism"', *Time and Society*, 5 (1996), pp. 275–300.
87 TNA, C6/384/70, 'Brocklesby v Waddington' (1697); TNA, C6/381/42, 'Brocklesby v Hey' (1697).
88 TNA, C6/381/42, 'Brocklesby v Hey' (1697), Answer of Thomas Braddyll.
89 Ibid.
90 Ibid., Answer of Nicholas Waddington and John Burton.

10s, and Stephens would cover the loss of £58 10s. Stephens paid £6 in cash and gave a note for the remaining £52 10s. in the name of another defendant, John Martin, which was to be satisfied on 17 September 1700. While Martin agreed it was a just debt, after six months of non-payment the plaintiff had Martin arrested by issuing a writ from the court of Common Pleas.[91] After several meetings, Martin desired the plaintiff 'forebear' the proceedings at law so he could satisfy his debt, which the plaintiff agreed to do. However, Barret claimed that since this agreement the two defendants had confederated in order to 'deceive and defraud' him and to 'share and divide' the sum of £52 10s, amongst themselves. Barret stated that the two defendants 'doe now pretend and give out in Speeches that the said Joshua Stephens is a Bankrupt ... and was a Bankrupt before the time the said note was given'. Ultimately, Barret stated that Martin was now fraudulently claiming all rights to the debts and credits of Stephens as the nominated assignee.[92] Continuing his complaint, Barret claimed to have not been informed of Stephens' bankruptcy until 'a considerable time after your Orator had arrested the said John Martin upon his said note'. To further complicate matters, Martin had subsequently arrested Barret for debt in a suit at King's Bench. Barret had placed the note in the possession of his solicitor, who had since died, and being unable to locate the note, he was unable to proceed at common law and so executed a suit in Chancery.[93]

In this bill, we can see how the plaintiff suggested that information and knowledge about the failure of Stephens had not been communicated in due course. Indeed, because of the delay in informing the plaintiff about the bankruptcy, coupled with the suspicions aroused by only claiming this was the case after Martin had been arrested, Barret believed that the failure was fictitious. However, it is the answer of John Martin that sheds light on the public nature of trade. Not only did Martin claim to be a genuine creditor of Stephens, but he also suggested that through his own naivety he had been the victim of fraud at the hands of the bankrupt. According to Martin, Stephens claimed that if he paid him a further £50, 'there was a business that he the said Stephens pretended he was concerned in which would be of great advantage to the Creditors towards satisfaction of his said Debts'.[94] While initially refusing to go along with the scheme, Martin felt sympathetic towards Stephens as 'he could not Trade or deale' due to the bankruptcy. In order to give 'encour-agement' to get his estate in order, and 'beleiving he would be as good as his word', Martin eventually issued Stephens a note for £50 on 17 August 1700.[95] In discussing the specifics of the bankruptcy, Martin claimed that he could not

91   TNA, C6/384/116, 'Barrett v Stephens' (1702–1706), Bill of Complaint.
92   Ibid.
93   Ibid.
94   Ibid., Answer of John Martin.
95   Ibid.

set forward the particular time when Stephens first became a bankrupt, or when he first informed the complainant that he was a bankrupt, but believed that 'all or most persons did know or might know the same the said Stephens's house and warehouse being shut up for a considerable time and the Commissioners having put in a messenger unto the said Stephens's house and warehouse'. Martin twice utilised the inability of Stephens to trade publicly to demonstrate that knowledge about his bankruptcy was commonplace within the wider community. With his shop and warehouse closed, it was the responsibility of creditors to decipher that Stephens was in financial difficulties and to take note of the public proceeding of the commission.

In *Hurt v Moss* (1730), the plaintiffs were two assignees of a woollen draper named Richard Moss, who in August 1727 became indebted to several individuals for over £1500. Being pressed by numerous creditors, finding his 'Credit low', and knowing that his estate would not cover his debts, Moss made several fraudulent assignments to keep his goods away from his creditors. The plaintiffs believed that any assignment made by the bankrupt was fraudulent, as on the 14 or 15 August 1727, Moss:

> totally failed in and left of his Trade and business and from that time his shop Continued shutt and he absconded and kept Close in an Upper Room in his Dwelling house for the space of about a Month after ward and did not appear abroad nor goe out of his said house except in the Night time for fear of being seen by or arrested at the suit of some of his creditors and about a Month after the said Richard Moss begun to keep his house as aforesaid he left and departed from the same in the Night time and he took himself to several private and secure places and there lived in a Secrett and Concealed manner on purpose and with an Intent to avoid his Creditors and to delay and defraud them of their just debts.[96]

The two defendants, John Moss, his son, and Elizabeth Moss – some other relation – claimed to be 'strangers' to most of the assignments, but insisted that during August 1727 Richard Moss 'kept his shop daily open as usual … and that he did not abscond and keep Close' until the 19 or 20 of August. While he had 'no Intention to defraud his Creditors', the defendants claimed that as Richard lived 'a very loose and disorderly life it was apprehended that unless some speedy Care was taken to secure his Effects he might waste the same to the prejudes of his Creditors and for that and no other reason (as these Defendants believe)' John Moss asked his father to assign over all of his real and personal estate and effects on the 18 and 19 August 1727.[97] Here, the timing of the assignment is accepted, but debates ensued regarding the timing

---

96 TNA, C11/2427/32, 'Hurt v Moss' (1730), Bill of Complaint.
97 Ibid., Answer of Elizabeth Moss and John Moss.

of Richard's absconding and when he removed himself from public view and ceased his public trading activities.

Returning to Thomas Goodinge, it becomes clear that the longer the time between the act of bankruptcy and the execution of a commission, the greater the opportunity to question the scope of the commission of bankruptcy. In *Wright v Cheshyre* (1725), the commission was executed some ten months after the initial act of bankruptcy, and unsurprisingly, there arose disagreements regarding the goods and estate that should fall within the jurisdiction of the commission. In their bill of complaint, the plaintiffs and assignees of Thomas Pindar, a hosier from Nottingham, clearly established the chronology of Pindar's failure. Having owed more than £2000, Pindar absconded and secreted himself from his creditors on 11 May 1724, with a commission of bankruptcy being issued on 2 March 1725. Furthermore, the plaintiffs claimed that the commissioners had specified that Pindar was a bankrupt from 11 May onwards and were seeking all goods that came into the hands of Thomas Cheshyre from that date. It appears that the plaintiffs were aware of the unusual delay between the initial act and the execution of the commission, as they seem to pre-empt any disputes by stating that Pindar was truly a bankrupt, 'some months before the date and sueing forth of the said Commission'.[98]

In his answer, Cheshyre agreed that a commission was issued around the time stated in the bill, but whether Pindar was declared a bankrupt by the commissioners he could not say, 'being a Stranger to the same'. Discussing the act of bankruptcy, Cheshyre claimed that Pindar 'did not commit any act of bankrupt whatsoever untill a month or two' after the date given in the bill. Cheshyre stated that Pindar left Nottingham on 11 May, and arrived in London on 13 May, where he appeared publicly in his warehouse. As such, Cheshyre insisted that he had several dealings with Pindar, providing him with silk and other materials, after 11 May.[99] Throughout this suit, the timing of when Pindar officially became a bankrupt, both legally and in the eyes of the community, is continually debated. Yet, it is Cheshyre's response which is illuminating, as looking back to the alleged point of failure, the defendant claimed that Pindar could not have been a bankrupt as he appeared openly and in public at his warehouse. While the plaintiffs had interpreted Pindar leaving Nottingham as a criminal act, Cheshyre understood this event as a normal part of his trading activity, as he appeared publicly in London and continued to engage in trade in an open manner. Ultimately, this final suit demonstrates how a single act could be interpreted in dramatically different ways, and as such, could be manipulated by either side in an attempt to create a coherent narrative regarding the motivations of individuals, as well as the timeline for failure.

98   TNA, C11/314/7, 'Wright v Cheshyre' (1725), Bill of Complaint.
99   Ibid., Answer of Thomas Cheshyre.

Conclusion

This chapter has analysed the narrative in pleadings surrounding a dynamic series of events that led to an individual failure. The ambiguities that arose within the law relating to certain aspects of the timing of failure became intensified in Chancery, as time itself became a contested concept. Indeed, parties vehemently debated the exact timing of certain events in relation to a commission of bankruptcy. Furthermore, a key theme that emerges is the manner in which specific actions could influence future aspects of the debt-recovery process. This is particularly true regarding the degree of risk, investment, and potential return involved in future dealings. As such, bankruptcy pleadings can inform us of multiple aspects of the temporality of trade, not just about the past, but also about opportunities and the assessment of outcomes in the future. The complexities of the bankruptcy process upset the ability to be able to look back and judge an individual's credibility, worth, and trustworthiness.

One way in which individuals tried to clarify such details was to discuss the public nature, public knowledge, and circulating information about every aspect of bankruptcy; ranging from the actions of the individual bankrupt to that of the knowledge of the commission as a 'matter of record'. The public nature of proceedings and the actions of individuals were utilised and manipulated in Chancery as an accusation or defence against fraud. Largely, such a focus centred around the duration in which trading activities were seen to be occurring within the public sphere. This led almost naturally into questions being raised about individuals, relating to the motivations behind undertaking certain acts, as the public nature of their activities set the background to accusations of fraud. Ultimately, the complexities of bankruptcy, and the ambiguities present in its procedure, upset how circulating judgements were communicated and known within the wider community, providing a more nuanced understanding of the multifaceted nature of failure within debt recovery.

4

Collaborative Narratives of Failure
in Country Depositions

The use of depositions as historical evidence is a divisive issue. This is possibly because it is this type of witness testimony that purports to record the spoken words of individuals from nearly all walks of life.[1] In her hugely influential book, *True Relations: Reading, Literature, and Evidence in Seventeenth-Century England*, Frances Dolan suggests that because of the complexities surrounding the process in which depositions were created, scholars who rely on them often accept that they are 'mediated' but privilege them as providing unique access to early modern 'voices'. According to Dolan, it may be more useful to 'recast mediation as collaboration'.[2] *True Relations* has certainly reinvigorated historiographical debate surrounding the 'unique voice' of witness testimony. Yet, this has largely been reserved for a gendered approach to the law, as scholars seek to analyse the obscuring filters created by the male-dominated legal profession. For example, in the introduction to a special edition – entitled 'Women Negotiating the Boundaries of Justice in Britain, 1300–1700' – Alexandra Shepard and Tim Stretton highlight the several boundaries that structured women's agency, and 'filtered their voices through male advisers and officials'. This collection of essays explores how women's abilities to negotiate legal jurisdictions, 'intersected with and were shaped by legal custom, regional difference, and broader social and cultural contexts'. Particular attention is paid to the collaborative processes that presented narratives within a legal setting, and the degree to which modern scholars can access the 'authentic female voice' of actors in the written documents that have survived.[3] This chapter engages with this ongoing and contentious debate by applying Dolan's line to narrative creation in the court of Chancery. In doing so, it demonstrates the ways in which narratives

---

1   Tim Stretton, 'Women, Legal Records, and the Problem of the Lawyer's Hand', *Journal of British Studies*, 58 (2019), p. 696.

2   Frances E. Dolan, *True Relations: Reading, Literature, and Evidence in Seventeenth-Century England* (Philadelphia, 2013), pp. 113–118.

3   Alexandra Shepard and Tim Stretton, 'Women Negotiating the Boundaries of Justice in Britain, 1300-1700: An Introduction', *Journal of British Studies*, 58 (2019), pp. 677–683.

of bankruptcy, failure, and personal decline formed an integral part of legal evidence in Chancery suits.

Broadly speaking, depositions were a chance for both sides of a dispute to interrogate witnesses, and gather evidence, to add weight to their legal claims. Lists of questions – known as interrogatories – were submitted by parties in the suit and their answers – called depositions – were transcribed by clerks of the court to be sealed, and if necessary, read out upon the hearing of the cause at a later date. In a similar manner to pleadings, questions were asked, and answers constructed, in order to conform to the legal requirements of the court. However, as a far wider range of material witnesses were examined at this stage of the legal process, depositions provide detailed personal accounts of an individual failure. By approaching these documents in a careful and considered manner – and by continuing to pay close attention to the processes and procedures that went into their creation – it is possible to reveal how the wider trading community clarified and described failure. This approach can provide us with myriad observations of the ways in which individuals chose to formulate such legal arguments in court, as well as the manner in which witnesses had previously engaged with a commission of bankruptcy, and subsequently the court of Chancery. It is striking how a number of witnesses revealed details surrounding the actions, attitudes, and emotional responses of those involved in financial failure, with particular reference to the physical and psychological strain that was placed upon bankrupts and their families. Rather than attempting to 'filter out' mediating legal authorities, I argue that scholars must pay close attention to how the work of certain individuals – such as legal experts, Chancery commissioners, and clerks of the court – has impacted on the creation of the final documents that have survived.

The thorough investigation conducted at the depositional stage of proceeding allows an exploration of the specific and evaluative language used in relation to failure. Heather Falvey has demonstrated the importance of paying attention to the relationship between the questions posed by parties in a suit and the answers provided by witnesses. By establishing the degree to which legal phrasing was initially presented in interrogatories and then repeated by a witness in the deposition, Falvey concludes that in terms of narrative reconstruction, inter-rogatories 'assume just as much significance as depositions'.[4] This chapter undertakes a similar approach by highlighting how certain witnesses answered particular questions in relation to economic and personal failure. Analysing specific words and phrases can illuminate how witnesses revealed details surrounding the actions, attitudes, and emotional responses of those involved in economic decline. This can provide unique access to the criteria used by

4   Heather Falvey, 'Relating Early Modern Depositions,' in Carl J. Griffin and Briony McDonagh (eds), *Remembering Protest in Britain Since 1500: Memory, Materiality and the Landscape* (Cham, 2018), pp. 81–106, p. 93.

early modern people to judge what they deemed to be respectable and credible actions in relation to the repayment of debts on the one hand, and fraudulent and criminal activity on the other.

In 1967, William Jones referred to the 'cathartic' role of the Elizabethan court of Chancery, as it sought 'to cleanse the conscience of the wrongdoer rather than to safeguard the excess interests of the wronged'.[5] More recent scholarship has paid attention to how individual emotions – such as anger, hope, remorse, empathy, and disgust – can be analysed for their relevance in legal proceedings.[6] A burgeoning scholarship has emerged analysing how emotions were layered through legal documents and procedure, allowing contested meanings relating to morality and wider social norms.[7] Indeed, historians of emotions have emphasised the need to place emotional language, terminology, and practices within the social and cultural contexts which produced them. Such emotions cannot be seen as universal and need to be historicised, especially within the legal jurisdiction and stage of proceeding from which they have been taken.[8] For example, Fay Bound has paid close attention to the ecclesiastical law of slander, and the jurisdiction of the Church courts at York, to demonstrate how specific words – 'anger', 'passion', and 'malice' – formed a core part of the accusation in question. Rather than simply being an incidental detail to a dispute, Bound shows how 'the imputation of a "passionate and malicious" mind became a central element in social and legal definitions of slander'.[9] A similar approach is undertaken in this chapter, as the specific words and phrases in Chancery depositions are analysed in the context of bankruptcy and failure.

In the second chapter, we saw how scholars such as Amanda Capern and Merridee Bailey have shown how emotions and emotional language were

5   W. J. Jones, *The Elizabethan Court of Chancery* (Oxford, 1967), p. 424

6   For a detailed discussion of emotions and the law, see Merridee Bailey and Kimberley-Joy Knight, 'Writing Histories of Law and Emotion', *The Journal of Legal History*, 38 (2017), pp. 117–129.

7   Katie Barclay and Amy Milka (eds), *Cultural Histories of Law, Media and Emotion* (New York, 2022), esp. part two; David Lemmings, 'Law', in Susan Broomhall (ed.), *Early Modern Emotions: An Introduction* (London, 2017), pp. 192–195; Merridee L. Bailey, 'Shaping London Merchant Identities: Emotions, Reputation and Power in the Court of Chancery', in Deborah Simonton (ed.), *The Routledge History Handbook of Gender and the Urban Experience* (London, 2017), pp. 327–337; Barbara H. Rosenwein and Riccardo Cristiani, *What is the History of Emotions?* (Malden, 2018).

8   Merridee L. Bailey, '"Most Hevynesse and Sorowe": The Presence of Emotions in the Late Medieval and Early Modern Court of Chancery', *LHR*, 37 (2019), pp. 1–28; Barbara H. Rosenwein, 'Worrying About Emotions in History', *American Historical Review*, 107 (2002), pp. 821–845; Peter N. Stearns and Carol Z. Stearns, 'Emotionology: Clarifying the History of Emotions and Emotional Standards', *American Historical Review*, 90 (1985), pp. 813–836.

9   Fay Bound, '"An Angry and Malicious Mind"? Narratives of Slander at the Church Courts of York, c.1660–c.1760', *History Workshop Journal*, 56 (2003), pp. 59–77, p. 63.

tactically selected in an attempt to gain a favourable outcome from the Lord Chancellor.[10] As Emily Ireland has argued, each Chancery case can be seen as a process of collaboration between numerous actors, 'all of whom contributed to the creation of a discrete emotional community'.[11] For Ireland, Chancery cases represent 'an isolated emotional community in which litigants, counsel, deponents, court officials and the Lord Chancellor engaged with the same emotions'.[12] Here, the focus turns to witnesses – working alongside plaintiffs, defendants, legal experts, and Chancery officials – in a wider pattern of narrative creation. Rather than attempting to isolate and analyse emotive accusations and responses as carefully constructed rhetoric – or exploring emotional content in and of itself – we can see emotions as part of an individual's financial and personal downfall. Indeed, while bankruptcy cases were not directly concerned with emotion – and emotion was not a part of the evidence of a suit – descriptions of emotion were a by-product of failure. While emotional descriptions were utilised in the court for strategic benefit, they can also inform us of wider perceptions of morality and credibility, as individuals attempted to look back and appraise the actions and words of those involved in personal, financial failure.

The chapter is divided into three sections. The first section provides a detailed overview of the commissioning, collection, filing, and reading – in public – of witness statements within the court.[13] The second section reviews the historiography surrounding the value of legal records as sources of evidence for early modern historians, and places these debates within the context of the creation of depositions, and the search for authentic or unique voices within legal sources. Two cases are then analysed in detail, demonstrating the way in which we can analyse lengthy and detailed statements made by witnesses in a particular suit. These two sections provide background and establish the methodology for the analysis which follows.

The final section builds upon the previous analysis by demonstrating how certain narratives began to be utilised as evidence in the court. Specifically,

---

10   Bailey, 'Most Hevynesse and Sorowe', pp. 1–28; Amanda Capern, 'Emotions, Gender Expectations, and the Social Role of Chancery, 1550–1650', in Susan Broomhall (ed.), *Authority, Gender and Emotions in Late Medieval and Early Modern England* (Basingstoke, 2015), pp. 187–209; Amanda Capern, 'Maternity and Justice in the Early Modern English Court of Chancery', *Journal of British Studies*, 58 (2019), pp. 701–716.

11   Emily Ireland, 'Conventional and Unconventional Emotions in the Eighteenth-Century English Court of Chancery: The Story of "Unhappy" Mary Bangs', in Katie Barclay and Amy Milka (eds), *Cultural Histories of Law, Media and Emotion* (New York, 2022), pp. 121–140, p. 122.

12   Ibid., p. 123.

13   Christine Churches, '"The Most Unconvincing Testimony": The Genesis and the Historical Usefulness of the Country Depositions in Chancery', *The Seventeenth Century*, 11 (1996), pp. 209–227.

witnesses sought to show how an individual had fallen from a respectable and credible position to that of a bankrupt, mirroring wider conceptions of morality, credibility, and ethical behaviour within the community. This section illuminates social and cultural attitudes to bankruptcy, failure, and personal decline, demonstrating how the public nature of status and reputation dictated a person's ability to function – both economically and socially – within the wider community. While there are certain similarities to previous chapters which reveal how and why the bankruptcy process broke down, at this stage of proceeding it is largely the witness statements which provide evidence of economic and personal failure. Focusing on the collaborative nature of witness testimony will show that the court of Chancery not only acted as a debt-recovery mechanism but it was also an institution which created social narratives of credit, debt, and personal failure, rather than just reflecting attitudes and assumptions from the wider society.

The Taking, Filing, and Cataloguing of Depositions

Witnesses in Chancery suits were examined in private, either by an officer of the court in London or by assigned commissioners in the country. If the parties lived within ten miles of London, then witnesses were required to attend on one of the Chancery Examiners at the Rolls Office. Parties outside this jurisdiction were examined in their local communities, and as Christine Churches has shown, by the late seventeenth century, the examining of witnesses by a Chancery commission was 'no novelty in any part of the country, and elementary prepa-rations for such an event were well understood and a matter of routine'.[14]

Plaintiffs and defendants had the right to nominate four commissioners, and to reject two named by the other party. Commissioners had to swear an oath to the court, whereby they would, to the best of their skill and knowledge, 'truly and faithfully and without partiality … take the Examinations and Depositions of all and every Witness and Witnesses produced'. They were also 'sworn to secrecy' in undertaking their duties and could not 'publish disclose or make known' the contents of the documents.[15] As such, commissioners had to swear the witnesses, privately examine them according to the interrogatories provided by each side, supervise the recording of witness statements by the clerk, and have the final documents sealed and returned to the court. The selection and rejection of commissioners was an important process for competing parties,

---

14   Ibid., p. 210.
15   The commissioners' oath and the clerks' oath were written on a small piece of parchment and attached to the top left of the interrogatories and depositions. Many of these oaths have not stood the test of time as they can easily be torn or fall off. Legible examples of writs and oaths can be found at TNA, C11/2331/23, 'Haill v Camp' (1748).

as commissioners would direct the clerks in the transcribing of answers. This could be of great advantage to a party in the wording of the deponent's evidence to the sense of the commissioner. Churches has shown the tactics involved in selecting commissioners within a cause, as references to 'kindness', 'friendship', their 'ability' as a commissioner, or whether or not pressure could be applied to a commissioner were all taken into consideration. The four remaining commissioners were either 'the least offensive ... or the most inept' to either side, which was an important process in attempting to gain a favourable outcome.[16]

Clerks were also required to swear an oath, whereby they would 'truly and faithfully and without partiality ... take and write down transcribe and Ingross the Depositions of all and every Witness', being similarly sworn to secrecy.[17] While relatives and attorneys of the parties – and others with an interest in the outcome of the suit – were ineligible to serve as officers of the court, it is not surprising that certain individuals acted as both a witness and as a clerk or commissioner.[18] Examples can be taken from my sample, as in *Finch v Robinson* (1742) Nathaniel Batty was sworn as a witness for the plaintiff before being sworn as a clerk; while in *Perrins v Gyles* (1736) Stephen Ashby was first sworn as a witness for the plaintiff, and later sworn as a commissioner of the court.[19] This not only demonstrates the localised nature of proceedings, but also suggests that certain individuals acting as clerks or commissioners were familiar with the details surrounding the suit. Indeed, Stephen Ashby found it necessary to complain that he was never 'acquainted with the merritts of the said Cause untill he was very lately informed by the Defendant Gyles that he was appointed a Commissioner therein and then this Deponent was shewn a Draught of Interrogatories a Coppy of the decretall Order in the said Cause and other Papers therein'.[20] The fact that Ashby complained that he was not given sufficient time to make himself acquainted with the details of the case suggests that this was the common practice. Ultimately, either side knew it was important to get at least one commissioner who was sympathetic to their cause, or there was always a risk that the deposition would not be taken fairly.[21]

In theory, the procedure for examining witnesses in the country was clearly defined. Questions were to be posed verbally with the deponent answering all in sequence before hearing the next, and not being allowed to leave the room until all had been completed. The clerk would then read the answers back and amend any drafts if necessary.[22] Throughout the seventeenth century, several

16 Churches, 'The Most Unconvincing Testimony', pp. 210–212.
17 TNA, C11/2331/23, 'Haill v Camp' (1748).
18 Churches, 'The Most Unconvincing Testimony', p. 210.
19 TNA, C11/2323/13, 'Finch v Robinson' (1742); C11/1934/9, 'Perrins v Gyles' (1736).
20 C11/1934/9, 'Perrins v Gyles' (1736), Deposition of Stephen Ashby.
21 Churches, 'The Most Unconvincing Testimony', pp. 210–212.
22 Ibid., p. 215.

Lord Chancellors found it necessary to publish collections of orders used in Chancery for the 'reforming of several abuses in the said court, preventing the multiplicity of suits, motions, and unnecessary charge to the suiters and for their more expeditious and certain course of relief'.[23] New interrogatories were not permitted to be inserted once examination had begun, and the court stressed the need for witnesses to be examined seriatim, taking one question after another in the order they were submitted, and to have no knowledge of future questions until the one posed had been answered in full. This was done to prevent 'perjury and other mischiefs often appearing to the Court'.[24]

Lord Chancellor Nottingham introduced penalties for inserting new interrogatories and ordered that commissioners were, 'not to take upon them to judge what interrogatories are pertinent and what not, but must examine upon them as they find them'.[25] Again, this was designed 'to prevent perjuries, cautelous and craft depositions, false and fraudulent examinations, and many other such mischiefs and abuses'.[26] One seventeenth-century tract questioned the objectivity of officers of the court, suggesting there was 'too much foul practice used in the taking of *Depositions*, wherein many *Commissioners* and Clerks on both sides, for the most part Act rather as Parties or Agents for the persons concerned, then as becometh *honest indifferent persons*, according to the trust reposed in them by the Court'.[27] This manner of collecting evidence was clearly viewed as being open to abuse and manipulation by parties in a suit, and accusations of collusion, fraud, and bias were commonplace.

Contemporary common law advocates and subsequent legal experts have demonstrated their disdain for this method of gathering evidence. As William Holdsworth has concluded, 'it may safely be said that a more futile method of getting at the facts of the case, than the system in use in the court of Chancery from the seventeenth century onwards, never existed in any mature legal system'. This method was 'productive of the most unconvincing testimony at the greatest possible expense'.[28] The distinction between matter of fact and matter of law had become well established in England by the sixteenth century. As Sir Edward Coke insisted, juries were not to answer questions of law, while judges were not to answer questions of fact. In Chancery, the Lord Chancellor

---

23   England and Wales Court of Chancery, *A Collection of Such of the Orders Heretofore Used in Chauncery* (London, 1649), further examples were printed in 1652, 1660, 1661, 1669, and 1676.
24   Ibid., p. 28.
25   Heneage Finch, Earl of Nottingham, *Manual of Chancery Practice, and Prolegomena of Chancery and Equity*, D. E. C. Yale (ed.) (Cambridge, 1965), p. 107.
26   Ibid., p. 110.
27   Philodemius Philostratus, *The Seasonable Observations on a Late Book Intitvled A System of the Law* (London, 1654), p. 21.
28   W. S. Holdsworth, *A History of English Law* (16 vols, London, 1926–1966), vol. 9, p. 353.

was to decide factual questions on the basis of depositions, meaning that the interrogatories and their subsequent answers frequently formed the basis of legal judgment.[29]

Upon completion, interrogatories and depositions were attached alongside a copy of the commissioner's oath, the clerk's oath, and a formulaic writ naming the assigned commissioners and stating the date of the examination and the date by which the sealed documents would need to be returned to the court.[30] However, there was also a clear disparity between the ideal manner in which to record depositions and the actual practice, as the strict regimen outlined above was rarely followed so precisely. Few deponents answered every question, and several chose to answer multiple questions at once. For example, in *Gould v Hannaford* (1746), Joseph Merchant, a thirty-five-year-old periwig maker from Devon, simply responded 'to the seventh Interrogatory only', and accepted that he was a witness to the execution of a deed.[31] Further ambiguity arose by the fact that certain clerks specified when deponents failed to answer questions, with remarks such as 'cannot depose', while leaving other questions blank.[32]

In common law, supplementary questions could be posed to witnesses in a cross-examination, resolving conflicting testimony or undermining and discrediting a witness. As the rules of equity forbade such a practice, much care and skill went into the framing of interrogatories by parties or their legal representatives in order to elicit responses favourable to their cause. Only on the date of publication – the day when depositions in a case were read aloud and 'published' in open court – were both sides formally permitted access to the statements of each other's witnesses. This was the first chance for a party to officially see the interrogatories posed by the opposing side, and the answers elicited from deponents.[33] If individuals felt that their personal concerns were not being addressed, they could submit interrogatories separate from the rest of the party. For example, in *Carril v Savage* (1729), the defendant George Savage administered a distinct set of interrogatories consisting of three questions relating to a bond made between the bankrupt, William Hayne, and another defendant, Kenard Delabere. Clearly, Savage felt this avenue of investigation required special attention.[34]

---

29   Barbara J. Shapiro, *A Culture of Fact: England, 1550–1720* (Ithaca, 2000), p. 11; see Barbara J. Shapiro, *Probability and Certainty in Seventeenth-Century England: A Study of the Relationship between Natural Science, Religion, History, Law, and Literature* (Princeton, 1983), esp. ch.5.
30   Writs were written in Latin before 1733 and English thereafter. The date for returning documents varied but it was usually between two to three weeks after a completed deposition.
31   TNA, C11/2791/3, 'Gould v Hannaford' (1746), Deposition of Joseph Merchant.
32   See TNA, C11/2331/17, 'Haill v Randall' (1746).
33   Henry Horwitz, *Exchequer Equity Records and Proceedings, 1649–1841* (Kew, 2001), p. 27.
34   TNA, C11/1368/4, 'Carril v Savage' (1729), Interrogatories submitted by George Savage.

In the other set of interrogatories posed by the remaining five defendants, we see three questions all begin with the same phrase: 'were you concerned in the Execution of a Comission of Bankrupt awarded against William Haynes in the Title of these Interrogatorys named and in what capacity did you act therein'. Each question then explored a specific aspect of the bankruptcy, including a bond executed by the bankrupt, the date the bankruptcy was proven, and finally, whether the commissioners of the bankruptcy deposed witnesses on a specific sum of money.[35] While this is an extreme example, it was not uncommon for successive questions to contain an element of repetition. In this manner, parties were ensuring deponents had no opportunity to avoid answering questions on specific topics, and by addressing a question from a slightly different angle, they ensured that they had attempted to cover every approach. One deponent, the solicitor John King, answered the above three questions simultaneously, further demonstrating the disparity between the ideal approach to examining witnesses set out by the court and the day-to-day practice in the country.[36]

Throughout the seventeenth and eighteenth centuries, several advice manuals and treatises were published outlining the correct manner in which proceedings in Chancery should be undertaken. The extent to which such time and care went into framing interrogatories is best illustrated by two publications that fall either side of the period under examination. The first is William West's *Symboleography*, a general practical treatise on English law under its several divisions.[37] This publication was extremely popular and came to be regarded as a work of legal authority. First published in 1590, the new edition of 1592 was reissued with further corrections eleven times between 1594 and 1647, while the second part of the new edition began in 1593 and was again reprinted ten times between 1594 and 1641. Neil Jones has described the work as 'the first printed systematic treatise on the writing of legal instruments, including not only precedents in conveyancing but also of indictments and proceedings in Chancery'.[38] West outlines the process through which interrogatories should be devised by parties, depositions should be transcribed by clerks, and how commissioners should oversee the process. It is striking that the appearance of Chancery depositions throughout this period aligns neatly with West's practical advice, which is charted in detail below.

The second source is the anonymous 330-page advice manual, *A Collection of Interrogatories for the Examination of Witnesses in Courts of Equity*, first published in 1775, with a second edition the following year, and a third edition in 1791. The author, 'An Old Solicitor', specifies 280 circumstances for framing

35   Ibid., Interrogatories submitted by William Hodges, Elizabeth Wood, Kenard Delabere, William Baggoll, and Frances Haynes.
36   TNA, C11/1368/4, 'Carril v Savage' (1729), Deposition of John King.
37   William West, *The Second Part of Symboleography* (London, 1627).
38   N. G. Jones, 'West, William (c.1548–1598)', ODNB.

interrogatories, boasting '*It is now only necessary to observe that the rapid sale of the first Edition is a proof of the utility of such a collection. To this Edition there are a considerable number of additions, which must render the work still more useful*'.[39] The practical nature of the publication as well as the author's experience and expertise are set out in the preface:

> The following Collection has been made out of many hundred draughts of Interrogatories, settled by some of the most eminent counsel, many of which the compiler kept by him in the course of his practice in the courts of Chancery and Exchequer; and the rest were furnished by several attorneys and solicitors of his acquaintance. And although it may possibly be objected, that the proofs in every cause must be adapted to its own particular circumstances, and that thereof there is no occasion for precedents of interrogatories; yet I think there is no weight in that objection.[40]

The similarities in the way in which these two documents – originally published some 185 years apart – set out the correct manner of framing the opening and closing interrogatories demonstrate the formulaic nature of Chancery depositions during this period. While the exact wording may differ slightly from one interrogatory to the next, nearly every bankruptcy deposition was initiated and concluded in the same way, as set forward in *A Collection*:

> *First Interrogatory.*
>
> Do you know the parties, complainants and defendants, in the title of these interrogatories named, or any, and which of them; and how long have you known them, or any, and which of them respectively? Declare the truth, and your knowledge herein.

> *Last Interrogatory.*
>
> Lastly, Do you know of any other matter, or thing, or have you heard, or can you say any thing touching the matters in question, in this case, that may tend to the benefit and advantage of the complainant [or defendant] in this cause, besides what you have been interrogated unto? Declare the same fully and at large, as if you had been particularly interrogated thereto.[41]

These examples were suitable for all cases at the depositional stage of proceeding, but a case involving bankruptcy may have specified in the first question how

---

39 *A Collection of Interrogatories for the Examination of Witnesses in Courts of Equity. As Settled by the Most Eminent Counsel*, 3rd edn (Dublin, 1791), preface.
40 Ibid., preface.
41 Ibid., pp. 1–2.

the parties knew the bankrupt if he were not named as a party in the cause. Where interrogatories and depositions survive in full, deponents' answers' can easily be cross-referenced to the original questions, enabling an understanding of how certain individuals navigated specific questions via the responses they gave. Yet, even when only interrogatories or depositions survive, these can be compared to similar documents in separate cases. We have already seen in the second chapter how the increased formalisation of the court enabled a greater expression by the composers of bills of complaint and their subsequent answers. This approach can be further extended in this chapter, as witnesses were provided with a platform, and granted a wide scope of expression, to discuss a particular failure. By paying close attention to the procedure outlined above, it becomes clear that several witnesses were not directly involved in a commission of bankruptcy, and were instead being examined upon a specific aspect of the bankrupt's life or failure.

The Collaborative Nature of Witness Testimony

When discussing narrative construction and the mediated nature of oral testimony within depositions, scholars routinely reference Natalie Zemon Davis' ground-breaking work on pardon tales in sixteenth-century France. Davis concludes that despite the legal process governing their construction, the letters of remission tendered by the supplicants 'are one of the best sources of relatively uninterrupted narrative from the lips of the lower orders', and reflect, 'where the documents allowed it, the supplicant's own language and ordering of events'.[42] In this manner, legal evidence can be utilised to illuminate widely held attitudes and beliefs, rather than as evidence of verifiable facts or historical accounts. However, as scholars now routinely approach these sources as 'fictive', there is a danger that this not only undermines the value of incidental details attached to the narrative, but according to Alexandra Shepard, 'leaves depositions curiously detached from the witnesses who provided them'.[43] Throughout Chancery depositions, it is fair to conclude that the answers of some witnesses to the same question are interchangeable. At the same time, there is an individuality about certain answers which cannot be attributed to the formulaic nature of the legal process. As Joanne Bailey succinctly concludes, 'Simply put, different people sound different'.[44]

42 Natalie Zemon Davis, *Fiction in the Archives: Pardon Tales and Their Tellers in Sixteenth-Century France* (Stanford, 1987), p. 5, p. 21.
43 Alexandra Shepard, *Accounting For Oneself: Worth, Status, and the Social Order in Early Modern England* (Oxford, 2015), p. 8.
44 Joanne Bailey, 'Voices in Court: Lawyers' or Litigants'?', *Historical Research*, 74 (2001), p. 393.

Within these documents, individual narratives concerning credit, debt, and bankruptcy can be accessed, but it is important to remember that such narratives were created through the legal process outlined above. This can raise certain methodological issues, and it is worth charting how historians have utilised depositions in an attempt to overcome such problems. Returning to *True Relations*, Dolan claims that historians 'who describe legal depositions as "fictions" or "stories" do so in order to acknowledge their limitations as evidence'. As Dolan concludes, 'many of us feel that we must suppress our knowledge of evidentiary problems to get on with the work at hand'.[45] In an attempt to overcome such mediating difficulties and access unique voices, scholars undertake a variety of strategies. For example, when scholars quote from depositions and remove legal formulae – often by replacing 'this examinant' or 'this deponent' with 'he' or 'she' – they are doing so because they feel that such formulae distract the modern reader.[46]

Explanations for this process are usually hidden away in notes, and rarely given a full and detailed discussion. Mirandor Chaytor states, 'narratives have been returned to the first person singular', while Garthine Walker repeats the phrase and further explains, 'examinations, depositions and petitions are rendered in the first rather than the clerical third person'.[47] Bernard Capp simply states he has 'chosen to avoid technical terms and modernize quotations in order to make the social and cultural world of our ancestors more readily accessible'.[48] Finally, Laura Gowing explains that 'legal forms have been removed from this quotation for clarity'.[49] These are attempts to return to a supposed pure form of a first-person narrative prior to the mediation of a clerk. While their intention is to obscure the reader's awareness of the clerk, this raises serious epistemological questions, as their final outcome is a creation in and of itself, rather than a return to origin.[50]

45 Dolan, *True Relations*, pp. 25–26.
46 Ibid., pp. 121–122.
47 Miranda Chaytor, 'Husband(ry): Narratives of Rape in the Seventeenth Century', *Gender and History*, 7 (1995), pp. 378–407, p. 401, n. 1; Garthine Walker, 'Rereading Rape and Sexual Violence in Early Modern England, *Gender and History*, 10 (1998), pp. 1–25, p. 20, n. 4; Garthine Walker, *Crime, Gender and Social Order in Early Modern England* (Cambridge, 2003), p. xv.
48 Bernard Capp, *When Gossips Meet: Women, Family and Neighbourhood in Early Modern England* (Oxford, 2003), p. vii.
49 Laura Gowing, *Common Bodies: Women, Touch and Power in Seventeenth-Century England* (New Haven, 2003), p. 210, n. 1; when using Chancery decree rolls, Neil Jones has stated, 'Manuscript sources in English have been punctuated and rendered into modern orthography', 'The Influence of Revenue Considerations Upon the Remedial Practice of Chancery in Trust Cases, 1536–1660', in Christopher Brooks and Michael Lobban (eds), *Communities and Courts in Britain, 1150-1900* (London, 1997), pp. 99–114, n. 1.
50 Dolan, *True Relations*, pp. 121–128.

Such discussions and attempts to return to first-person narratives centre on the reliability of the clerk, the accuracy of transcriptions, and the authenticity of original speech. Discussing the work of scribes in the consistory court, Laura Gowing has claimed that 'clerks wrote, making a lengthy, clumsy, but technically unimpeachable statement'.[51] Lawrence Stone has insisted that the result of transcription in the ecclesiastical courts, 'is a full, and sometimes more-or-less verbatim, account of what was said by dozens, or hundreds, of persons, protagonists, witnesses, lawyers, and judges, who gave evidence or argued a given case. As a result we can eavesdrop on the conversations of men and women of all sorts and conditions.'[52] For Stone, the reliability of the clerk allows the historian to recreate the early modern courtroom and almost act as a fly on the wall, retelling the stories they have overheard. Garthine Walker uses the same terminology as Stone, describing these accounts as being recorded 'more or less verbatim', while Miranda Chaytor goes further, arguing that despite altering witnesses' statements – such as placing them in the third person – clerks 'wrote at the plaintiff's diction, changing nothing and omitting nothing. Or so the internal evidence of these narratives suggests.'[53] While it is impossible to check a clerk's accuracy – or the degree to which the final transcription reflected the direct speech of the deponent – this last statement seems overconfident and rather unlikely, as accuracy must have varied from clerk to clerk, and certainly between jurisdictions.[54]

Within these discussions, the role of the clerk has been defined as a transcriber, which firmly places them after the creation of the original narrative. However, as Dolan reminds us, clerks were not simply receivers of testimony who recorded accurately or otherwise, but rather shaped 'the statement before and as it is solicited, dictated, and revised'.[55] Similarly, parties and their legal representatives carefully formulated the questions, deponents responded to the questions posed, and clerks transcribed the answers; all of which took place within the overarching legal framework of the court. As such, there is a need to pay attention to the specific circumstances of the production of legal

---

51   Laura Gowing, *Domestic Dangers: Women, Words and Sex in Early Modern London* (Oxford, 1998), pp. 45–46.
52   Lawrence Stone, *Broken Lives: Separation and Divorce in England 1660–1857* (Oxford, 1993), p. 4.
53   Walker, 'Rereading Rape and Sexual Violence in Early Modern England', pp. 378–407; Chaytor, 'Husband(ry): Narratives of Rape in the Seventeenth Century', p. 381; This terminology is employed in other disciplines as well. Paul Glennie and Nigel Thrift describe depositions as a 'near verbatim source for non-elite utterances', Paul Glennie and Nigel Thrift, *Shaping the Day: A History of Timekeeping in England and Wales 1300–1800* (Oxford, 2009), p. 193.
54   Dolan, *True Relations*, p. 120.
55   Ibid., p. 120.

documents in order to fully understand their creation. While there were certain similarities in the process and procedure of collecting and presenting evidence to early modern courts, scholars either routinely highlight these similarities to make comparative analysis easier, or fail to adequately explain the complex differences between jurisdictions.

The court of Chancery had specific rules governing how evidence was to be collected in the country, and while this regimen was not always followed as closely as possible, many aspects were unique to the court. These specificities alter the way the document was created and the manner in which we can interpret such sources. Returning to Natalie Zemon Davis' work, it needs to be stressed that Davis deals not only with a sixteenth-century foreign court, but also with individuals presenting a judicial supplication in order to persuade the king and courts of the extenuating circumstances that would lead to a pardon. This document creation bears little or no resemblance to the variety of depositions that occurred throughout a wide range of local and central courts, as well as occurring at differing stages of a criminal or civil proceeding and across centuries of medieval and early modern examination.

Finally, some caution should also be exercised over the use of the word collaboration, which is seen as synonymous with such terms as 'cooperation' or working 'in partnership' with other parties. To an extent, this is true. It is clear from the previous section that several individuals worked together to create depositions. However, it cannot be said that these individuals were working towards the same goal or intended outcome, as they would have had different, and often competing aims. Furthermore, we can never be certain as to who contributed what to the finalised narrative, presented to us in the written documents that survive. We should accept that the *voice* that we *hear* has been created by the court – and the people utilising the court – under examination. With this in mind, it is worth analysing two cases, and particularly the accounts of two witnesses, to illustrate the methodological approach that will be employed in the final section.

In *Hoar v Darloe* (1737), both sets of depositions centred on the discovery of a bag of gold in a family home in Penzance, Cornwall in 1737. The plaintiffs were the assignees of the bankrupt, Thomas Darloe, and the defendants were the bankrupt's brother, William Darloe and his wife Susannah. Thomas Darloe previously lived in the house with his wife, Ellen, who had subsequently died. After Ellen's death, the bankrupt's brother William took over Thomas' trade and moved into the house. Mary Douglass, who was originally a servant for Thomas, stayed on to clean the house for William, and was the individual who discovered the bag of gold. While the case centred on who held legal ownership of the gold for the purposes of the post-bankruptcy distribution of goods, Mary Douglass provides a detailed account of the discovery of the gold. In the plaintiff's third interrogatory, they asked:

Did you or any other person find and where particularly in the said House and whether in any Chest of Drawers … [a] purse pocket or Fobb and was any money or any other thing and what contained therein … was the same Gold or silver or both and what Number of pieces of each might the same contain or what Quantity might the same be and of what there of at any time and when after you delivered the same in whose Custody did you or did you not see the said Money told or telling over if yea what did such person in whose Custody you saw the same say to you or any one else in your presence concerning the same and what did such person do when you saw the said Money telling.[56]

The defendants asked a similarly straightforward question: 'Do you know any thing touching a bag of money being found in an old Chest of Drawers … and when and by whom was the same found and how much Money was Contained in the Said Bag'.[57] This demonstrates that both sides of the dispute sought statements from Mary outlining the discovery of the gold. Mary answered the plaintiffs' questions first, and so provided a much more detailed account, which is worth quoting at length:

on Drawing out the Drawers which were First in Number in Order to Clean the same this Deponent Discovered a Bag of Money lying between the under most Drawer but one upon the Bottom that Parted that same Drawer from the under one it being a false Bottom which Bag being made of yellow Canvas and about the length of a Quarter of a Yard was Pinned with Two Pins One of which this Deponent taking out in order to Open the Bag Found the same to be Gold which by the Bulk and Weight of it this Deponent Doth verily Believe was more than Two hundred and Fifty Pounds and this Deponent Crying out that she had Found a Bag of Money the Defendant Susannah then being in the same Room with the Defendant William her husband Drinking Tea or Coffee she the Defendant Susannah Snatche the said Bag out of this Deponents hand and lockt up the same instantly in a side Cubbart in the same Room where they usually kept their Cash but at the time of taking it from this Deponent as aforesaid Pretended that the said were Leads such as are usually Worn in Womens Gowns Sleeves tho at the same time when this Deponent had Pulled out one of the Pins a Broad piece of Gold Tumbled out of the said Bag and had Fallen to the Ground If the Defendant Susannah had not Catcht it in her hand.[58]

Mary goes on to detail the contents of the bag, which were all gold, and some 'was Old Coin some Picies Thick, some Thin, some Broad, some Small … that

---

56   TNA, C11/412/20, 'Hoar v Darlow' (1737), Interrogatories submitted by John Hoar and John Smith.
57   Ibid., Interrogatories submitted by William Darloe and Susannah Darloe his wife.
58   Ibid., Deposition of Mary Douglass.

the said money was not tarnished but looked very bright and seemed to this Deponent not to have lain above a year in the place where the same was found'. Mary claimed that she and her husband William then retired to their bedroom, and about ninety minutes later they came down the stairs, and 'through a small hole in the wall', they spied the Defendants William and Susannah Darloe examining the money. When they entered the living room, Susannah 'Flung her Apron over the bag' to conceal the contents, 'whereupon this Deponent told the Defendant Susannah she need not Throw her Apron over it to hide it, for that she this Deponent saw it was all Gold and that she would Swear it'.[59] Mary concluded her deposition by stating that several days later:

> this Deponent Applied to the Defendant William Darloe she having Bought a pair of shoes and Clogs and a hat, for Money to Pay for them and told him she hoped that he would Give her Money to Pay for them out of the Bag of Gold which this Deponent had Found but he Refused to do so and Bid her Go to his Wife the Defendant Susannah which this Deponent accordingly did and she the said Susannah likewise Refused and Told her twas a Lie for that it was no Gold she had Found but that it was Lead that belonged to her Cousins Gowns sleaves and thereupon this Deponent Discovered the finding the said Gold to the said Thomas Darloe after which the said Defendants William Darloe and Susanna his wife offered this Deponent to give her two Guineas upon condition she would say no more nor make any further discovery of finding the said money which this Deponent refused to accept.[60]

What is clear in this case is that Mary Douglass was called as a witness to provide her own account of a specific historical event relating to a sole bankruptcy. Both the plaintiffs and the defendants presented interrogatories that appear to have been constructed solely for the deposition of Mary, who was neither a named party in the suit nor a creditor or debtor in the commission of bankruptcy. Specific words and phrases were stated in the interrogatories and then repeated in the depositions. We see reference to the chest of drawers, the bag of money, and a description of the quantity and quality of the pieces of gold. Yet, the degree of individuality surrounding this recollection is striking. Mary provides much more detail, describing the layout and number sequence of the drawers, the colour of the bag and how it was fastened with pins, the defendants drinking tea or coffee, their refusal to reimburse her for work clothes, and finally, the failed attempt to bribe her. As such, it appears that Mary maintains a degree of agency over her account, and detailed and particular statements such as these can shed light on social perceptions of bankruptcy and failure.

59   Ibid., Deposition of Mary Douglass; for a discussion of the convention and legitimacy of peep holes, see Dolan, *True Relations*, p.146.
60   Ibid., Deposition of Mary Douglass.

The second case, entitled *Hopkins v Newton* (1718), concerned the bankruptcy of an ironmonger named John Hopkins, who was engaged in the failed renovation of up to sixteen houses in Bull Street, Birmingham. The plaintiffs asked whether Hopkins did 'abscond and conceal himself to avoid being arrested for debts', and if he 'at any time and when make his Escape from the Bayliffes after he was arrested'.[61] In her response to this question, Anne Chatwin, who was a tenant of Hopkins, stated that the bankrupt kept house, absconded, or 'went in and out of the same privately and very early or very late' to avoid being arrested. Furthermore, Hopkins' doors were 'diligently watch'd and taken care of by his wife and servant maid', while Hopkins' wife spoke 'with Tears' that she feared 'all they had would be seized'.[62] Chatwin stated that on one occasion, and in order to avoid the bailiff, Richard Banner, Hopkins:

> Ran out of his own dwelling house or yard into this Deponents dwelling house and went up Stairs and Immediately afterwards the said Richard Banner came to this Deponent's door enquiring for the said Hopkins And the said Banner did in a Violent manner burst and break open the door of this Deponents dwelling house and came in and ran upstairs after the said Hopkins and brought him down into the Kitchen.[63]

Upon pressing the bailiff as to whether Hopkins had been arrested, Chatwin deposed that Banner had forgotten the arrest warrant and so shortly after left her house, 'saying that he would return presently and desired this Deponent to keep and detaine the said Hopkins'. While Hopkins returned to his own house, Chatwin stated that 'in a few weeks after that attempt or escape … another Bayliff did arrest the said Hopkins and took him to Warwick Gaol as this Deponent hath heard'.[64] Again, this deposition demonstrates an extremely detailed account of what appears to be a lucky escape for the bankrupt. We see reference to the emotional strain placed on family members, as the bankrupt's wife spoke 'in tears' at the constant fear of seizure, as well as the need to 'diligently' lock their doors and the eventual 'violent' attack Hopkins encountered. Even though Hopkins had successfully managed to avoid his creditors for over two years, this deposition demonstrates the constant threat to a bankrupt of arrest, as creditors continued to press for repayment.

What is clear in both of these cases, is that two women – one a servant and one a tenant –were called as witnesses to provide their own account of specific historical events relating to a single bankruptcy. In both examples, the

---

61   TNA, C11/1330/22, 'Hopkins v Newton' (1718), Interrogatories submitted on behalf of the plaintiffs.
62   Ibid., Deposition of Anne Chatwin.
63   Ibid.
64   Ibid.

witnesses were not named as parties in the suit, and neither were they explicitly mentioned as creditors or debtors within a commission of bankruptcy. It is not necessary to debate whether it is Mary Douglass' or Anne Chatwin's authentic, spoken, recollection of events we are interpreting. Instead, while there are clearly individual words, sentences, and descriptions encompassed within these documents, we can analyse and interpret them as being collectively created by the people involved in the legal process and presented to us in the written documents that survive. While scholars have attempted to highlight, edit, or even remove complex legal formulae in order to gain access to the unique voices of deponents, we can see here that such an endeavour is at best misguided, and at worst methodologically unsound. The legal process outlined above means that the court was not simply reflecting narratives about credit, debt, and failure, but was rather an active agent – alongside plaintiffs, defendants, witnesses, and legal experts – in creating narratives at this stage of the proceeding.

With this in mind, we are able to analyse the particular and evocative words, phrases, and idiosyncratic details employed in depositions, in order to illuminate attitudes towards bankruptcy within the wider community. Nearly forty years ago, Jim Sharpe argued that the law in early modern society reflected social and cultural norms and was central to early modern popular culture.[65] Since then, an established scholarship has shown how the law was a core element of everyday life. For example, Katie Barclay and Emily Ireland have stated that the law did not just account for statute law, trials, and judicial decisions, but can also be seen 'in the ways that ordinary people applied, interpreted, reinterpreted, and contested it in their daily lives. Such reworkings of the law, in turn shaped legal practice'.[66] During this period, Dolan has claimed that 'legal culture was popular culture', while Christopher Brooks has suggested that the law was one of the principal discourses through which early modern people

65   J. A. Sharpe, 'The People and the Law', in Barry Reay (ed.), *Popular Culture in Seventeenth Century England* (London, 1985), pp. 245–246; see also Carolyn Steedman, 'Lord Mansfield's Voices: In the Archive, Hearing Things', in Stephanie Downes, Sally Holloway, and Sarah Randles (eds), *Feeling Things: Objects and Emotions Through History* (Oxford, 2018), pp. 209–228; Katie Barclay, *Men on Trial: Performing Emotion, Embodiment and Identity in Ireland, 1800–1845* (Manchester, 2018); Frances Dolan, *Dangerous Familiars: Representations of Domestic Crime in England 1550–1700* (London, 1994); Douglas Hay, 'Master and Servant in England: Using the Law in the Eighteenth and Nineteenth Centuries', in William Steinmetz (ed.), *Private Law and Social Inequality in the Industrial Age: Comparing Legal Cultures in Britain, France, Germany and the United States* (Oxford, 2000), pp. 227–264.
66   Katie Barclay and Emily Ireland, 'The Household as a Space of the Law in Eighteenth-Century England', *Law and History*, 7 (2020), pp. 98–126, p. 103.

conceptualised society.[67] Witnesses used legal and economic terms – such as 'absconding' – in numerous ways to establish that an individual had acted in a fraudulent, deceitful, and criminal manner. Analysing the use of these terms can inform us of how such judgements were made by wider society, particularly in relation to the public nature of the actions of debtors.

Narratives of Bankruptcy, Failure, and Decline

Appraisal and the Bankruptcy Process
Shaw v Mellor (1716) is a case which highlights the construction of inter-rogatories and depositions in detail. The plaintiffs asked whether before 1700 the deceased bankrupt, Middleton Shaw, did 'Voluntarily abscond himself on purpose to avoid payment of his Debts', or whether he went abroad 'to avoid payment of his Debts'.[68] Several deponents confirmed that the bankrupt absconded after cases were initiated in the common law courts for the recovery of numerous individual debts. Thomas Salt, the bankrupt's servant, stated that he was 'not paide his servants Wages which came near to Forty pounds'. As such, he took out an action against Shaw and received a judgment in his favour, but 'for some time before and ever since the said judgment was obtained', Shaw absconded and he had 'not yet received any satisfaction for the debt'.[69] Similarly, Thomas Henton claimed that once the bankrupt absconded he never 'used or Exercised his former Trade or any other Imployment as formerly ever since beeing … greatly in debt and fearfull of being arrested'.[70] In their fifth interrogatory, the defendants asked 'what business or imployment did he [the bankrupt] at any time follow and when and for how long did he at any time and when and for how long seek his living by buying and selling of any and what goods and merchandizes'.[71] Interestingly, of the eight deponents who answered, none answered that question. In a similar manner to the previous chapter, we see specific elements of bankruptcy being discussed – namely the accusation of absconding abroad – but here, it is the witnesses who were providing detailed background to the failure of a now deceased individual.

The bankruptcy of Edward Halliday was litigated across several suits in Chancery.[72] In one of his responses, Halliday stated that his wife, family, and

---

67   Dolan, *True Relations*, p. 120; Christopher W. Brooks, *Law, Politics and Society in Early Modern England* (Cambridge, 2008), p. i.
68   TNA, C11/899/7, 'Shaw v Mellor' (1716), Interrogatories submitted by the Plaintiffs.
69   Ibid., Deposition of Thomas Salt.
70   Ibid., Deposition of Thomas Henton.
71   Ibid., Interrogatories submitted by the Defendants, John Mellor and Henry Buxton.
72   For a detailed discussion of the indebtedness of the Halliday family, see Aidan Collins, 'The Interconnected Nature of Family Indebtedness: The Halliday Family of Frome, Somerset (1733–1752)', *Enterprise and Society* (open access online, 2023), pp. 1–27

servants were all 'privy to this deponents goeing away Absconding or hiding himself', providing an insight into the family dynamic of absconding and economic failure.[73] In another case, the plaintiff John Phelps asked whether at the time of balancing the accounts, Halliday was 'not generally looked upon and Esteemed as a man of creditt and fortune and worth more than Suffcient to pay his just debts'.[74] Four deponents – including the bankrupt himself – repeated the phrase almost verbatim.[75] Thomas Ames, for example, stated that Halliday was 'generally looked upon and esteemed as a man of Creditt and fortune and worth much more than sufficient to answer his Just debts'. As a very considerable creditor, Ames felt that Halliday was 'was worth sufficient to Pay his Just Debts even after the time he first absconded'.[76] While this answer raises questions about when Ames would ever see Halliday as unable to fulfil his demands, the other deponents agreed that he had a sufficient estate to satisfy his debts. While the repetition of the phrase could raise questions regarding the individuality of each response, plaintiffs and defendants employed specific and relevant terminology to elicit answers that spoke to an individual failure. In this example, the use of the term 'Esteemed as a man of creditt and fortune' as set out in the interrogatory demonstrates that the plaintiffs were seeking to establish the solvency and financial capability of Halliday before he absconded. As the consensus was that Halliday was a substantial man of credit who could fulfil his demands, his absconding is identified as the exact moment he failed in his moral and financial duties.

We can see similar remarks about the financial solvency of bankrupts at the time of their failure in other cases. The bankruptcy of Tobias Lambert was litigated across two suits in Chancery. In response to a question about the 'probability or Improbability' of Lambert recovering specific debts, Henry Hall, a 39-year-old cloth worker, stated that Lambert 'remarked that one of them was bad and that others would pay half and … observing there were Scotch men in the said Schedule who had no Residence and could not be Found … the said Scotch men Generally came to his house every Two Months or six weeks'.[77] In Hope v Salmon (1724) the bankrupt, John Sabb, claimed that another defendant, Robert Salmon, had agreed to sell certain goods for his 'wifes Subsistence in this Deponents absence but instead thereof hath kept the same or Converted the same to his owne use'. On Christmas Day 1722, Sabb absconded and sought

73   TNA, C11/2790/24, 'In the Matter of Halliday' (1741), Deposition of Edward Halliday.
74   TNA, C11/2790/23, 'In the Matter of Halliday' (1741), Interrogatories submitted by the Plaintiff.
75   Ibid., Deposition of Robert Haywood, Deposition of William Dorrington; C11/2790/24, 'In the Matter of Halliday' (1741), Deposition of Edward Halliday, Deposition of Thomas Ames.
76   TNA, C11/2790/24, 'In the Matter of Halliday' (1741), Deposition of Thomas Ames.
77   TNA, C11/2769/14, 'Denison v Paine' (1722), Interrogatories on the behalf of the Plaintiffs; Deposition of Henry Hall.

refuge in the Mint for four months. While there were debates surrounding the legitimacy of the bill of sale, Sabb declared that the 'true Intent' of executing the bill was 'for the benefitt of his Creditors in Generall and to Enable Salmon to Support this Deponents Wife and five Children in the time of this Deponents withdrawing himself'. Finally, Sabb stated that Salmon was indebted to him in the sum of £10, but when he absconded he 'strucke out' of his book in order to discharge Salmon for repayment.[78]

These cases demonstrate the complex nature of indebtedness as bankrupts were known to be creditors and debtors in the early modern economy. Tawny Paul has shown how 'desperate debts', or debts that held a low probability of being repaid, were a common part of the credit system. For Paul, extending credit was more of an obligation than a calculated risk which depended on an assessment of trust and reliability: 'in a consumer economy that demanded credit, a tradesperson's calculations may have been less about whether they *could afford* to extend credit, and more about whether they *could afford not to*'. The information that creditors ascertained about their debtors appeared limited, and traders 'seemed to know remarkably little about the people to whom they extended credit'.[79] Certainly, this appears to be the case in the bankruptcy of Tobias Lambert, as not only were debts struck off, but the limited information surrounding the debtors in Scotland suggests an obligation to lend, rather than a carefully considered decision to lend based on trust and credibility. Again, these issues only come to light once Lambert failed and was unable to recoup the money owed to him.

In a similar example, the bankruptcy of William Stainer was litigated across several suits in Chancery, as while he had a single commission of bankruptcy taken out against him, he was also involved in a commission with his co-partners, Richard Presland and Thomas Jones. In one case, the assignees asked whether in September 1732 Stainer was a trader on his own account and was 'esteemed a person of Good Creditt and Reputation and of good Substance was such his Separate Trade Considerable or not'. One witness claimed that in September 1732, and for ten years previously, Stainer traded as a draper on his own account, and had 'a Good trade and Character' and was seen 'to be a person of Good Stock Credit and substance This Deponent being during all that time his next Door Neighbour'.[80] Hannah Holding was Stainer's servant for eight years and agreed that until the joint commission of bankruptcy was

---

78   TNA, C11/2642/6, 'Hope v Salmon' (1724), Answer of John Sabb. For a detailed discussion of the trading activities of Sabb, see Aidan Collins, 'Bankrupt Traders in the Court of Chancery, 1674–1750', *Eighteenth-Century Studies*, 55 (2021), pp. 65–82.
79   Tawny Paul, *The Poverty of Disaster: Debt and Insecurity in Eighteenth-Century Britain* (Cambridge, 2019), p. 39, p. 83.
80   TNA, C11/1876/28, 'Vaughan v Edwards' (1734-1755), Deposition of (illegible).

issued, he was seen as a 'person of Good Credit and Substance'.[81] In contrast to the Edward Halliday case above, the assignees were attempting to establish Stainer's reputation and credibility in regards to him as a 'person', and not just his credit and fortune. It is a much more individual and personalised appraisal of respectability than simply his ability to repay debts.

Martha Stainer, the bankrupt's wife, again stated that Stainer was of good stock, credit, and reputation, but blamed the co-partnership for his bankruptcy. When he traded on his own account he was 'very successful', having already paid the defendants several hundreds of pounds in satisfaction of his debts.[82] William Shepheard, a draper, and James Blakeway, a mercer, stated that Stainer was trading on his own account and was seen to be of good credit, reputation, and substance, but linked this directly to his trading activities in Shrewsbury. Shepheard stated that Stainer, 'had the Most Considerable Trade or business in that way of any one of that Trade in Shrewsbury on his own separate Account', and the stock in his individual shop was valued at £469 7s 8d and four farthings.[83] Blakeway claimed that Stainer had 'as good a retail trade as most of the Drapers in Shrewsbury'. He also stated that the defendant said to him 'you Rogue if you Don't pay me my Money according to your Bond I will sue you or to that Effect'.[84] We see the reputation of the same bankrupt come to be linked to his trading reputation, and the size of his business, in a particular town. Indeed, some responses provide further instances of how the initial failure had occurred and the way in which the bankruptcy was dealt with. Even when stock words and phrases were repeated, we see how witnesses still held a degree of scope to provide their own narrative account of past events.

Blakeway stated that after he and two other defendants had purchased goods from the bankrupt, they agreed to allow Stainer 'meat and drink for himself and his poor small family'. This amounted to 'less than two Shillings and Six pence a day which was agreed and allowed by the assignee'.[85] Both the bankrupt and his wife confirmed the agreement, with Martha stating that her husband was employed to sell his own shop goods, being paid the 'necessary Subsistence for his Trouble'. After Stainer had paid Blakeway £70 15s, and a further £5 1d, Blakeway provided him with forty shillings 'to buy necessary provision for his Family'.[86] William Shepheard claimed that the three defendants employed him and authorised him as an agent, to 'sell and Dispose' of the bankrupt's goods, for which he was paid 2s 6d per day. However, Shepheard was eventually 'Removed from the said Imployment as the said Defendants thought

81   Ibid., Deposition of Hannah Holding.
82   Ibid., Deposition of Martha Stainer.
83   Ibid., Deposition of William Shepheard.
84   Ibid., Deposition of James Blakeway.
85   TNA, C11/2318/32, 'Vaughan v Edwards' (1735), Deposition of James Blakeway.
86   TNA, C11/2785/28, 'Vaughan v Bowdler' (1735), Deposition of Martha Stainer.

that two shillings six pence a Day was too great an Expence'.[87] Finally, one of the co-bankrupts, Thomas Jones, deposed that 'he hid himself for sometime but afterwards came and Surrendred himself to the acting Commissioners'.[88] In these suits, we see similar aspects of the bankruptcy process being discussed as in the previous chapters – absconding, a provision for the bankrupt, the inter-connected nature of family indebtedness, and discussions of the bankrupt's credibility – but we also see a more specific and deliberate use of language being deployed.

Particular words and phrases were selected by plaintiffs and defendants to elicit particular responses. At the same time, deponents were allowed a wide scope to respond to a range of closed and open-ended questions as they saw fit. In *Durling v Clarke* (1722) the plaintiffs were assignees of Richard Hooper. The suit centred around the vocation of Hooper, and whether he was one quarter owner, a bargemaster, or simply a cost bearer of a barge called the 'Great Dove' which belonged to the sole defendant, Francis Clarke. Several deponents stated that the going rate for a return journey from Oxford to London was between thirty and thirty-five shillings. Francis Davis, a butcher, stated that Clarke had claimed that Hooper was 'the fittest man in Oxford to make a Bargemaster'.[89] In contrast, Nicholas Tirrold simply said that the bankrupt was a cost bearer who earned a wage, and he had 'never heard of the said Hooper being partner with the Defendant in any share of a barge with him and the said Hooper was not looked upon to be a man in very good Circumstances in the world nor fit to be a partner in a barge but as he was a costbearer he made a great bustle and talked big'.[90] Similarly, another deponent simply stated that Clarke had called Hooper a 'Rascall'.[91] Here, we can see deponents deploy contrasting words to present the bankrupt as either a legitimately employed bargemaster who was well-versed in the trade, or a rascal and a cheat who liked to exaggerate his abilities and credibility. The appraisal being undertaken was related to skill in a particular trade and the narratives surrounding this failure directly relate to Hooper's ability to undertake that skill.

In *Houlding v Legood* (1735), the assignees of William Gosling, who had a drapery and grocery business, named the bankrupt, his wife Mary, Benjamin Legood, and James Wilson as defendants. All that survives are the interroga-tories and depositions that were taken on behalf of the defendants. Legood had asked two individuals – Richard Young, a linen draper and grocer, and James Dunbar, a linen draper – to appraise the goods of the bankrupt. Young and Dunbar were chosen because of their expertise in the linen trade, and in

---

87 Ibid., Deposition of William Shepheard.
88 TNA, C11/1876/28, 'Vaughan v Edwards' (1734–1755), Deposition of Thomas Jones.
89 TNA, C11/2302/19, Durling v Clarke (1722), Deposition of Francis Davis.
90 Ibid., Deposition of Nicholas Tirrold.
91 Ibid., Deposition of Thomas (illegible).

May 1733 they sold some goods to James Wilson for £150. While the goods were valued at between £170 and £176, they were sold at a lower price because Wilson, 'took the same goods together and agreed to pay the said One Hundred and fifty pounds for them some short time after the delivery thereof which saved in this Deponents Judgement as much or more than the Difference in regard to the Charge and trouble of retailing them in a small Country Village where they stood'.[92] One deponent, William Taylor, stated that Legood wanted him to be present to oversee the removal of the goods of the bankrupt as a servant was thought to be trying to seize the goods for the benefit of the bankrupt and to the prejudice of Legood. Similarly, James Morris, a servant of Legood, stated that his master ordered him to enter Gosling's premises at three or four in the morning, to maintain possession of several goods in his house and warehouse. Obeying orders, Morris 'entered and continued for Eleven Days together and that he lay in the said Goslings house during all that Time'.[93] This is a remarkable account of the lengths that a creditor went to in order to seize control of an individual's estate. While background details to this suit are sparse, there were several competing claims on the bankrupt's estate, as the assignees sought to identify and incorporate it within the commission.

Similarly, in *Barstow v Ashurst* (1733), the plaintiff-creditors of Thomas Harrison asked the defendants, 'have you or any other Person or Persons by your order been Diligent in applying to the Several Persons who were indebted to the Estate of the said Bankrupt for the several sumes by them oweing respectively and have you used any and what meanes to receive and Gett in the same'.[94] In response, William Watkinson stated that 'he hath by himself and other persons used all imaginable diligence in applying from time to time to the several persons who were indebted to the Estate of the said Thomas Harrison the bankrupt for the several sums by them respectively owing and has caused several persons who were able to pay but neglected the doing thereof to be sued and recovered the money owing by them'. Due to several debtors being insolvent, gone to parts unknown, or having subsequently died, Harrison 'did not think it prudent in him nor that he was under any obligation to enter such or multiplicity of suits for the recovering those debts the success whereof is not only incertain but the Expence greater than what this Examinant thought proper or apprehends himself under any Obligation to bear'.[95] It appears that the risk outweighed the reward in the pursuit of this particular debt.

In *Perrins v Gyles* (1736), Evard Roberts, a wherryman from Worcester, claimed that he only knew the bankrupt – a public house owner called William

---

92   TNA, C11/1929/21, 'Houlding v Legood' (1735), Deposition of Richard Young.
93   Ibid., Deposition of James Morris.
94   TNA, C11/1928/12, 'Barstow v Ashurst' (1733), Interrogatories submitted by the plaintiffs.
95   Ibid., Deposition of William Watkins.

St Clere – for twelve months about nine or ten years earlier. During this time, Roberts suggested that St Clere frequently asked him to send a letter or note to a defendant named John Gyles, which requested him 'to send him some more money and at other times to lend him some more money and to send the same by this Deponent'. Gyles subsequently lent St Clere several sums amounting to roughly £100, during which time the bankrupt 'followed his said Business publickly and openly and at that time this Deponent kept a wherry between Worcester and Gloucester which was the reason he was Imployed in the Business aforesaid and this Deponent cannot say when the said Saint Clere became a Bankrupt but at that time there was no suspicion of his being a Bankrupt as this Deponent knows or has heard of'.[96] Similarly, Thomas Giles – who appears to be a relative of the defendant having known him from his 'Infancy' – claimed that roughly ten years earlier John Gyles lent the bankrupt several sums of money, amounting to £50 or £60. However, 'he knows not when the Defendant Saint Clere became a bankrupt nor did this Deponent hear he was a Bankrupt till Master John Hunt the Complainants Sollicitor in this Cause told him so', which was in 1730 or 1731. In this case, it is the public activities and the circulating knowledge – or lack thereof – which determine the bankrupt's credibility at the time of his failure.

A similar account is put forward in *Carril v Savage* (1729), whereby two deponents provide insights into the bankrupt's behaviour, which they deemed to be tell-tale signs of dishonesty and his desire to abscond. The plaintiffs were three assignees of William Hayne, a deceased mercer from Gloucester. They asked a question which was aimed directly at Hayne's servant, Mary Westbury, and whether in August 1726, she did:

> live as a Servant with him at that time, or how otherwise came you to be Conversant and acquainted with him And did the said William Haynes upon any and what day in the said Month of August or at any time before to your knowledge or belief Abscond from his dwelling house or cause himself to be denied to any and what Creditor as you know or believe and upon what day did he first Abscond or cause and order himself to be denied to any and what Creditor or Creditors ... or commit any other Act of Bankruptcy to your knowledge or belief and what have you heard.[97]

Mary's response is worth quoting at length:

> about twelve of the Clock in the afternoon of the said Wednesday the said William Haynes absconded and left his dwelling House in Gloucester ...

96   TNA, C11/1934/9, 'Perrins v Gyles' (1736), Deposition of Evard Roberts.
97   TNA, C11/1368/4, 'Carril v Savage' (1729), Interrogatories submitted by the plaintiffs, Thomas Carrill, Samuel Worrall, and Samuel Pawling.

and this Deponent helped him put on his great Coat just before he went to his House but at that time did not suspect his Intention or design of going of until the next day she was informed thereof … in the night time of the Saturday … the said William Haynes came again to the dwelling House but upon his return this Deponent was ordered by her Mistress the said William Haynes Wife to deny that the said William Haynes was at home to anyone who should enquire for him.[98]

The inclusion of Haynes putting on his 'great Coat' just before he left the house appears to be a deliberate inclusion to suggest that he had an intention to leave for an extended period. While Mary Westbury claimed that initially she did not suspect her master of absconding, the fact that he did not return until late in the evening, coupled with the order from her mistress to deny entry to any visitors, provides a clearly defined timeline of the events in question. John King answered the same question and gave a similar account. He stated that on Wednesday 6 August Haynes was being pressed for money, but that he 'would not answer their Demands but that he would go off or words to that Effect and saith before that day this Deponent never heard or was informed by the said William Haynes or any other person whatsoever that he was in bad circumstances'.[99] The combination of witness statements provided evidence of an identifiable date and timeline of an individual failure, and the dishonest and disreputable actions of Haynes.

Similarly, in *Wickes v Marshall* (1745), the plaintiffs were assignees of Isaac Knott, and the depositions were taken in Norwich, Norfolk. The plaintiffs sought to identify a specific date, an exact time, and a defined timeline of failure. They asked whether Knott:

was in the Judgement of the said Commissioners acting under the said Commission proved or declared a Bankrupt under all or any of the Statutes concerning Bankrupts; Were you and who else a Witness or Witnesses to or concerning the Act or Acts of Bankruptcy committed or ordered or done by the said Bankrupt and when and upon what day of the month and in what year were such acts committed ordered or done and what were such acts or orders and how do you know the same and in what relation did you stand in respect to the Bankrupt Declare what you know remember or can recollect concerning the said Act or Acts of Bankruptcy with the Exact time when with your Reasons at large and particular Circumstances thereof.[100]

98   Ibid., Deposition of Mary Westbury.
99   Ibid., Deposition of John King.
100   TNA, C11/2336/30, 'Wickes v Marshall' (1745), Interrogatories submitted by the Plaintiffs.

Three of the five defendants responded directly to this question. Jacob Ramsbotham, a thirty-year-old wool comber, explained that he knew the bankrupt well as he was previously his apprentice. When he was examined by the commissioners, he stated that on a Friday in July 1736 a fellow servant named Sarah Beckham provided him with a note from his master. The note did, 'order and direct this Deponent to deny him to any of his Creditors and other persons who should come to enquire for him and to inform such creditors or persons that he was not at home'. As such, he informed several visitors that Knott was not home, despite him being 'in his said dwelling house in perfect Health to all appearance and not under any Fatigue or Interruption of Business'. While Knott concealed himself for the entire day, 'the next day and for some few Days afterwards went abroad as usual and until sometime in the first week in August when he totally confined himself to his House'.[101] Beckham corroborated Ramsbotham's version of events and clarified that the Friday on which Knott kept house was 23 July 1736, and repeated the phrase that he was 'to all appearance in perfect Health'.[102]

Finally, Thomas Warkhouse, a fifty-year-old esquire, deposed that he was himself a commissioner. The commission declared Knott a bankrupt according to the wording of the statutes and stated that he committed his first act of bankruptcy on 23 July 1736.[103] We have previously seen how a deponent could have been a commissioner for the court, but in this case Warkhouse was a commissioner in a commission of bankruptcy. His knowledge of the previous bankruptcy process is used as testimony to provide a specific timeline of failure. Such details and specificities can only be seen at the depositional stage of proceeding as it is the witnesses, rather than the parties in a suit, who provide such compelling narratives. Furthermore, we see different ways in which individuals looked back to appraise the actions and words of a single failure. Being in good health, there was no legitimate reason why Knott would remain in the house for an extended period of time, especially as he had previously gone abroad in the normal course of his business.

The court of Chancery provided a platform for a range of witnesses to be interrogated in a particular case. These statements were then transformed into evidence so that the court could identify and establish failure – as a social construct at law – to mediate in social and financial affairs. While plaintiffs and defendants used carefully selected language to elicit particular responses, deponents still had the ability to provide individual and unique narratives based upon their own interpretations and experiences. This analysis adds a new dimension to cultures of appraisal, worth, and interpersonal credit, and the work of Craig Muldrew, Alexandra Shepard, Margot Finn and others,

---

101 Ibid., Deposition of Jacob Ramsbotham.
102 Ibid., Deposition of Sarah Beckham.
103 Ibid., Deposition of Thomas Warkhouse.

by demonstrating the complex and multifaceted nature of debt-recovery in Chancery. Ultimately, the ways in which individuals looked back and described and debated the actions and words of bankrupts came to rely on the individual circumstances of the case. This could include, but is not limited to, financial solvency, the (in)ability to repay debts, family support networks, the circulation of knowledge, public or private actions, expertise in trade, or unique characteristics such as the need to put on a large coat and the health of the individual in question. These ways of appraising the past came to be used to judge reputation, credibility, and morality and shed new light on our understanding of personal economic failure.

Failure and Personal Decline
As well as detailing the numerous ways in which appraisals were made, several suits spoke in greater detail about the personal decline of the bankrupt himself. Returning to the bankruptcy of Tobias Lambert, the plaintiffs in *Dodson v Denison* (1722) asked whether before 13 November 1719 Lambert did 'on what day or night and in what month and year and on what hour of the Day or Night abscond secret and Conceal himself or Cause or order himself to be secreted or Concealed from or deny'd to any and which of his Creditors or any and what other person or persons ... that Came to endeavour to Arrest him'. Depositions from Tobias Lambert, his wife Sarah, and their three children all confirm that Tobias ordered his family to deny entry to any of his creditors.[104] Sarah stated that leading up to her husband's failure, her husband kept himself concealed, and he 'only Sometimes peeped out into the Shop ... But neither Stayed or Satt downe there as she Remembers, being afraid of an arrest or Dunn from Some of his Creditors'. She recalled several creditors coming to demand repayment, including a Robert Dennison, who was so outraged at her husband's failure to repay him that he suggested Lambert 'had the devil in him'. Tobias corroborated his wife's account, and confirmed that Dennison said he had 'the devil' in him.[105] He further stated that while he 'Sometimes did curiously look into his Shop' he did so 'but with fear of being arrested and made no long stay' and 'never appeared so publick in his trade as he did before'.[106]

In response to the same question, a family friend and 'perriwiggmaker' named Edward Brogden specified that on 15 November he went to see Lambert at his home, where he seemed very 'pensive and melancholy'. He asked 'what the matter was with him and if any Losses had happened'. He realised that Lambert was experiencing severe financial difficulties, as he recalled that if Lambert, 'at any time before had lost Ten or Twenty pounds usually told this Deponent of

104   TNA, C11/2762/22, 'Dodson v Denison' (1722), Interrogatories submitted by Thomas Denison and Robert Denison.
105   Ibid., Deposition of Sarah Lambert.
106   Ibid., Deposition of Tobias Lambert.

it they being so very Intimately acquainted'. However, according to Brogden, upon this occasion 'it was A Great deale worse, for that he had been Casting up his Books the week before and he Could not make both ends meet and also that he had received one or more threatening Letter or Letters from some or One of his Creditors at London', and might be forced to flee the next morning. While Lambert did not flee, Brogden estimated his debts to be approximately £2500, and under the strain of such pressures Lambert fell 'Crying to this Deponent'.[107] In this instance, Brogden's portrayal of bankruptcy can be seen as an ongoing decline in Lambert's economic, psychological, and emotional health.

Further depositions seem to confirm this description of Lambert's decline. For example, the defendants asked, 'of what Creditt and Reputation was the said Tobias Lambert as to his Trade … did he appear publickly and attend his shop and Business'. In response, Christopher Heblethwait, a saddler from Leeds, stated that when he entered Lambert's shop, the bankrupt's wife Sarah was working, but the pair failed to come to an agreement on the sale of certain goods. As such, Lambert entered the shop about nine o'clock with 'his Stockings untyed and his Cravatt Loose about his neck, and Sold to this Deponent the Goods'.[108] Heblethwait's decision to mention the state of Lambert's dress in his formulation of the bankrupt's credit and reputation is a notable inclusion. Being in a state of undress was both an attack upon established social hierarchies as well as being a clear signifier of psychological decline during the period. Tawny Paul has shown how popular prints often showed the dishevelled nature of individuals upon the point of their arrest and imprisonment. As Paul concludes, 'symbols of masculine social debasement were prominent in visual representations of debtors, and they communicated debasement through the self-presentation of indebted bodies'.[109] Clothing held symbolic value as a marker of social standing and was considered a valuable financial resource that could quickly and easily be pawned, sold, or traded.[110] Lambert's failure is also presented in his decline from a respectable position to that of a dishevelled individual.

Responding to a similarly worded question in the second suit, Henry Hall recollected that prior to his demise, Lambert used to walk 'publickly before his

---

107 Ibid., Deposition of Edward Brogden.
108 Ibid., Deposition of Christopher Heblethwait.
109 Paul, *The Poverty of Disaster*, p. 201, see also Tim Hitchcock, *Down and Out in Eighteenth-Century London* (London, 2004), pp. 97–123; Simon P. Newman, *Embodied History: The Lives of the Poor in Early Philadelphia* (Philadelphia, 2003); John Styles, *The Dress of the People: Everyday Fashion in Eighteenth-Century England* (New Haven, 2007), ch.2.
110 See Jonathan Andrews, 'The (un)Dress of the Mad Poor in England, c.1650–1850. Part I', *History of Psychiatry*, 18 (2007), pp. 5–24; Part II, *History of Psychiatry*, 18 (2007), pp. 131–135.

shop Door in the street' and according to his usual Custom he would regularly 'shake this Deponent by the hand, and Desire him to walk into the house and Drink with him, which this Deponent did, and stayed with him two or three hours'. Since his failure, however, this had become a rare occurrence.[111] Within these depositions, Tobias Lambert is depicted as not only voluntarily removing himself from social ties by keeping house and absconding, but also as being in a serious decline of his physical, economic, and mental health. The bankrupt is portrayed at his lowest point, as a desperate man and one who is separated from the accepted norms of society.

Bernard Capp has argued that emotional public displays – and especially outbursts of anger – were discouraged in early modern England.[112] However, as Linda Pollock has shown, displays of anger were culturally significant, as 'displaying anger could be a source of pride', while in other circumstances 'it could be regretted'.[113] While the history of emotions in legal sources is still a relatively new topic, Merridee Bailey has shown how individuals in Chancery 'selected from emotional norms to suit their circumstances'.[114] In this case, we see the dichotomy between the private and public elements of emotional responses to failure. We are not seeing emotions presented as they truly were, but rather we see the ways in which individuals looked back and interpreted emotional responses to individual failures. Creditors were seen to take their anger out on Lambert in a public manner, while the bankrupt was either hidden away in the private sphere or appeared in public as a poorly dressed melancholic failure. In this sense, the construction of the emotional narrative is simply another way in which individuals judged reputation and creditworthiness.

Indeed, emotional constructions can function in dynamic and multifaceted ways. In certain instances, Pollock has argued that emotion could be a 'responsible reaction'.[115] While it appears that Tobias Lambert did genuinely suffer a decline in his material and personal circumstances, by demonstrating a downward emotional trajectory, he and several witnesses were showing the 'correct' way to respond, by demonstrating a sense of remorse, guilt, and material hardship at the unfortunate situation he had found himself in.[116] As Muldrew has shown, bonds of credit 'were conceived of as both social and emotive relationships'.[117] Ultimately, taking risk is emotional, and the

111   TNA, C11/2769/14, 'Denison v Paine' (1722), Deposition of Henry Hall.
112   Capp, *When Gossips Meet*, pp. 204–205.
113   Linda Pollock, 'Anger and the Negotiation of Relationships in Early Modern England', *Historical Journal*, 47 (2004), pp. 567–590, p. 574.
114   Bailey, 'Shaping London Merchant Identities', p. 335.
115   Pollock, 'Anger and the Negotiation of Relationships in Early Modern England', p. 582.
116   Bailey, 'Most Hevynesse and Sorowe', pp. 1–28; see also Kuehn, 'Reading Microhistory', pp. 512–535.
117   Muldrew, *The Economy of Obligation*, p. 152.

failure to repay debts can manifest itself in emotional experiences, actions, and descriptions of past events. Tawny Paul has argued that 'the emotional basis of trust becomes apparent during moments when credit broke down'.[118] Emotional displays and descriptions were a by-product of unconscionable actions and accusations of acting in an immoral manner. And of course, these actions needed to lead to a clearly defined remedy that the court could enact. While Chancery did not elicit or invite emotions as a form of evidence, it received them because parties and witnesses were part of a social and cultural environment whereby emotional experiences and reactions were commonplace. As Bailey succinctly concludes, 'debt was harrowing'. Those involved in failure felt unfortunate, victimised, or targeted. In this sense, 'people *feel* injustice, and it is this that carries emotional meaning'.[119] According to Joanna Bourke, emotions 'mediate between the individual and the social', aligning people to the wider community.[120] The collaborative nature of Chancery depositions demonstrates the ways in which emotional norms and responses were transformed into compelling narratives to add evidence to a personal, financial failure within the court.[121]

   In sixteen cases the interrogatories explicitly mentioned absconding, and twelve cases refer to a decline in terms of an individual's credit, trust, reputation, or circumstances. However, in certain suits, more emotive words and phrases were used. Returning to *Hopkins v Newton*, the creditors asked whether the bankrupt John Hopkins was in 1705 and 1706, 'known or generally reputed to be a thriving man' or whether he was known 'to abscond and withdraw himself'. Here, the creditors were seeking to establish what the common assessment of Hopkins was during this period, suggesting that Hopkins' credible or deceptive behaviour would be well known to the trading community. However, they also asked whether Hopkins was 'reputed to be in a flourishing condition or did he conceal himselfe soe that it was difficult to speak to him or procure him to be arrested'.[122] In this situation the creditors saw these two actions as mutually exclusive: a person can either be seen to be acting in a credible manner, appearing publicly and continuing with their trade, or they can be acting in a deceitful manner by concealing themselves from public view. In this context, the use of the term 'thriving' was commonly associated with an individual who increased their worldly and physical estate by honest, sincere, and generous causes. Commentators made reference to the English proverb, 'Ill

118   Paul, *The Poverty of Disaster*, p. 115.
119   Bailey, 'Most Hevynesse and Sorowe', p. 23.
120   Joanna Bourke, 'Fear and Anxiety: Writing About Emotion in Modern History', *History Workshop Journal*, 55 (2003), pp. 111–133, p. 117.
121   Bailey, 'Most Hevynesse and Sorowe', p. 26.
122   TNA, C11/1330/22, 'Hopkins v Newton' (1718), Interrogatories submitted on behalf of the plaintiffs.

gotten goods seldom thrive', which was built upon Mark 8:36: 'For what shall it profit a man if he shall gain the whole world, and lose his own soul?'[123] To 'thrive' or to 'prosper' were generally taken as the same thing, and men who sought to achieve this not only had increasing estates, but were sound in mind and soul.[124] By attempting to make the deponents choose between Hopkins as a thriving man or one who absconded, they were portraying him as an extremely deceitful individual, who at no point had acted in a trustworthy manner.

In *Andrews v Vaughan* (1734), the plaintiffs asked whether between 1719 and 1721 the bankrupt did 'begin to sink in the world'. Of the four witnesses – three of whom answered this question – only Thomas Blayney repeated the term 'sink'. He suggested that between 1719 and 1721 the bankrupt held a 'very good creditable reputation', and it was not until 1729–1730 'when it was reported he began to sink in the world'.[125] During the early modern period, the term 'sink' was used in relation to moral and ethical religiosity, and to sink in the world meant to lapse or degenerate into some inferior moral or social condition.[126] For example, Phillip Goodwin promulgated the need to act in a Christian manner throughout the entirety of the week, condemning those who were provident and diligent, 'yet decay and sink in the world' by not respecting the Sabbath.[127] In his *Caution Against Ill Company* (1705), James Ellesby preached against those who can see the correct path but choose alternatives: 'Christians who have all the Helps and Encouragements to become the *Best* of Men and excel all the World beside, should yet Sink and Degenerate beneath the *Basest* and *Vilest* of Mankind'.[128] Using the example of a Captain Wilkinson – who had become impoverished and imprisoned due to his outstanding debts and poverty – one anonymous tract highlighted the disparity between respectable, credible individuals and the plight of those who have fallen from grace. While Captain Wilkinson was once 'a loyal subject, or an honest man', he was now 'sunk in the world' and came to town to put himself in 'some new way of life' and regain his respectability.[129] By using the term 'sink' in their interrogatory, the plaintiffs were insinuating that not only had the bankrupt declined in financial terms, but he had also fallen below the accepted standards of moral, religious, and neighbourly conduct.

123   Jennifer Speake (ed.), *Oxford Dictionary of Proverbs* (Oxford, 2015), p. 162.
124   James Donaldson, *The Undoubted Art of Thriving* (Edinburgh, 1700), pp. 1–3.
125   TNA, C11/1931/3, 'Andrews v Vaughan' (1734), Deposition of Thomas Blayney.
126   OED; Phillip Goodwin, *Dies Dominicus Redivivus* (London, 1654), p. 230; James Ellesby, *A Caution Against Ill Company* (London, 1705), p. 63.
127   Phillip Goodwin, *Dies Dominicus Redivivus; OR; The Lords Day Enlivened* (London, 1654), p. 230.
128   James Ellesby, *A Caution Against Ill Company* (London, 1705), p. 63.
129   *Animadversions On Capt. Wilkinson's Information* (London, 1682), pp. 5–10.

In *Buckworth v Peart* (1730), the plaintiff and creditor of the bankrupt carefully constructed nineteen lengthy interrogatories. Of these, the tenth question asked whether a Captain Michaele was reputed to be a 'ready moneye man and a person of good Circumstances in the World or of ability to purchase the reale Estate' of the bankrupt.[130] This was an explicit reference to the availability of Michaele's disposable money. Ready money was seen as distinct and separate from estate, goods, and credit. Within this case, the plaintiff was seeking to establish whether Michaele was in a position to purchase the estate of the bankrupt, or whether it was fraudulently assigned in order to prevent the creditors from gaining access to it. Only one deposition survives, whereby a fifty-five-year-old gentleman named Henry Morris simply answered a question relating to a deed and a letter of attorney regarding the transfer of property. However, in a further five suits, reference is made to the bankrupt's 'circumstances', a term that was largely associated with material and worldly goods, rather than credit or trust. In his treatise on the subject, Isaac Watts suggested that being of 'low circumstances in the world' was diametrically opposite to being rich, while Humphry Smith stated that 'Men of very low Circumstances in the World' were 'utterly destitute of any secular Advantages'.[131] Within these suits, we see further reference to attempting to establish the bankrupt's 'estate', 'fortune', or 'stock and substance', meaning that creditors sought to determine the physical, material, and financial valuation of individual worth. Throughout these examples, we see the formulation of language in interrogatories change according to the specific details of the case. Chancery depositions referred to the private emotions of individuals – and the relationship between individuals – alongside the wider social implications of failure in the trading community.[132]

While the language used to denote financial failure reflected a decline of personal circumstances, we can see narratives concerning the deterioration of mental health come into play. Michael MacDonald has argued that by the early seventeenth century, the language of madness had become 'rich and pervasive ... words and phrases about insanity were part of the common coinage of everyday speech and thought, negotiable everywhere in England and not restricted to a small circle of medical and legal experts'.[133] The early modern period exhibited a specific and deliberate use of language, so much so that to ramble, or speak too quickly, quietly, or loudly were tell-tale signs of mental

130   TNA, C11/1931/30, 'Buckworth v Peart' (1730), Interrogatories submitted on behalf of Everard Buckworth.
131   Isaac Watts, *Discourses of the Love of God* (London, 1729), p. 235; Humphry Smith, *The Divine Authority, and Usefulness, of Ecclesiastical Censures, Asserted* (Exeter, 1708), p. 4.
132   Bailey, 'Shaping London Merchant Identities', pp. 327–337.
133   Michael MacDonald, *Mystical Bedlam: Madness, Anxiety, and Healing in Seventeenth Century England* (Cambridge, 1981), pp. 122–123.

disorder. MacDonald's case study of the medical practitioner Richard Napier has shown how financial hardship could directly lead to mental anguish, as somewhat unsurprisingly, 'debt was by far the greatest single source of anxiety'.[134] It is interesting to see MacDonald use economic metaphors to discuss popular culture and the narratives surrounding insanity, as economic and mental decline were closely connected.

While more research needs to be conducted to effectively link bankruptcy to narratives of insanity, some preliminary observations can be made from the analysis above. It was the observations and anxieties of family members, neighbours, and the wider community which formed the social structure and the defining process of *both* lunacy and bankruptcy. While the taint of madness may have been more severe, the attachment of the label 'mad' or 'bankrupt' had a seriously detrimental effect on a person's social reputation and standing within the community. A debtor had no control over the initiation of a commission of bankruptcy, while those with perceived mental disorders had a similarly limited control over their fate. Jonathan Andrews has shown how 'it was not the insane, but their friends and parishes' who negotiated for their admission.[135] As the Restoration poet Nathaniel Lee declared upon his committal, 'they said I was mad; and I said they were mad; damn them they outvoted me'.[136] Those declared insane and those declared bankrupt had their situation determined to them from without, and the build-up to such determinations could follow similar paths.

Throughout Chancery depositions, we are often confronted with an individual bankrupt who had fought long and hard to remain solvent. This process of economic decline is often mirrored in discourse concerning insanity, as the terms surrounding madness were used to refer to a build-up of behavioural signs rather than a specific action.[137] For example, excessive solitude was a deviation from the accepted norms of society, alienating individuals from their community. A reputable trader would need to be seen to be acting in a public manner at certain agreeable times. As such, a private and solitary individual – whether absconding from creditors or showing signs of melancholy – was seen to be disrupting socially accepted norms. Across several depositions, we see narratives concerning economic, personal, and mental decline formulated and presented in numerous ways, as individuals sought to look back and appraise the actions and words of those involved in debt recovery.

---

134   Ibid., 67.
135   Jonathan Andrews, 'The Politics of Committal to Early Modern Bethlem', in Roy Porter (ed.), *Medicine in the Enlightenment* (Amsterdam, 1995), pp. 6–63, pp. 42–43.
136   Quoted in Roy Porter, *Mind-Forg'd Manacles: A History of Madness from the Restoration to the Regency* (London, 1987), p .2.
137   Peter Rushton, 'Lunatics and Idiots: Mental Disability, the Community, and the Poor Law in North-east England, 1600-1800', *Medical History*, 32 (1988), pp. 34–50, p. 37.

Conclusion

In her work on maternity and justice, Amanda Capern has argued that the legal rhetoric used in Chancery, 'observed certain rules of maternal performance that fashioned speech acts according to the strategic legal needs of the case in the arena of Chancery and in direct relation to its jurisdiction'. As such, the words used could not be directly transferrable to other jurisdictions in order to 'prove' an individual's character, because as Capern summarises, 'the cases were about different things'.[138] While there was a specific and deliberate use of language in relation to maternity in Chancery, so too was there a specific and deliberate use of language in relation to bankruptcy, failure, and decline within the court. In any adversarial process there is never one set and accepted plot, story, or script, to which we can gain access. Instead, individual narratives can be accessed, but it is important to remember that such narratives were created through the legal processes outlined above. By paying close attention to the procedure put in place for asking questions, providing answers, and recording the process, it becomes apparent that Chancery was not only a court that mediated in social and financial affairs, but was also an institution which helped to create narratives.

I have argued that the scholarly endeavour to try and uncover the unique voices of deponents is misguided, especially if this comes at the expense of acknowledging the active role of commissioners, clerks, and witnesses. However, this does not mean that we cannot identify and analyse the specific, evaluative, and particular language used in Chancery depositions. Indeed, we have seen how rich and evaluative language was used in order to comment on the physical, emotional, and psychological turmoil of bankruptcy and its effect on those who experienced such failure. Witnesses commonly provided detailed – and often lengthy – descriptions of specific activities, providing an insight into the process of appraisal of those embroiled in debt-recovery. The words used to denote failure and decline mirrored wider conceptions of morality, credibility, and ethical behaviour within the community, as bankrupts were depicted as degenerating from a respectable position to that of an untrustworthy individual. However, these were not necessarily stock phrases and conventions that were conveniently used to conform to legal requirements. Rather, we see the formulation of language change according to the specific details and history of the case, highlighting the fact that creditors, debtors, witnesses, and others involved in the process maintained a high degree of control over their use of specific words and phrases.

---

138   Capern, 'Maternity and Justice in the Early Modern English Court of Chancery', p. 707.

Through the process of analysing the words and phrases used in the formulation of narratives concerning economic failure, we can illuminate wider attitudes towards personal decline. The appraisal of a debtor came to rely on a wide range of factors relating to their actions and words, which had wider ramifications for our understanding of the assessment of worth, status, and credibility in wider society.

5

The Finality of Enrolled Decrees

As a court of equity, Chancery was committed – in principle at least – to thoroughly investigate individual complaints and render appropriate relief based upon the concepts of conscience, fairness, and justice. Once a cause came to be heard in open court, the presiding judge would make their decision – known as a final decree – which would be recorded verbatim by a register of the court in the entry book.[1] The parties then had the option to enrol a decree, whereby the text from the entry book was prepared on paper in the form of a docquet – a formal memorandum or register of a legal judgment – setting out the decree verbatim. After the docquet was checked by the initiating party's Six Clerk – or his deputy – then it was signed by the Lord Chancellor.[2] This chapter undertakes a detailed analysis of enrolled decrees to demonstrate the way in which Chancery dealt with the complex and multifaceted nature of competing claims on a bankrupt's estate. While the previous chapters have focused on how plaintiffs', defendants', and witnesses' written accounts were transformed into a compelling narrative in an attempt to persuade the court, this chapter focuses on the decision-making processes of the judges. We will see how the judges interpreted equitable principles of justice in order to mediate in social and financial affairs.

The summaries of the case highlight what the court felt were the pertinent legal issues to be decided, while the legal decision was presented orally, and transcribed by a clerk. As such, the documents that survive had been created by the bureaucracy of the court. In this manner, decrees need to be treated as a distinct source from the preceding chapters, as the narrative presented is entirely that of the institution of the court, representing the legal ideal of equity and justice. This is in stark contrast to the preceding chapters, whereby documents were created and utilised in written form by a wide range of individuals, such as parties to the suit, legal representatives, witnesses, and local and central officers of the court. These are complicated documents, as the presiding judge would summarise the previous stages of proceeding before providing a legal decision

---

1   Series C33 at TNA.
2   Henry Horwitz, *A Guide to Chancery Equity Records and Proceedings 1600–1800* (Kew, 1995), p. 85.

on how the case would proceed or conclude. There is often an assumption that a final decree would finalise the central issue at hand. However, it is unhelpful to think of a decree in early modern Chancery creating a clearly defined winner and loser in such a way that the case could be closed in a neat and tidy fashion. This is especially true in bankruptcy suits where, in many circumstances, the collection and distribution of goods or an estate was ongoing.

In attempting the difficult task of trying to define a 'dispute', the legal anthropologist Simon Roberts has suggested that 'we could treat as disputes those occasions where one feels he has suffered an injury, sees another as to *blame* and confronts him with *responsibility*'.[3] This notion of a dispute, whereby one party assigns blame and subsequently seeks some sort of redress against a guilty or responsible party, seems to be commonly applied to legal cases. In modern usage, the terms 'legal dispute' and 'legal case' seem to be used as synonyms for one another, especially in civil jurisdictions. However, the fact that many Chancery cases did not end in a distinctly definitive manner is well known to modern scholars. Henry Horwitz states that it was not uncommon for hearings to end 'without a definitive resolution, at least in detail'.[4] As a Chancery commission explained before parliament in 1826:

> The judgement for a plaintiff in a court of equity is not, as in a court of law, simply a decision upon a definite point in his favour; but, in almost all cases in which he succeeds, the decree to which he is entitled, embraces several points, finally disposes of some, and directs various enquiries or accounts, with a view to the determination of others; and it is not easy nor always possible for the Registrar to write down at once full minutes of such a decree as ought to follow the judgement which the court has given.[5]

While enrolled decrees constitute the final stage of a proceeding in Chancery, they cannot provide a form of narrative closure to cases involving failure. Despite scholars being aware that many cases did not conclude in such a fashion, they still suggest that the court declared a winner and a loser. For example, Horwitz uses the terms 'winning party' or 'losing party' throughout his publication on Chancery records and practice.[6] Similarly, William Jones frequently discusses

---

3 Simon Roberts, 'The Study of Dispute: Anthropological Perspectives', in John Bossy (ed.), *Disputes and Settlements: Law and Human Relations in the West* (Cambridge, 1983), pp. 1–24, p. 7, my italics.
4 Horwitz, *A Guide to Chancery Equity Records*, p. 22.
5 *Parliamentary Papers* (1826), xv 16.
6 A useful example can be found in the following sentence: 'we find at least as early as the 1690s that Masters, in taxing costs, would on occasion make provision (by consent) that if the *losing party* paid the assessed costs promptly, the *winning party* would forego enrolment, with the result that the *losing party* might reduce its obligation by the amount that an

the 'winning attorney' or the 'successful party'.[7] In reference to bankruptcy suits, this notion is unhelpful, and in many examples incorrect. With multiple parties claiming a legal right to recover debts – often through an estate, goods, or paper instruments – the court was frequently placed in the position of arbitrator, assessing each individual claim and attempting to render a fair and equitable judgment for each individual.

Steve Hindle has shown how there was a 'spectrum of outcomes to dispute in early modern society'. Courts of equity worked alongside informal agreements and arbitration in a wider pattern of conflict.[8] Often, this was not a linear process and involved individuals interacting and engaging with a range of formal and informal processes. While Craig Muldrew has demonstrated how increasing levels of indebtedness led to a 'culture of reconciliation', social disputes still needed the injection of public authority to come to some form of resolution.[9] In Chancery, a suit could be referred to a Master to determine a specific aspect of the case, while a definitive point of law could be tried in the common law courts. Once determined, the case could return to Chancery, meaning that the final stage of proceeding is far more complex than many scholars have recognised.

The use of Chancery decrees and final decisions has been dominated by legal experts. However, Eileen O'Sullivan has argued that contemporary lawyers often misuse history and present the evolution of the law as a linear process. O'Sullivan believes that the reality is far more complex, as the law is unstable, unpredictable, multifaceted, and needs to adapt to societal pressures. There are numerous examples of courts – especially appeal courts – coming to different conclusions, or alternatively, coming to the same conclusion, but for different reasons.[10] Broadly speaking, legal historians have utilised the records of Chancery to demonstrate how the substantive context of the law and the equitable jurisdiction of Chancery were formed and developed over time. Largely, this has been done by analysing law reports and the secondary literature,

---

enrolment would otherwise have cost', Horwitz, *A Guide to Chancery Equity Records*, p. 24, my italics.

7   W. J. Jones, *The Elizabethan Court of Chancery* (Oxford, 1967), pp. 297–300.

8   Steve Hindle, 'The Micro-Spatial Dynamics of Litigation: The Chilvers Coton Tithe Dispute, *Barrows vs Archer* (1657)', in Lobban, Begiato, and Green (eds), *Law, Lawyers and Litigants in Early Modern England*, pp. 140–163.

9   Craig Muldrew, 'The Culture of Reconciliation: Community and the Settlement of Economic Disputes in Early Modern England', *The Historical Journal*, 39 (1996), pp. 915–942; Steven Hindle, 'The Keeping of Public Peace', in Adam Fox (ed.), *The Experience of Authority in Early Modern England* (Basingstoke, 1996), pp. 213–248.

10   Eileen M. O'Sullivan, 'Law and Chaos: Legal Argument as a Non-Linear Process', in Andrew Lewis and Michael Lobban (eds), *Law and History* (Oxford, 2004), pp. 433–452.

rather than archival records.[11] David Yale, for example, has provided detailed introductions to Lord Chancellor Nottingham's decisions and writings on Chancery practice. Describing Nottingham as the 'father of systematic equity', Yale analyses the ways in which the process and jurisdiction of the court came to be governed by settled rules under Nottingham's tenure.[12] In this manner, Yale outlines the evolution of Chancery from a court of conscience to a court of equity, utilising specific cases to illustrate how definitive rules – such as how a court of equity cannot relieve a careless individual – came to be established.[13] Mike Macnair has demonstrated the development of early modern conscience, equity, and the jurisdiction of English bill procedure in comparison to the common law system. During the early modern period, Macnair argues that 'we should not imagine that there was a clearly drawn demarcation line between law and equity'.[14] Similarly, Michael Lobban has analysed parliamentary papers, pamphlets, popular literature, caseload statistics, and secondary sources to link nineteenth-century debates surrounding Chancery reform to issues of evidence, procedure, jurisdiction, and high legal politics.[15]

Legal scholars who undertake archival work and use final decrees in their research, often do so to demonstrate how a particular topic developed within the court. Discussing the construction and execution of trusts in Chancery, David Foster has used archival material – alongside case law and law reports – to demonstrate how the intention of the settlor was just one of several competing factors, 'which combined to determine the outcome of a legal dispute'.[16] Similarly, Edith Henderson incorporated enrolled decrees and the decree and order books in her research to explain how and why cases relating to the rights to land were litigated in the early history of the court.[17] Building on the declaration of John Baker that, 'the origin of the trust … cannot be traced from

---

11   Several scholars have published reviews of landmark cases in equity, see Charles Mitchell and Paul Mitchell (eds), *Landmark Cases in Equity* (Oxford, 2012), especially ch.1–5.

12   Yale, *Lord Chancellor Nottingham's Chancery Cases*, vol. 1, p. xlv.

13   Ibid., vol. 1, p. xciv.

14   Mike Macnair, 'Common Law and Statutory Imitations of Equitable Relief Under the Later Stuarts', in Christopher Brooks and Michael Lobban (eds), *Communities and Courts in Britain, 1150–1900* (London, 1997), pp. 115–131, p. 131; Macnair, 'Equity and Conscience', pp. 659–681.

15   Michael Lobban, 'Preparing for Fusion: Reforming the Nineteenth-Century Court of Chancery (part 1)', *LHR*, 22 (2004), pp. 389–427; Michael Lobban, 'Preparing for Fusion: Reforming the Nineteenth-Century Court of Chancery (part 2)', *LHR*, 22 (2004), pp. 565–599; Michael Lobban, 'The Chancellor, the Chancery, and the History of Law Reform', *LHR*, 22 (2004), pp. 615–617.

16   David Foster, 'Construction and Execution of Trusts in Chancery, c.1660–1750', *The Journal of Legal History*, 40 (2019), pp. 270–297.

17   Edith G. Henderson, 'Legal Rights to Land in the Early Chancery', *The American Journal of Legal History*, 26 (1982), pp. 97–122, p. 117.

the law reports', Neil Jones has undertaken extensive archival research and analysed over 300 trust cases from the decree rolls between 1536 and 1585.[18] As Jones surmised, the study of trusts had largely been thematic, 'paying little attention to why trust cases came to litigation, or to how the court responded from case to case'. By analysing a body of trust litigation, Jones sought to consider 'the nature of trust property; the causes of litigation; questions of proof; and the court's responses to trusts litigation'.[19] Jones sees the evidence of litigation as 'a fruitful and essential historical source', which sheds light on 'hundreds of unreported trust cases in the decades following the passage of the Statute of Uses'.[20] Ultimately, Jones has undertaken archival research and uncovered non-reported cases to provide an overall picture of the nature of trust litigation in Chancery.

Yet, while legal scholars have incorporated final decrees in their work to differing degrees, few scholars outside of this field have done the same. Since Maurice Beresford's overview of the usefulness of Chancery decree rolls as a source for economic historians – and despite the digitisation process of the University of Houston's Anglo-American Legal Tradition – enrolled decrees are a dramatically underused resource for economic, social, and cultural historians.[21] Largely, scholars utilise the decree and order books to understand the procedural elements of cases, or as Horwitz suggested, 'to fill in gaps in the history of the case for which the relevant documentation cannot be traced'.[22] Few scholars have undertaken substantial analysis of enrolled decrees, and no work has been conducted on bankruptcy cases in the court using this final stage of proceeding.[23] This chapter attempts to bridge this gap by demonstrating how judges worked through competing claims in bankruptcy suits. In doing

18   J. H. Baker, 'Why the History of English Law Has Not Been Finished', *Cambridge Law Journal*, 59 (2000), pp. 62–84, p. 79, n. 51.

19   N. G. Jones, 'Trusts Litigation in Chancery After the Statute of Uses: The First Fifty Years', in Matthew Dyson and David Ibbetson (eds), *Law and Legal Process: Substantive Law and Procedure in English Legal History* (Cambridge, 2013), p. 104.

20   N. G. Jones, 'Trusts for Secrecy: The Case of John Dudley, Duke of Northumberland', *The Cambridge Law Journal*, 54 (1995), pp. 545–555; see also Jones, 'The Influence of Revenue Considerations', pp. 99–114; N. G. Jones, 'Tyrrel's Case (1557) and the Use Upon a Use', *The Journal of Legal History*, 14 (1993), pp. 75–93; N. G. Jones, 'The Use Upon a Use in Equity Revisited', *Cambrian Law Review*, 33 (2002), pp. 67–80; N. G. Jones, 'Wills, Trusts and Trusting from the Statute of Uses to Lord Nottingham, *The Journal of Legal History*, 31 (2010), pp. 273–298.

21   M. W. Beresford, 'The Decree Rolls of Chancery as a Source for Economic History, 1547–c. 1700', *EHR*, 32 (1979), pp. 1–10; 'AALT Chancery Final Decrees', University of Houston, stable URL: http://www.uh.edu/waalt/index.php/Chancery_Final_Decrees (accessed 25/03/2024).

22   Horwitz, *A Guide to Chancery Equity Records and Proceedings*, p. 96.

23   Beresford, 'The Decree Rolls of Chancery as a Source for Economic History', pp. 1–10.

so, it is vital to pay close attention to the specific details surrounding the suit in question. Only by unravelling these complex, multifaceted, and vehemently debated cases can we reveal the specificities of the debt-recovery process and how bankruptcy intersects with wider issues concerning the trading community.

The chapter is divided into three sections. The first section outlines the difference between final and enrolled decrees, attempting to account for the variations in the levels of enrolment from the fifteenth century. Attention is then turned to establishing the practical implementation of equitable principles of justice, illustrating the problems that arose when applying these legal ideals to a growing case load. The second section analyses the documents themselves, discussing the finality of bankruptcy suits by placing enrolled decrees alongside the concept of appropriating blame and clarifying the degree to which parties left the process as 'winners' or 'losers'. This section illuminates the way in which Chancery intersected with other courts and legal jurisdictions in the debt-recovery process. The final section seeks to establish what we can learn about bankruptcy and the broader conception of failure in Chancery from this stage of proceeding. Particular attention is paid to the appeals process up the legal hierarchy, and the complex relationship between debt recovery, courts of equity, and the common law courts. Ultimately, this chapter provides a unique perspective on our understanding of failure, as it highlights how the judges sought to grapple with equitable principles of justice, foregrounding the analysis and interpretation of the court in the ongoing and complex operation of bankruptcy.

The Implementation of Equitable Principles of Justice

While all final decrees were recorded in the entry book, until the decree was enrolled it only had the force of an 'interlocutory order', meaning it could be altered upon a rehearing or occasionally upon a motion.[24] In order to contest an enrolled decree, a party had to initiate a more formal reconsideration by way of submitting a bill of review. The scope of a bill of review was limited to those who were parties to the original bill and could only be submitted to remedy an error in law, or to present newly discovered evidence.[25] The only other option was to petition the House of Lords to appeal the enrolled decree. As both processes would involve considerable time and expense, enrolment could create a substantial barrier to any attempt to reopen the cause.[26] In this sense, The National Archives' online description explains that enrolled

24   *The Practical Register in Chancery* (London, 1714), pp. 123–125.
25   Holdsworth, *A History of English Law*, vol. 9, p. 368.
26   Horwitz, *A Guide to Chancery Equity Records and Proceedings 1600–1800*, p. 23.

decrees provide 'a permanent and authoritative record of final judgements of the court of Chancery'.[27] Horwitz elaborates, suggesting that enrolled decrees reinforced the court's decision, thereby gaining 'a greater degree of finality'.[28] However, there is a danger in overstating the definitive finality of decrees, enrolled or otherwise.

Certainly, an enrolled decree did provide some sense of finality in comparison to a final decree or order, and in certain circumstances parties in a suit would refuse to act until they had been ordered by the court to do so. For example, in a complex case concerning a will and the disposal of several lands and tenements in Chertsey, Surrey, a defendant named Thomas Webster stated that he had not, 'Intermeddled with the said Trust or Joyned in any Deeds or Conveyances relating thereto being unwilling soe to doe without the Decree of this Honourable Court'. Webster stated that he was willing to sign and join in any agreements that 'this honourable Court should direct'.[29] However, a final decree was not as conclusive as is often believed. If a bill of review failed, then it could be subject to appeal up the legal hierarchy: from the Master of the Rolls to the Lord Chancellor, and above the Lord Chancellor to the House of Lords. Furthermore, the Lord Chancellor could rehear an appeal, and as William Holdsworth states, 'it thus appears that the impossible attempt of the court to produce a perfect decree prevented any kind of decent finality'.[30] Michael Birks elaborates, and states that from the standpoint of jurisprudence, the judgment of any court should be 'perfected immediately after the judge has pronounced his decision'. In practice, however, this ideal is not easily attainable, especially in a court of equity. It was not until 1954 that the court clarified at what moment in time its decisions become irrevocable. In *Re Harrison*, the point at issue was whether a judge of the Chancery Division held the power to alter or reverse – before the judgment had been formally entered – an oral and decisive judgment in open court. It was decided that a judge did have the power to recall an order before it had been perfected, which was later confirmed by the Court of Appeal.[31] This decision shows that throughout the history of the court, the exact moment whereby a case was concluded was not clearly defined.

The extent to which decrees were enrolled varied dramatically throughout the early modern period. For most of the Elizabethan period, final decrees were not automatically enrolled, and Jones has shown how in the second half

27   TNA, 'Chancery and Supreme Court of Judicature, Chancery Division: Six Clerks Office and successors: Decree Rolls' online description for C78 and C79 series, stable URL: http://discovery.nationalarchives.gov.uk/details/r/C3638 (accessed 25/03/2024).
28   Horwitz, *A Guide to Chancery Equity Records*, p. 23.
29   AALT, C78/1795 no.1 [75], 'Goodfellow v Webster' (1724).
30   Holdsworth, *A History of English Law*, vol. 9, p. 369.
31   Michael Birks, 'The Perfecting of Orders in Chancery', *Cambridge Law Journal*, 13 (1955), pp. 101–112, p. 101.

of Elizabeth's reign enrolment showed signs of falling into disuse. However, it was during this period that there was the beginning of the notion that for decrees to be effective, they had to be written down in one form or another. In this sense, Jones believes that litigants became reluctant to enrol decrees, as adequate records were already being kept by the register in the entry books. It was becoming apparent that enrolment was an unnecessary expense.[32] This led to a degree of legal ambiguity, as it was always possible for decrees, enrolled or otherwise, to envisage the possibility of further proceedings at law. This has led Jones to conclude that the Elizabethan period was one of uncertainty: 'Entries of decrees jostle with those of final decrees, some were enrolled, and many were not.' In 1597, and in an attempt to clarify such ambiguity, Lord Chancellor Egerton ordered that a decree was not binding unless it was drawn up and enrolled, which set the precedent for the formality and finality of decrees throughout the seventeenth century.[33]

By the late seventeenth century, it began to be common to speak of enrolled decrees as being of a similar authority to a judgment in the common law courts. Lord Chancellor Nottingham placed an emphasis on giving decrees in equity the same force as judgments at law, a course which had involved building equitable rights upon common law rights.[34] However, Nottingham realised the potential for the abuse of enrolled decrees, in cases where they were employed as a tactical manoeuvre to discourage the opposing party from bringing an appeal. As such, Nottingham cautioned against hasty enrolments, as it may 'prejudice [the] defendants' rights to be heard and put him to a bill of review which may not always fit his case'.[35] In a suit from 1674, an order was made, and the enrolment undertaken, without giving the opposing side an opportunity to question the order. Nottingham set aside the enrolment as irregular, stating 'a court of conscience shall never confirm an award made against conscience'.[36] In a curious case from 1674, it was resolved that the plaintiff may have a bill of review to reverse a decree made for him if it be less beneficial to him than in truth it ought to have been.[37] As Nottingham explained, while an enrolled decree could only be reversed or altered by a bill of review, any mistakes that were demonstrative, such as an 'error in arithmetic by miscasting, or mistaking the date, or the like', could be rectified without submitting a new bill.[38] For example, in a case from 1677, the final decree had accidentally omitted two previous orders made by the court. Nottingham ordered the decree to be

32   Jones, *The Elizabethan Court of Chancery*, pp. 296–297.
33   Ibid., p. 299.
34   Yale, *Lord Chancellor Nottingham's Chancery Cases*, vol. 1, p. 195.
35   'Robinson & Barton' (1675), in Ibid., vol. 2, p. 207.
36   'Burges v Skinner' (1674), in Ibid., vol. 1, p. 31.
37   'Vanderbende & Levingston' (1674), in Ibid., vol. 1, p. 86.
38   Finch, *Manual of Chancery Practice, and Prolegomena of Chancery and Equity*, p. 129.

enrolled *de novo* with the previous orders inserted in the enrolment.[39] While Nottingham desired enrolled decrees to be built upon, and have the same force of judgment as the common law, he was careful not to impress an excessive rigidity that would render the concepts of conscience and fairness inaccessible.

While the seventeenth-century conception of the status and importance of enrolled decrees is unquestioned, there was a dramatic decline in the number of decrees being enrolled throughout the eighteenth century. Horwitz has shown that between 1627 and 1636 the average number of enrolments was roughly 180, which had decreased to about ten per annum between 1785 and 1794. This dramatic fall in enrolled decrees seems to have been an eighteenth-century phenomenon, as between 1685 and 1694, the average number of enrolled decrees was approximately 170, out of a case load roughly comparable to the 1620s.[40] Within the date range of this book, the fall in the number of enrolled decrees is substantial, averaging around 184 for the five-year period of 1674–1678, before falling to just under 43 for the five years up to 1750.[41] As Birks has concluded, by the second decade of the eighteenth century, for all practical purposes, enrolment had already 'fallen into desuetude'.[42] When attempting to account for such an alteration, Horwitz concludes that why such a decline occurred 'is not altogether clear'.[43] What is certain is that the court itself was discouraging enrolment from the turn of the century, despite the loss of fees for some of its officers. Practice manuals of the later eighteenth and early nineteenth centuries suggest that the reason for such an approach was the additional expense to the parties of altering enrolled decrees concerning financial matters.[44] As enrolled decrees decreased, re-hearings became more common, again causing further delays. Ordinarily, a decree had to be enrolled within six months of the date of the final decree, but the court did enable decrees to be enrolled after the six-month period, and as enrolment became less common, the length between the date of the final decree and the enrolment lengthened. In this manner, it is also relevant that after 1725, the House of Lords would refuse to accept an appeal if the enrolment had occurred more than five years previously.[45]

39 'Todd & Nicholson' (1677) in Yale, *Lord Chancellor Nottingham's Chancery Cases*, vol. 2, p. 588.
40 Horwitz, *A Guide to Chancery Equity Records*, pp. 27–28.
41 Averages calculated from 'Chancery Final Decrees', AALT: University of Houston, stable URL: http://www.uh.edu/waalt/index.php/Chancery_Final_Decrees (accessed 25/03/2024).
42 Birks, 'The Perfecting of Orders in Chancery', pp. 106–107.
43 Horwitz, *A Guide to Chancery Equity Records*, pp. 27–28.
44 For a detailed discussion see Ibid., pp. 23–24.
45 Ibid., p. 23, n. 43, p. 85.

The Finality of Bankruptcy Cases

While it is difficult to compute the exact length of cases within my sample – as often the enrolled decree did not specify the date of the first bill – a crude estimation shows that the average duration was over four years, with the shortest being concluded within a year, and the longest lasting over twelve years.[46] This aligns with the level of litigation and the duration of cases outlined in the introduction, as while the number of bills submitted to the court began to decline during this period, the time that it took for the court to conclude a suit increased dramatically.[47] This meant that the court continued to be overburdened in its application of equitable principles of justice.

Definitive Outcomes
Broadly speaking, a plaintiff's bill may have been upheld, or it may have been dismissed, and there are examples of both within my sample. In a bill submitted in Easter term 1697, but not concluded until 21 November 1709, the sole plaintiff Charles Booth took aim at the entirety of the bankruptcy process. Booth named the three commissioners, two assignees, the bankrupt James Boswell, and finally a debtor of the bankrupt, William Awbury, as the defendants in the suit. In his bill, Booth claimed that there were several dealings between Awbury and the bankrupt, and after coming to an account on 26 November 1696, Awbury assigned a note to the bankrupt for an outstanding debt of £65. On 2 December 1696, the bankrupt applied to Booth for a cash loan of £200, and as a part-security for the debt Boswell assigned the note over to Booth, as well as 'nine Watches a small box of rings and diamond Case box' worth an additional £50. Shortly after this transaction Boswell absconded, and a commission of bankruptcy was taken out on 27 February 1697. However, the crux of the case centred around Booth's attempts to redeem the original note to satisfy the £200 debt due to him from the bankrupt. Ultimately, Awbury claimed that there was previously a £40 discount that needed to be deducted from the £65 note, and as the rest of the defendants were involved in the ongoing commission of bankruptcy, they refused to redeem the entirety of the note, preferring instead to pay the creditors a fair and proportional dividend from the bankrupt's estate. When the cause came to be heard in open court,

---

46   The date of the decree is the date upon which the suit was heard and concluded in open court, not the date upon which it was enrolled upon parchment. The year of the case is also the year in which it was decided.

47   Henry Horwitz and Patrick Polden, 'Continuity or Change in the Court of Chancery in the Seventeenth and Eighteenth Centuries?', *Journal of British Studies*, 35 (1996), p. 53.

no counsel appeared for the defendants, 'though they were duely served with subpenas to heare judgement'.[48]

It was ordered that Awbury should pay the plaintiff the full £65 plus interest, as well as his costs for the suit in Chancery, which were to be calculated by a Master. It was further ordered that the assignees should pay out of the bankrupt's estate the remainder of the £200, together with interest. In default of such a payment, the plaintiff was 'to keep and enjoy the Watches Rings and other things' previously mentioned. Finally, the defendants were to pay the complainant for their 'default of Attendance', which meant they were fined for not appearing to have the suit heard, which presumably would not have helped their case.[49] This is a relatively rare example of the plaintiff securing an absolute victory. Not only did Booth redeem the full amount due on the note, but he was able to secure repayment from the bankrupt's estate for the remainder of the outstanding debt. The final decree also included any interest due, as well as the entirety of the costs of proceeding in Chancery. Ultimately, this suit demonstrates that the defendants suffered an outright loss. The order to pay the opposing side's costs can, to a certain extent, be seen as the court appropriating blame, and seeking to render appropriate equitable relief. What is clear in this suit is the level of complexity over the details of the case. While this example could have simply been used to demonstrate an outright victory and loss, it is only the analysis of the complexities surrounding the bankruptcy process, and the particular details around the note, that informs us of how the court came to make final decisions.[50]

In contrast, there are examples where the plaintiffs' suit had been dismissed outright. In a fairly straightforward case decided on 9 May 1693, the plaintiffs were creditors of a deceased bankrupt named Edward Larkin. The bill of complaint was submitted in Trinity term 1690 – after a commission of bankruptcy had been taken out some three to four months previously – and stated that the bankrupt was indebted to several individuals for over £600. The plaintiffs claimed that a defendant named Nicholas Crisp was indebted to the bankrupt for £400, and that during his lifetime Larkin held a sixty-acre estate in Kent. Put simply, the plaintiffs were claiming a legal right to the estate, as well as the £400 due from Crisp, in order to satisfy their outstanding debts. On the opposing side, the three named defendants – including the bankrupt's widow – argued that the plaintiffs held no right to the estate or any debt due

48   This was the common procedure, whereby after a ruling a Master would calculate the costs to be paid by specified parties, as well as any interest due on paper instruments. Throughout this chapter, unless otherwise stated, costs and interest would be calculated by a Master after the final judgment.

49   AALT, C78/1719, no. 12 [135], 'Booth v Awbury' (1709).

50   Another example of an outright victory for the plaintiffs can be seen in AALT, C78/1346, no. 5 [68], 'Robins v Forward' (1711).

from Crisp, as it should be the legal property of his executors. Ultimately, the Lord Chancellor dismissed the bill without costs, demonstrating that the plaintiffs held no equitable right to the estate, or the subsequent debt due to the bankrupt's executors.[51]

In a complex case whereby the assignees of John Hinde – a bankrupt and co-partner of Thomas Kirwood, both goldsmiths – sought to recover over £17,000 owing to the partners from several defendants, the court 'Declared that there was noe Cause to give the Complainants any Releife on their said bill'. The bill stood 'absolutely dismissed out of this Court but without cost but if the Complainants shall not Acquiesse in the said Order but shall give the Defendants any further trouble touching the matters in question then the Complainants are to pay the Defendants their costs'.[52] The specific details about the rationale and reasoning behind these decisions are sparse, and as Neil Jones has shown, without law reports it is difficult to establish why certain mechanisms were employed and decisions were made.[53] However, these examples clearly demonstrate that, on occasion, a suit could be categorically won or lost. The order to pay costs can be seen as an attempt to appropriate blame to the losing party, as it demonstrated that in a court of equity the plaintiff's bill or the defendant's answer were seen to be in opposition to equitable principles of justice. In contrast, if no costs were assigned, then this simply meant that there was no basis to apply equitable relief to that party. As we see in the second example, while there was no right to any redress in Chancery, if the complainants continued to give the defendants 'any further trouble', then blame would be appropriated in the form of paying their costs at law.

In an extremely complex case heard in 1728, the suit centred around the dealings of a bankrupt vintner and tavern keeper named John Guy. The bill of complaint was submitted in Easter term 1724, and the creditor-plaintiffs claimed that they sold the bankrupt port and wine worth roughly £112. While Guy frequently promised to satisfy the debt, the plaintiffs claimed that 'there was little reason to doubt thereof in regard the said Guy had been left by his late Father and was then in possession of a considerable real estate of Inheritance to the value of one hundred pounds per Annum'. Guy also held a considerable personal estate, had recently received a marriage portion of £1000, and was 'in possession of a very good Tavern Trade'. Sometime in 1616, a wine trader named Richard Mead 'sold to Guy several large quantities and parcels of Wine in pipes and hogsheads at much larger prices than the value of the same and

---

51   AALT, C78/2061, no.12 [51], 'Dunmall v Crispe' (1693); another example of an outright dismissal can be seen in AALT, C79/78 no. [145] 'Child v Metcalfe' (1719).

52   AALT, C78/957, no.3 [33], 'Browne v Hind' (1694).

53   N. G. Jones, 'The Influence of Revenue Considerations Upon the Remedial Practice of Chancery in Trust Cases, 1536-1660', in Brooks and Lobban (eds), *Communities and Courts in Britain, 1150–1900*, pp. 99–114.

often times at such price as he himself pleased to rate them'. Guy became indebted over £1100 to Mead, who eventually executed a warrant of attorney against the bankrupt and had his 'wines and Goods so taken in Execution Inventoried and appraized after his own manner by persons unskilled in the nature and true value of wines and other goods thereby seized'. After appraising the goods at a lower value, Mead sold them for £637 1s 6d, to a merchant named Thomas Allen, but 'without any proper Bill of Sale or any thing more than a memorandum'. The plaintiffs took out a commission of bankruptcy and received an indenture of the bankrupt's goods on 20 December 1722, claiming that the goods seized were worth more than £1000. When Richard Mead attended the commission, he gave 'Evasive Answers' and either reassured the plaintiffs that they would receive their debts or offered £100 or 100 Guineas for their demands. Ultimately, the plaintiffs sought the 'aid and assistance' of the court to compel the defendants to answer and to come to an account for their dealings with the bankrupt.[54]

In his answer, Richard Mead stated that he sold the bankrupt several quantities of wine, but the last dealing he had was on 9 May 1715, and he provided a schedule of these transactions. On 20 March 1716, the two came to an account and concluded that the bankrupt was indebted to Mead for £134 11s 8d. Mead denied the plaintiffs' accusations and claimed that in December 1716, the bankrupt was severely indebted to several individuals and owed him £810. He was informed by Guy's wife and mother-in-law, that he 'was got into ill Company and was likely to be ruined'. Mead claimed that at the time of his dealings with Guy, he was not a bankrupt and he denied that Guy was 'in good Credit or that he kept a Tavern of Fish street hill or any other place on the contrary he believed the said Guy left of keeping house and trading' in 1716. The Master of the Rolls heard the case and 'upon long Debate of the Matter and hearing the Deposition taken before the Commissioners of Bankrupt … the said Defendants answer and the proofs taken in the cause read and what could be alleged by Councel on both sides his honour saw no Cause to give the Complainants any Relief in Equity'. The plaintiffs' bill stood absolutely dismissed.[55]

Multifaceted Outcomes

While the examples above demonstrate an outright winner, it was far more common for this not to be the case, and bankruptcy cases remained multi-faceted, even in the decision-making process. *Hardie v Brooke* was decided by the court on 27 January 1685 and concerned the costs relating to the recovery of the bankrupt's estate. The decree provides a clear example of how the court

54   AALT, C78/1812, no.3 [7], Standert v Mead (1728).
55   Ibid.

decided what pertinent facts of the case needed to be decided: 'The Cause comeing to bee heard in open Courte … in the presence of Councell learned on both sides the substance of the Complainants bill and the defendants Answers thereto appearing to bee in effect…'. After summarising the details of the bill and answers, 'and upon long debate of the matter and … what could bee then alleadged on either side', the court was able to render its decision. The Lord Chancellor decreed that the complainants' charges were allowed, and out of a total of £629 claimed by the plaintiffs, they were entitled to £300, which would be shared equally among the bankrupt's creditors.[56]

Furthermore, a defendant named Robert Bretton was to pay his contribution money within three months and, 'come in as a Creditor for profitt and losse unto the said Dividend and each other Dividend'. Another defendant, Robert Langley, was to pay contribution money and come in as a creditor. However, 'the Defendant Langley being dissatisfied with the said order or Decree Petitioned his Lordshipp … Complaineing that the said order was in several poynts mistaken'. The Lord Keeper appointed counsel on both sides to attend him on 21 January, but the court found no need to alter the decree. Finally, the assignees were to be paid their charges before Langley was to come in as a creditor, whereas the commissioners were to pay back any excess – having already received £80 for their work – that was not allowed by the Master.[57] Here, we can see the court working through complex claims on a single estate, involving five plaintiffs and nine defendants. The plaintiffs gained a marginal victory, securing £300 from a possible £629, while several defendants were permitted to enter the commission of bankruptcy once they had paid their contribution money and the costs of the assignees and commissioners had been settled. This case is an excellent example of the way in which the court directly mediated in a failed commission of bankruptcy to repair the debt-recovery process. Indeed, the commission was ongoing, and creditors had three months to pay their contribution and officially enter to receive a dividend. While the case was finalised and the decree enrolled, the process would have continued outside of the jurisdiction of the court.

Cole v Mackrill is a lengthy and complex case, which is worth working through in detail to illustrate the complexities of bankruptcy and the multi-faceted nature of final judgments. The bill of complaint was submitted in Trinity term 1733 and the cause was decided on 24 January 1738. The plaintiffs in the suit – Christian Cole and William Wilkinson – were two assignees of John Thomson, who was described as a 'warehouse keeper to the Charitable Corporation for Relief of Industrious Poor'.[58] The plaintiffs claimed that

---

56   AALT, C78/910, no.8 [13], 'Hardie v Brooke' (1685); this decree is repeated in a separate entry, C78/920, no.11 [15] 'Hardie v Brooke' (1685).

57   AALT, C78/910, no.8 [13], 'Hardie v Brooke' (1685).

58   While this appears to be the same John Thomson who worked for the Charitable Corporation and was discussed in the second chapter in 'Charitable Corporation v Chase'

Thomson committed an act of bankruptcy on 12 October 1731, and a commission was executed six days later, on 18 October. As well as the bankrupt, the suit named four defendants: Thomas Mackrill, Giles Biggot, Claude Johnson, and Thomas Barnes. The bill stated that Thomson was entitled to a mortgage of the estate of William Cordwell in the County of Kent, as an indenture had been made 'on or about the Sixth day of October' 1731. Once the property was in his possession, Thomson assigned over the mortgage to the defendant Mackrill in consideration of the sum of £2485 12s 6d. Only £1000 was paid up front by Mackrill, who provided three promissory notes for the outstanding balance, all of which were dated 6 October 1731. The notes were specified for the following amounts and due dates: £500 three months after 6 October 1731, £500 after six months, and £485 12s 6d, after nine months. As the indenture and the three notes were executed six days prior to any act of bankruptcy being committed, they were seen to have been executed for a genuine and valuable consideration. The assignees were claiming a full right to the notes, as Mackrill had refused to come to an account with the ongoing commission to satisfy the debt. Furthermore, two defendants, Giles Biggot and Claude Johnson, claimed that two of the notes had been assigned to them, again for a valuable consideration. In contrast, the plaintiffs claimed that if any such assignment did occur, then it was fraudulently enacted, occurring *after* the bankruptcy of Thomson.[59]

As well as the multiple claims to the promissory notes, the decree also explained that there had previously been an action brought by Biggot in a common law case against Mackrill. According to Mackrill, 'the said Biggot produced such Evidence to prove the Indorsement by the said John Thomson the Bankrupt before any Act of Bankruptcy'. This led to the jury finding a verdict against Mackrill for the note, specifying a payment of £485 12s 6d, as it had in fact been honestly made for a valuable consideration. In his answer, Biggot said he was 'a Stranger' to any transactions made between the bankrupt and Cordwell, but 'had heard' that about 7 October 1731, Mackrill gave a note to the bankrupt, who subsequently endorsed it, before finally producing it to Biggot on 11 October 1731. It was on this date that Biggot discounted £22 18s, from the note, and 'Denyed that at the time of discounting the said note he knew or was informed of the Bankruptcy of the said Thomson and believed he publickly appeared in Business some days after the said Transactions'. When Biggot applied to Mackrill, he refused payment, so Biggot was forced to bring

(1735), this enrolled decree does not relate to the same case, as William Wilkinson was named as a plaintiff in this case and a defendant in the previous one. Similarly, there is no mention of Christian Cole in the previous case, and as is explained below, this case was revived by a bill in 1736; AALT, C78/1797, no.4 [4], 'Cole v Mackrill' (1737).

59   AALT, C78/1797, no.4 [4], 'Cole v Mackrill' (1737). This suit was actually heard in 1738, according to the Gregorian calendar.

an action against Mackrill and obtained a verdict in common law for payment of his debt and costs at law. Similarly, Claude Johnson suggested that on 29 December 1731, he received a note that was again dated 7 October, signed by Thomas Mackrill, and endorsed by the bankrupt. Yet, both Mackrill and the bankrupt had refused to satisfy the note. As such, the two defendants denied that the assignees held any legal right to the two notes, as they were made honestly at a time when Thomson was not a bankrupt. Finally, the bankrupt answered and gave an account that was similar to that of the plaintiffs, as William Cordwell had executed a mortgage of an estate in Kent to him for securing £2000 plus interest, which in October 1731 Thomson then assigned to Mackrill for the sum of £2186.[60]

This case is clearly complex, and in several instances difficult to follow. Yet, as we look at the path that the suit took between its introduction in Chancery and its eventual completion, we see a number of interesting developments. At some point during the suit, the defendant Thomas Barnes died, and the suit was abated. When the case was revived – by a bill of revivor submitted in Michaelmas term 1736 – we find that William Wilkinson remained the sole plaintiff and assignee, as Christian Cole had also died. The new bill sought to name Mary Barnes, widow of Thomas Barnes, in the place of her deceased husband, which was accepted by the court and the suit went forward. Somewhat unsurprisingly, Mary Barnes provided an answer similar to that of her husband's previous statement, and suggested she was 'an absolute Stranger to all such Transactions and knew nothing' about the details of the case. In Hilary term 1737, Samuel Grove submitted a supplementary bill in which he sought to be named sole assignee to the bankrupt's estate, as Wilkinson declared himself 'desirous to be discharged from his said Trust'. This was accepted by the court, and the cause – containing the original bill of complaint, the bill of revivor, the supplementary bill, and depositions of witnesses – came to be heard by Sir Joseph Jekyll, Master of the Rolls. We see the court meticulously work its way through the specific details before attempting to come to a fair and equitable decision.

Turning to the decision of the court, we see the multifaceted nature of the final judgment. It was ordered that the bill stood absolutely dismissed against Mary Barnes, with her costs to be paid by the plaintiff. Similarly, the suit was dismissed against the defendant Claude Johnson, although he was ordered to pay forty shillings towards the cost of the suit. It was further ordered that the bankrupt Thomson was to 'Deliver the said note admitted to be in his hands to the said Complainant in the Same Condition as the said note was delivered to him'. This meant that the plaintiff, as assignee of the bankrupt, was to redeem one of the notes that was initially given to the bankrupt by Thomas

60   Ibid.

Mackrill. It was referred to a Master to see exactly what amount of principal money and interest was due on the note, and the plaintiff was to pay the cost of this suit 'relating thereto'. It was also ordered that the complainant and the defendant Biggot were to proceed to a trial in the court of King's Bench, upon the following issues: first, to determine when the money on the note claimed by Biggot was paid to the bankrupt; and secondly, to establish whether Thomson was a bankrupt on or before the time of such payment.

As we have seen throughout, and as is clearly illustrated in this case, the exact timing of bankruptcy was an identifiable matter of fact and would determine what debts could be legally claimed by the assignee. The decree concluded by stating that the 'Consideration of all further directions is hereby reserved until after the said Tryal is had when either party is to be at Liberty to resort back to the Court as they shall be advised'.[61] There are no further details regarding the trial in the decree. It could be possible that the trial never took place, or if it did take place, the parties never returned to Chancery. What is certain is that the decree was formally enrolled, and no further details of this common law case survive in this source. What we see in this decree is that it is difficult, if not impossible, to establish a clearly defined winning and losing party. The complainant's bill was dismissed against some defendants, and was upheld against others, while costs were assigned on an individual basis. Therefore, it is completely inappropriate to attach notions of blame upon such an entangled and interconnected conclusion, as the court attempted to arbitrate and meticulously work through each individual claim.

Chapman v Tanner was decided on 10 November 1684.[62] The plaintiff, Jasper Chapman, was one of the assignees of Nathaniel Tanner, and named the bankrupt's son – also Nathaniel Tanner, who was the executor of his mother's estate – alongside the other assignees and creditors of the bankrupt's estate. The plaintiff claimed that during his lifetime the bankrupt owned an estate in Wiltshire, which he mortgaged to several individuals as a security for money lent. While the decree worked through the specificities of the estate and each individual transaction, the plaintiff stated that in October 1673 Tanner committed his first act of bankruptcy and that a commission of bankruptcy was taken out on 15 July 1674. After this date, there was 'noe course being taken by him to pay his debts by sale of his Estate or other Wise though often applyed unto For that purpose and his Creditors by personal securities and simple Contracts'. As such, Tanner had refused to sell the lands to pay his father's debts and was continuing to defraud his creditors. Furthermore, Chapman accused the defendants of allowing the bankrupt to live on the property and to

61   Ibid.
62   AALT, C78/758, no.1 [172], 'Chapman v Tanner' (1684), the AALT has the first named defendant as Nathaniel Turner, but as this is the bankrupt's son, it is certainly Nathaniel Tanner.

receive the rents and profits from the estate, failing to pay the full contribution money, and refusing to let the assignees have full access to the estate.

The court found that a deceased defendant named Nathaniel Ridley, 'by the direction and advice of the said John Coxe … did obstruct and hinder the Playntiffe and the said other Defendants Assignees from entering upon' and gaining access to the property. The court agreed that the bankrupt was able to receive the rent and profits from the estate. Because of the complexities of the case, and the fact that creditors were seen on both sides, the court worked through the individual credits and debts relating to the bankruptcy of Tanner, his estate, and how his son acted as executor. The Lord Chancellor ordered that the plaintiff was allowed the equity of redemption on the property, and that the estate was to be put to the full use for the benefit of the creditors. Under oath, all defendants were to provide the ongoing commission of bankruptcy with any pertinent documentation they held in their possession. Again, we see that the defendants were treated individually and subjected to specific orders. While Coxe was ordered to repay £150 and costs, Jasper Chapman was to be paid the annuities due to him, but without any interest that had accrued. It was further ordered that 'if any doubt or difference shall hereafter arise touching the distribution of the said Bankrupts estate then the said partyes are to resort backe to the Court for his Lordshipps further order and Direction'.[63]

In *Denn v Kindon* (1707), the plaintiffs, Cornelius Denn and William Stead, were assignees of Arthur Dent, a merchant dealing in woollen cloth from London. The plaintiffs named Henry Kindon, who was the executor of Henry Kindon, as the sole defendant. On 23 August 1704, a commission of bankruptcy was taken out against Dent, who was indebted in the sum of several hundred pounds. The plaintiffs claimed that the defendant 'pretended that he had several great Demands against the estate of the said Arthur Dent and particularly that he had … a judgement in the Court of Queens Bench for four thousand pounds upon two seperatt bonds'. Put simply, the plaintiffs did not believe that the bankrupt was ever indebted to Kindon in such large sums. While the defendant accepted that Dent was a bankrupt, he argued that he was declared a bankrupt on 23 August 1703 and not 23 August 1704. The Lord Keeper ordered that the defendant was to deduct two fifths of the £188 allowed for interest on the account dated November 1701 but was to come in as a creditor in the commission of bankruptcy for £300.[64]

What we see in these cases is that Chancery had developed a specific procedure for arbitrating in complex transactions and settling financial affairs between multiple parties. Michael Lobban has argued that such a function made the court 'chronically inefficient'.[65] While juries in common law cases

---

63 Ibid.
64 AALT, C78/1484, no.4 [24], 'Denn v Kindon' (1707).
65 Lobban, 'Preparing for Fusion (part 1)', p. 394.

could answer specific questions outlined in the pleading, effectively taking decision-making processes away from the judges, in Chancery the entirety of the work was done by the officials of the court. While administrative cases – and especially bankruptcy cases involving numerous creditors – provided a sizeable income for the court, they took up very little of the judge's time. Frequently, such cases were delegated to the Masters who were tasked with reporting on complex financial issues and matters of account. As Lobban concludes, 'whenever questions were raised on a defendant's answer that required fuller investigation, where accounts were to be taken or titles investigated, the judge's decree could not be final, but there would be a reference to a master to make the relevant inquiries'.[66] The most striking examples of the complex and multi-faceted nature of decrees can be seen in cases where a Master had included his report, demonstrating how the formal authority and expertise of the court were required to clarify the specific details of indebtedness.

Chancery Masters' Reports
In *Richardson v Richardson* (1696), the plaintiff, Randolph Richardson junior, was previously in a co-partnership in the trade of dry salter with his father, Randolph Richardson senior, and Sackford Gonson, who had subsequently been declared a bankrupt. Richardson named the three commissioners – Thomas Gooding, Robert Wilkinson, and John Weaver – and two assignees – William Richardson and Humphrey Gonson – as defendants. The plaintiff claimed that Gonson absconded on 20 December 1692, and a short while afterwards William Richardson took out a commission of bankruptcy against him. The commissioners seized £1000 worth of goods to satisfy Gonson's debts, which amounted to roughly £6500. The assignees had the goods appraised and sold, but the plaintiff claimed that the assignees 'pretended' to have bought the goods themselves at the appraised value, but they were in fact 'worth much more'. Ultimately, the plaintiff claimed that these transactions were fraudulent, as the 'Commissioners or Assignees ought to be in no better condition against the said Complainant than Gonson [the bankrupt] could have been'. As such, Richardson demanded to be let in as a creditor and to force the defendants to come to an account for what goods of the bankrupt they had in their possession.[67]

In their answer, the two assignees stated that they appraised the bankrupt's work goods at £747 2s 1d, and his household goods at £38 15s 1d, and claimed to have only bought a few items at a fair price. The case was referred to a Master to take an account of the partnership between the plaintiff and the bankrupt from 1 January 1690 until the bankrupt absconded on 20 December 1692.

66   Ibid., p. 393.
67   AALT, C78/2011, no.5 [87], 'Richardson v Richardson' (1696).

While the Master was making his assessment, the commission of bankruptcy was forbidden from conducting any business and paying out further dividends. Again, we see the complexities of a bankruptcy case in Chancery, as not only were there multiple creditors, but also disagreements about what goods and stock belonged to the co-partnership, and what belonged to the bankrupt.[68]

The Master made his final report on 14 July 1693 and meticulously worked through the accounts of the company and the credit and debts of the bankrupt from 1 January 1690 until 29 September 1692, when Richardson senior broke off the co-partnership. The Master found that the company held £1725 11s 11d, in cash and stock, and a further £6384 9d was due in unpaid debts. In total, the company held £8109 12s 8d, in assets. On the other side, there was a total of £2540 15s 1d, owing from the company, including £500 due to the plaintiff himself. When the bankrupt absconded on 30 December 1692, there was a total of £6717 2s 4d in company assets. Finally, the Master found that the bankrupt:

> for the most part received and collected the debts due to the said Joint stock and I do find that the said Sackford Gonson since the first of January one thousand six hundred and ninety received several debts and sumes of mony due to the said joint stock which he did not bring to Account or into the Cash of the said Joint stock the particulars whereof I have sett downe in the schedule hereunto annexed and also that he took out of the cash of the said joint stock since that time several sumes of mony upon pretence to pay of debts owing from the said joynt stock which were never paid.

Overall, the bankrupt was found to have 'embezilled' a total of £1929 17s.[69] The court ordered that the plaintiff was to receive the £500 due to him plus interest from the defendants within six weeks, and the joint stock in the hands of the commission was to be paid to the creditors of the company, with the plaintiff's costs in the case to be paid by the defendants.[70]

In a case decided on 1 August 1718, the plaintiff was a London merchant named Thomas Willis, who was also the sole assignee of Henry Heginbotham junior. The bill of complaint stated that the bankrupt absconded and committed an act of bankruptcy in June 1712, and named the bankrupt alongside his father, also Henry Heginbotham, as the only defendants. The plaintiff claimed that as part of a marriage portion, Heginbotham senior was expected to receive £400, and that from certain properties that he held in Lancashire and Cheshire, he was to pay his son an annuity of £20 per annum. However, the annuity had not been paid for the past nine years, and the father owed £720 to several individuals, for which he made his son liable upon several bonds. As such, the

68   Ibid.
69   Ibid.
70   Ibid.

son, 'sometime after with his own money' paid a number of these original creditors in discharge of the bonds. The father had 'prevailed' on the rest of the creditors to prove their bonds before the commission of bankruptcy, so that the bankrupt's estate would satisfy his own, personal debt. Ultimately, the plaintiff claimed that the father was in fact indebted to his son, and any bonds were 'obtained by fraud and Surprize and the bankrupt being under the influence of the Father' had executed the bonds without knowing their content.[71]

In their separate answers, the father claimed he was a creditor to his son and wished to enter the bankruptcy process, while the bankrupt claimed to be a creditor to his father. The Lord Chancellor referred the matter to a Master to take an account of who stood as a creditor, and who as a debtor. It was ordered that the father was to be examined under interrogatories and 'come to an Account' before the Master for any of his son's estate which had 'come to his hands or to the hands of any other person for his use'. It was further ordered that the Master should look into the father's answer and 'examine and Certifye whether the Defendant Heginbotham Senior was bound therein for the proper debt of the Defendant Heginbotham Junior or on what account'. Furthermore, the Master was to 'examine and Certifye what Bonds the Defendant Heginbotham Senior and Junior were Jointly bound in att the time of the Defendant Heginbotham Juniors marriage'. If anything should 'appeare Doubtfull' to the Master, he was to 'Report the same Specially to the Court'. The Master submitted his detailed report on 7 May 1718, which was included in the enrolled decree. The father held £18 9s of the bankrupt's goods in his possession and owed the bankrupt for thirteen years of arrears of annuity, at the rate of £20 per annum, occurring from 24 January 1704 to 24 January 1717, which totalled £278 9s 2d. However, the father had 'paid taxes for the Estate out of which the said Annuity doth Issue' at the rate of two shillings in the pound, which amounted to £26. With the taxes being deducted, the father owed a total of £252 9s 2d, to the bankrupt. The father did also 'serve and Assist' the bankrupt in trade for four years from 24 January 1704, for which the Master allowed the rate of £40 per annum. This meant that £160 was deducted from the original £252 9s 2d, leaving £92 9s 2d, due to the bankrupt. Finally, the father 'did lay out and pay for the use' of his son £22 11s 10d, which left a total of £69 17s 4d, to be paid to the bankrupt from his father.

On the other side, the Master found that on 17 November 1704, the bankrupt borrowed £300 on bond, which was still due. The Master thought this 'fit to Allow' and computed interest until 17 March 1712 – which was the time when the bankrupt first failed – being eight years and four months at 6 per cent, which amounted to £150. This made a total of £450 to be deducted from the £69 17s 4d, owing from the father, which meant that a final total of £380 2s 8d,

71   AALT, C78/1396, no.4 [99], 'Willis v Heginbotham' (1718).

was due from the bankrupt son to the father. Finally, the Master found that the two defendants were jointly bound in numerous bonds to several people from the time of the son's marriage. As such, the Lord Chancellor ordered that the Master's report stand ratified, and that the father was to enter the commission of bankruptcy as a creditor, while the plaintiff was to pay the father's fees and costs in Chancery.[72] In this instance, it appears that the assignees miscalculated the bankrupt's credit and debts, as the father was actually a creditor to the bankrupt, rather than a debtor. Here, we not only see the multifaceted nature of the final judgment of the court, but we again see the interconnected nature of credit networks being played out in Chancery. We see a complex series of indebtedness within a family network, as the originally autonomous commission of bankruptcy came to Chancery for aid and assistance.[73] It is clear that such credit networks had already been formed, and were so complicated in their very existence that they required the expertise and formal authority of the court to untangle them, clearly establishing the roles of creditors and debtors, as well as the specific amounts due.

Herne v Humphreys was heard on 11 May 1708. The plaintiffs were the assignees and creditors of William Sheppard, Joseph Bragg, and John Sheppard, co-partners and goldsmith bankers from London. The plaintiffs named the bankrupts alongside five other defendants in a suit that centred around the fraudulent bankruptcy of the company. The plaintiffs submitted their bill in Michaelmas term 1705 and explained that on 3 February 1700, the co-partners became bankrupt and held debts above £100,000. The bill claimed that the commission had found the three bankrupts had 'removed their moneys and Effects by night' and had 'made several Fraudulent Conveyances on purpose to defraud their Creditors and were found Bankrupt'. The three bankrupts had made a 'secret confederacy' between themselves and Robert Lancashire, hiding assets and their estate and pretending that he was indebted to them for £25,000. Lancashire had died, and the defendants named his executors, William Humphreys and his wife Ellen, in an attempt to locate and distribute the bankrupts' estate for their creditors' satisfaction.[74] The defendants denied that any transactions were fraudulent and accepted that the three co-partners were severely indebted. They stated that in February 1700, William Sheppard 'being sensible that it was Impossible for him and his partners to keep upp their creditt advised with that said Robert Lancashire about the management of himself and his Estate'. After this meeting, the bankrupts decided that the only way to secure a specific debt and 'conceal it from any Commision of Bankruptcy' would be for the partners to execute a release to Lancashire.[75]

---

72   Ibid.
73   See Collins, 'The Interconnected Nature of Family Indebtedness', pp. 1–27.
74   AALT, C78/1428, no. 2 [54], 'Herne v Humphreys' (1708).
75   Ibid.

The court agreed that the three partners became bankrupts on 3 February 1700 and worked through the specific debts due to the assignees and the creditors of the bankrupts from this date. The court found that the account book of the partners – dated 15 September 1690 – and a specific bill of exchange were sufficient evidence, and that Robert Lancashire was indebted to the bankrupts in the sum of £2685 8s. The Lord Chancellor decreed that the defendants were to be examined under interrogatories by a Master to gain a greater understanding of the dealings between themselves and Lancashire. Under oath, all parties were to produce 'all Books of Account notes papers memorandums and writing' which they held in their possession. It was furthered ordered that all parties were to proceed to a trial in the court of Common Pleas in London, to determine 'who hath the Right of the Equity of Redemption of the said Stock now mortgaged or pawned'. While the issue was to be tried by special jury, the court ordered that, under oath, William Sheppard was to provide a list of the company's creditors, and that 'noe Creditors or relation of a Creditor of the Defendants the bankrupts or either of them unto be of the Jury'. Finally, the parties were 'att liberty to make objections against any that … be offered to be of the jury'.[76]

One final example of the complexities of competing claims on accounts can be seen in *De La Chambre v Marten*, whereby the Master struggled to identify specific details relating to the account of a bankrupt named Samuel Harrison. The bill of complaint was submitted in Hilary term 1708 and the creditor-plaintiffs named John Marten – a surgeon – and Joshua Stevens and William Clarke – both warehousemen – as defendants, all of whom resided in London. The bill claimed that in 1705 and being 'in Want of money to pay some Bills of Exchange', the defendants, 'under pretence of kindness but takeing Advantage of Harrisons necessities proposed to lend such mony as he had occasion for' at 6 per cent interest. Harrison subsequently deposited goods worth twice the value in the hands of the defendants who took out a commission of bankruptcy on 7 October 1705 and promised to discharge the bankrupt if he cooperated fully. The plaintiffs and the other creditors found themselves outside of the dynamic of the commission and complained about not receiving any satisfaction upon their debts. The court ordered the defendants to come to an account with the Master for what goods had come into their possession and whether the goods were genuinely sold, or fraudulently conveyed. The Master found that the goods specified in his schedule came into the hands of the defendants, 'but the time When to Whom or for What the said goods were sold doth not Appeare to me'. The defendants were found chargeable and were to pay the plaintiffs specific amounts. John Marten was to pay £405 10s 6d, to the plaintiffs, but not being happy with this outcome Marten filed two separate exceptions to the Master's

76   Ibid.

ruling. While a detailed analysis of appeals and exceptions is discussed below, in this instance both petitions were overruled, and Marten was ordered to pay interest on the £405 10s 6d, with the defendants paying the costs of the plaintiffs' proceedings in Chancery.[77] Ultimately, the fact that the Master could not specify details relating to the bankruptcy and the dealings of Harrison adds further evidence to the complexities and difficulties involved in identifying and clarifying failure in the court. Cases where a Master was delegated to report on such complex issues provide definitive examples of the court attempting, but in many instances struggling, to identify failure as a social construct in law to mediate and arbitrate in complex financial disputes.

The Appeals Process

From the sample of forty-three enrolled decrees, eleven had been appealed in one form or another. Of these appeals, eight were entirely unsuccessful, two were successful, and one had elements of both success and failure within it. Several appeals were dismissed in a fairly prompt manner. In a suit decided in 1703, a defendant named Mary Ashfield refused to satisfy a mortgage of her late husband, as she claimed the repayment contained 'very unconscionable Interest being Allowed upon Interest many times over to make upp the said two thousand three hundred and thirty five pounds'. Ashfield hoped to prove that the demanded repayment was 'Interest and Interest upon Interest', and argued that she 'should not pay more for the Redemption thereof then the principall sumes originally lent and the simple Interest'.[78] However, the Lord Chancellor ordered that the Master's report – which stated that the amount due was actually far higher, standing at £3214 9s 9d – should be confirmed, unless the defendants appealed within eight days. Within this period, Mary and her new husband, Anthony Ashfield, submitted their appeal to the court to have the cause reheard. While the defendants' counsel offered 'diverse reasons for Discharge of the said Order', they failed to pay the necessary £10 costs to have the cause reopened. Their appeal was dismissed outright, and the Master's report stood confirmed.[79] In a similarly straightforward case concluded on 30 January 1685, the Lord Chancellor originally decreed in favour of the nine defendants. However, the sole plaintiff, John Loggin, filed exceptions to the order and paid the necessary costs to have the cause re-examined. In direct and unambiguous language, the court found 'noe Cause or ground of Equity to releive the Complainant', and subsequently, 'noe Cause to Alter the

77 AALT, C78/1658 no.1 [10], 'De La Chambre v Marten' (1713).
78 AALT, C78/1485, no.8 [5], 'French v Ashfield' (1703).
79 Ibid.

said former order'. The plaintiff was ordered to pay an additional £5 in costs directly to the defendants.[80]

These two suits demonstrate straightforward examples whereby the appeal had initially been entered and then rejected outright. But again, there were more complex instances of appeals. In an intricate case decided on 21 October 1745, over twenty creditors of Sir Stephen Evance submitted their bill against several administrators and assignees of Evance and his business partner, William Hales, who were also co-bankrupts in a separate commission of bankruptcy.[81] The suit was referred to a Master, to account for the size and substance of goods and estate that were in the possession of the defendants, as well as to assess the contribution money paid by creditors in the two commissions of bankruptcy. It was ordered that because of the sheer scale of the indebtedness of these two goldsmith bankers, creditors were at liberty to come forward and prove their outstanding debts. In a lengthy report, Master Bennett meticulously specified the exact debts due, the contribution monies paid by creditors, and the outstanding costs to each individual defendant for the multiple suits executed in Chancery. However, before the report could be ratified, there were 'Several Setts of Exceptions' submitted by the plaintiffs, other creditors of the bankrupts, and four defendants.

While the exact details of these exceptions, and the conclusions made, are too numerous to effectively work through in detail, a few examples can provide a general picture. The defendants claimed that in the first schedule of account, the Master had reported that £350 was due to Edward Woodcock on bond, as he was an assignee of Thomas Coleborn in an unrelated commission of bankruptcy. The exception was made that in fact only £337 2s 7d, was due. Similarly, Sarah Clough was reported to be owed £200 on bond, whereas the defendants claimed that there was only £181 14s 1d due from Evance's estate. On complex financial issues such as these, some exceptions were allowed, some overruled, and some compromised. Interestingly, the estate was so large that the costs of the suit were to be paid by Evance himself.[82] While this clearly demonstrates that Evance's estate was large enough to cover the expenses, it again shows that the concept of appropriating blame for such financial losses was not appropriate in Chancery. Within this decree, it is the appeals process

80   AALT, C78/916, no.1 [80], 'Whitaker v Loggin' (1691).

81   Sir Stephen Evance appears frequently in discussions of eighteenth-century finance, see Larry Neal, *'I Am Not Master of Events': The Speculations of John Law and Lord Londonerry in the Mississippi and South Sea Bubbles* (New Haven, 2012); Jessica Richard, *The Romance of Gambling in the Eighteenth-Century British Novel* (London, 2011); Stephen Quinn, 'Gold, Silver, and the Glorious Revolution: Arbitrage Between Bills of Exchange and Bullion', *EHR*, 49 (1996), pp. 473–490; Henry Lancaster, 'Evance, Sir Stephen' (1654/5–1712), ODNB.

82   AALT, C78/1814, no.12 [24], 'Bromley v Child' (1745).

that has enabled us an insight into the aim and decision-making procedure of the court. We can see the court trying to render an equitable remedy that suited the majority of the creditors of the bankrupt; compromising, rejecting, or accepting exceptions to the Master's appraisal of outstanding debts.

In *Sadlier v Pashley*, the bill of complaint was submitted in Hilary term 1718, and came to be heard on 14 April 1722. The plaintiffs – Giles Sadlier a merchant and James Coulter a linen draper, both from London – were assignees of a chapman named Samuel London and named eight men as defendants. The plaintiffs claimed that in January 1717, and for a long time before that, the bankrupt bought several large quantities of linens and velvets and was over £13,000 in debt; £800 of which was owed directly to Sadlier, and £500 to Coulter. Having 'mett with losses and disappointments in the world', London became 'disabled to make payments of the said debts thereupon'. On 12 January, London was arrested and made a composition with his creditors to release him. However, once he was released, London 'concealed himself in his house and caused himself to be denyed to his creditors soe as that he could not be seen or spoken to by any of them by which meanes he did about the same tyme become a bankrupt'.[83] In March 1717, the bankrupt held a meeting with his creditors, and:

> pretended that the greatest part of his Estate lay out in debts due to him which he should be able to gett in within sixteenth months and that the same would be sufficient when gott in to pay off all his debts and therefore proposed to the Complainants and his said other Creditors that if he might have his liberty to goe about to gett in his debts he would give them Bonds to pay one moiety of their debts within eight months after the date thereof and the other moiety thereof att the end of sixteen months.[84]

While the creditors accepted this proposal, on 30 October 1717 a creditor outside of this agreement brought an action in the common law courts and received a judgment for £300. Since that time, London and his family had left their house and continued to abscond, forcing the plaintiffs to take out a commission of bankruptcy on 4 November 1717. Having examined the bankrupt and his wife, Sarah, the commissioners discovered that after his bankruptcy, Sarah – withoutthe privity of her husband – delivered large quantities of goods in return for money. For example, she provided several parcels of lace and other goods worth £2328 19s to Thomas Pashley to secure a sum of £858. The plaintiffs claimed that the defendants continued to defraud the creditors of the bankrupt, either denying that any goods were transferred, reducing the value of the goods

---

83   AALT, C79/15 [26], 'Sadlier v Pashley' (1722).
84   Ibid.

received, or stating that they took goods from Sarah when she was trading on her own account as a feme sole trader.[85]

In their response, the defendants claimed that since their marriage, Samuel allowed his wife 'to carry on her said trade in her owne name as she had been a Feme sole and entrusted her to buy and sell Goods in her owne name'. As such, the defendants claimed that Sarah was able to raise and use credit on her own account. One of the defendants denied any knowledge of Samuel committing an act of bankruptcy, for if he had known, he 'would not have dealt with the said Sarah London in any manner whatsoever'. After the pleadings and deposi-tions were entered, the case was sent to a trial at the court of Common Pleas in Middlesex to determine the specific date that Samuel London first became a bankrupt. The jury found that London became a bankrupt on 16 October 1717, and the Master was tasked with determining the transactions of those who dealt with the bankrupt before and after his bankruptcy for the post-bankruptcy satisfaction of debts. Ultimately, the plaintiffs wanted the bankruptcy to be declared in January 1717 so that they could claim a legal right to a much broader range of goods. However, as the bankruptcy was declared ten months later, the case was eventually dismissed with costs, and any goods or transac-tions which occurred after October 1717 were to be given to the plaintiffs as the assignees of the commission of bankruptcy.

The plaintiffs filed an appeal and paid £10 to have the cause reheard, but lost the appeal with the £10 given over to the defendants.[86] This case is illuminating for what it reveals about the decision-making processes of the court, and how other social and economic aspects intersect with bankruptcy in Chancery. An established scholarship has shown how feme sole traders held an independent economic and legal status and could be sued for debt in numerous jurisdictions. Marjorie McIntosh has shown how litigation concerning feme sole traders in urban centres often centred around the woman's independent activities, whereby she would be held responsible for the accumulation of her own debts.[87] However, in bankruptcy proceedings, we can see the inability to clearly identify and separate individual working activities, whether that be in the form of a

85   Ibid.
86   Ibid.
87   See Marjorie Mcintosh, 'The Benefits and Drawbacks of Femme Sole Status in England, 1300–1630', *Journal of British Studies*, 44 (2005), pp. 410–438; Karen Pearlston, 'What a Feme Sole Trader Could Not Do: Lord Mansfield on the Limits of a Married Woman's Commercial Freedom', in Kim Kippen and Lori Woods (eds), *Worth and Repute: Valuing Gender in Late Medieval and Early Modern Europe: Essays in Honour of Barbara Todd* (Toronto, 2011), pp. 309–333; Amy Erickson, 'Coverture and Capitalism', *History Workshop Journal*, 59 (2005), pp. 1–16; Brian W. Gastle, '"As if she were single": Working Wives and the Late Medieval English *Femme Sole*', in Kellie Robertson and Michael Uebel (eds), *The Middle Ages at Work: Practicing Labor in Late Medieval England* (Basingstoke, 2004), pp. 41–64.

co-partnership, within a family unit, or more broadly in terms of business and personal liability.[88] We also see detailed descriptions of imprisonment for debt, absconding and keeping house, compositions for the satisfaction of debts at a later date, common law litigation, the timing of failure, and perceptions of credibility, honesty, and trustworthiness. The court had to work through these aspects of a case and come to a fair decision based upon equitable principles of justice.

One appeal is worth analysing in detail, as it was successfully taken to the pinnacle of the legal hierarchy, whereby the House of Lords overturned a previous decision made by the Lord Chancellor.[89] This complex case – that involved several suits in multiple jurisdictions – is explained in an extremely lengthy enrolled decree. In a bill submitted on 20 June 1732, the two plaintiffs were assignees of John Ward, who had debts exceeding £60,000 owing to multiple creditors. The plaintiffs named the bankrupt's son, Knox Ward, alongside his wife, Elizabeth, and nine other defendants. The bill claimed that Ward held several lands and establishments in Essex and Middlesex which far exceeded his debts, but had fraudulently concealed his estate by assigning it to numerous defendants. For example, in 1725 he purchased the office of Clarencieux King at Arms for over £3000 and a premises named Pimlico for £2000, both of which were deposited in the name of his son. The plaintiffs demanded that the defendants individually come to an account for any of the estate of the bankrupt that remained in their possession. After several pleas and answers were presented to the court – whereby a common defence was that Ward had not committed an act of bankruptcy, or was not a 'trader' under the wording of the statutes – the suit came to be heard on 4 December 1736.[90]

The petitioning creditor who sued out the commission, George Surtees, was owed £112 on a promissory note dated 7 July 1730. The plaintiffs and assignees claimed that an act of bankruptcy was committed as far back as 1725, with one being definitively proven in 1726. However, the counsel for the defendants stated that as an act of bankruptcy was proven in 1726, and that 'John Ward appeared to be a bankrupt in 1726', he was incapable of legally providing a note to Surtees in 1730. Therefore, the bankrupt was unable to contract a debt, or provide a legitimate note, after he had committed an act of bankruptcy. As such, the commission was taken out by a person who was not a genuine creditor. At this juncture, the Lord Chancellor agreed with the defendants and dismissed the plaintiffs' bill without prejudice, meaning they were free to resubmit a new

---

88   Margaret Hunt, *The Middling Sort: Commerce, Gender, and the Family in England, 1680–1780* (London, 1996), p. 23.

89   For the law reports relating to the Chancery and House of Lords Cases, see LX, 'De Gols v Ward' (1734), Court of Chancery, 25 ER 758; 'De Gols v Ward' (1737), House of Lords, 1 ER 740.

90   AALT, C78/2067 'De Gols v ward' (1739), no.1 [67].

bill if they pleased. However, being 'Dissatisffyed' with the decree, the plaintiffs submitted their appeal to the House of Lords. The summaries of the appeals, taken from law reports, are worth quoting at length. The plaintiffs argued that:

> if an act of bankruptcy, secretly committed by a person continuing in a public course of trade for several years afterwards, should be allowed to overturn a commission carried on by the whole body of the bankrupt's creditors, who had joined the commission, by seeking relief under it, and not impeached or opposed by one single creditor, it would be of dangerous consequence to trade and credit; for by these means, the several acts made for the relief of creditors might, in many instances, become a snare and delusion, instead of a relief and protection to them. And if this doctrine should be established, it would greatly deter creditors from taking out commissions, which are attended with very great expence, for they never can be sure that a prior secret act of bankruptcy has not been committed; it would also be the highest encouragement to dishonest debtors to commit secret acts of bankruptcy, on purpose to protect them from commissions, or to render them fruitless. That though an act of bankruptcy disables the bankrupt from contracting a debt with another person to the prejudice of creditors, prior to the act of bankruptcy, if they insist on their priority; yet the bankrupt may contract a debt, not only to charge his person, but even his effects, if they are sufficient to pay the whole, or if the prior creditors do not insist on a preference. And if they wave their preference, and allow such, person to be a creditor, neither the bankrupt himself, nor any of his confederates, are at liberty to say he is not a creditor.[91]

On the other side, the defendants argued that the commission of bankruptcy was:

> not maintainable ... for no commission can issue, but upon the petition of some person, who has by law a right to sue for it; and every commission issuing otherwise, and all the proceedings under it, are illegal and void. None have a right to sue out a commission but creditors, and such creditors only who can be intended to be defrauded by the bankruptcy: but this cannot be the case of those who do not become creditors till after the act of bankruptcy is committed, unless a man can abscond to avoid creditors when he has none. Besides, those who become creditors after the bankruptcy committed, cannot be admitted to prove their debts, or receive a dividend with the rest under the commission issued; and it would be an absurdity to allow a man to be a petitioning creditor, and yet not capable of relief under the commission he applies for.[92]

---

91   LX, 'De Gols v Ward' (1737), House of Lords, 1 ER 740.
92   Ibid.

The appeal was heard in the Lords on 22 and 23 February 1737, and it was unanimously decided that the decree of dismissal be reversed: 'It should seem that an act of bankruptcy, if once plainly committed, can never be purged.'[93] In this instance, it appears that the Lords interpreted the statutes for the benefit of the creditors, and for the maintenance of trade and credit. The suit was to be reheard in Chancery on the merits of the case, which occurred on 30 and 31 October 1738.[94]

The Lord Chancellor ordered that the parties were to proceed to a trial in the court of King's Bench, to answer the question: 'Whether John ward became a bankrupt on or before the 13 day of June 1729'. The jury established that Ward became a bankrupt on 26 August 1725, which was over five years before the commission of bankruptcy was taken out on 20 November 1730. Maintaining his concern with the distance between the two events, the Lord Chancellor sought clarification from the common law judges, 'on what Act of Bankruptcy the said Verdict was founded'. In his final decree of 14 December 1739, the Lord Chancellor declared that

> it appeared to him by the information of the Judges of the Court of Kings Bench before whom the said issue was tried … That no Evidence was given on the said Tryall of any Act of Bankruptcy committed by the said John Ward on or before the twenty-sixth day of August One thousand Seven hundred and twenty Five besides the making and Executing of the said Indentures.

The indentures were dated 25 and 26 August 1725, and were the 'Ground on which the Jury Founded their Verdict'. Having been informed by the Lord Chief Justice of the King's Bench – on behalf of himself and the rest of the judges who heard the case – the Lord Chancellor accepted the date given by the common law verdict and declared that all indentures and deeds mentioned in the Chancery suit were executed *after* the first act of bankruptcy on the 26 August 1725. As such, they were 'Executed by the said John Ward without any real and Valuable Consideration and were deceitfully contrived with intent to defraud the just Creditors of the said John Ward'.[95]

The Lord Chancellor further ordered, 'that all the said conveyances, assignments, and other deeds, except the said marriage articles, and indenture of the 13th June 1729, should be set aside in respect of the plaintiff, and the other creditors of the said John ward' for the benefit of his creditors. Ultimately, the specified indentures and deeds, as well as any of the estate of the bankrupt in the possession of the defendants, were to be handed over to the plaintiffs as assignees of the bankrupt. Knox Ward was ordered to pay the plaintiffs' costs,

93 Ibid.
94 AALT, C78/2067 'De Gols v ward' (1739), no.1 [67].
95 Ibid.

both in Chancery and for the trial in King's Bench. Such was the duration and complexity of this suit that all parties were 'at Liberty to apply to the Court from time to time as Occasion shall require' in order to conclude the repayments.[96]

This case is striking for several reasons. Firstly, we get to see the complexities and the multiple jurisdictions that a bankruptcy suit could take, involving Chancery and the King's Bench, as well as an appeal to the House of Lords. Secondly, the Lord Chancellor can be seen working in collaboration with the common law judges to come to a conclusion on a definitive question of fact regarding the date of the act of bankruptcy. At the same time, the House of Lords overruled his initial decree and allowed the plaintiffs to have their cause reheard by the court. Thirdly, this case seems to have taken a remarkably long time to reach a conclusion, as the first act of bankruptcy was committed in 1725, but the suit was not finalised until 1739. Parties were still permitted to prove their debts before a Chancery Master as the suit was ongoing, and even when a final decree had been ordered – and subsequently enrolled – the court still acknowledged the complexities of the bankruptcy process, enabling individuals to return to the court for aid in gathering and reclaiming their debts. Fourthly, this suit is a rare example of a successful appeal occurring outside of Chancery. While initially the suit was decided in the absolute favour of the defendants, after the House of Lords reversed the dismissal and reopened the case, the cause was eventually decided on the side of the plaintiffs, with a sole defendant being charged the entirety of the costs in Chancery and the common law. Finally, we have already seen how crucial the exact timing of bankruptcy was to the debt-recovery process. In this example, the jury established a far earlier chronology of failure, which meant that any action taken by the bankrupt after this date – i.e. an execution of a deed, indenture, or mortgage – was seen to be legally invalid. The combination of these specific and interesting details can only be gathered and fully understood at this final stage of proceeding by unravelling and working through the case in its entirety.

In another complicated case, we can see the degree to which a decree could be appealed, as any aspect of the final judgment could be contested. This suit was decided on 13 February 1713 and the two plaintiffs, William Riley and William Applebee, were assignees of Elizabeth Dye, who owned a coffee house and a stagecoach in Oxford. Alongside the two assignees was a third plaintiff named Mary Hartwell, who was a widow and executrix of Elizabeth Dye's brother, Richard Hartwell. In November 1702, Dye asked her brother to be her coachman, paying a wage of five shillings per week – on top of his room and board – to run journeys between Oxford and London. The plaintiffs claimed that Hartwell worked for his sister for the space of six years, but 'never received any wages', instead being content 'to let them rest in the hands of his said sister

---

96   Ibid.

hopeing it might be a kindnesse to her in her way of trade not doubting but she had been in good Circumstances and would have paid him when requested'. It was suggested that Hartwell lent his sister the sum of £10, sold her a 'fatt hogg' worth £2 12s 9½d, and 'kept A child' of Dye's for above six years, for which he was owed £8 per annum. Being owed more than £150, and being indebted to the sum of £100, Hartwell demanded satisfaction from his sister on 16 December 1708. In lieu of cash, Dye provided some household goods, horses, and her stagecoach to Hartwell, who subsequently agreed to sell the goods to the two named defendants, John Stonell and Richard Wise for £178. However, Hartwell died leaving his wife Mary as sole executor of his estate, and never received any payment for the goods, which remained in the defendants' possession.[97]

What is interesting in this case is the way in which the defendants were accused of manipulating the bankruptcy process, and taking advantage of Richard Hartwell's death, to avoid paying their debts. The plaintiffs' bill concluded by suggesting that the defendants achieved this by playing one side off against the other. They refused to pay Mary Hartwell by claiming she had no right to the debt, as Elizabeth Dye was 'a Bankrupt and Absconded before the making the said Deed of Bargaine and Sale'. If this were the case, then the goods in their possession would be liable to a future commission of bankruptcy. In response to the accusation that Dye had committed an act of bankruptcy, Mary Hartwell took it upon herself to execute a commission, so that she could prove herself a creditor and satisfy the debt due to her. The commission subsequently found Dye a bankrupt, accepted contribution money from several creditors, assigned the two plaintiffs as assignees, and granted Dye a certificate of conformity, discharging her from future liability. When the assignees sought repayment from the defendants, they pretended that Dye was not a bankrupt, and claimed that the goods belonged to Richard Hartwell's executrix Mary, 'And soe put it off from One to Another and paid noe body'. Growing increasingly frustrated, the plaintiffs initiated a suit in the common law courts. However, being restrained by the technical rigidity of procedure, Elizabeth Dye was not permitted to be a witness, and so the bankruptcy could not be proven. Therefore, the plaintiffs sought redress through Chancery.[98]

In their answer, the defendants claimed that they were unaware that the plaintiffs were either assignees, or the executor of Richard Hartwell, and suggested that the most Hartwell was owed from Dye was £10. On 2 December 1712 the cause came to be heard, and the court ordered that the parties should proceed to a trial at law in the next assize at Oxford. The central issue to be decided was to establish if, and when, Elizabeth Dye became a bankrupt. After such a trial, 'either party was at liberty to report backe to the Court whereupon

97 AALT, C79/80, no.[36], 'Riley v Stonell' (1713).
98 Ibid.

such further Order should be made as should be Just'. However, the defendants were dissatisfied with the decree and appealed, asking for the cause to be heard in Chancery, rather than at common law. Upon a rehearing, the Lord Chancellor saw 'noe Cause to give the Complainants any reliefe in equity' and dismissed the bill. It was ordered that the plaintiffs were to pay the entirety of the costs for the suit, and that the £10 deposited by the defendants for their appeal was to be returned.[99] This suit demonstrates that any part of a decree could be appealed. In this instance, the defendants were not appealing a final judgment of the court, but rather seeking to prevent the cause returning to the common law courts, preferring instead a hearing in Chancery. From this appeal process, we gain an insight into a specific complexity of bankruptcy procedure, as it was possible to play one side off against another and manipulate the situation so as not to satisfy outstanding debts. While the defendants were unsuccessful in their appeal, we see their arguments presented in a plausible manner, which is especially the case as it was the court which was summarising the pertinent details and arguments of both sides.

In a similar suit, the three plaintiffs were the assignees of Robert Williamson, and named the bankrupt alongside four other defendants. The plaintiffs were claiming a legal right to an estate which had been mortgaged between two sets of defendants; Robert and Faith Clarkson on the one hand, and John Rayner on the other. The enrolled decree summarised that a previous order had been made for this specific detail to be tried at the assize in Nottingham, whereby the plaintiffs were to proceed in an action against Robert and Faith Clarkson. The central question to be asked of the jury was whether the disputed property was assigned between the two defendants for a valuable consideration, or was enacted fraudulently to prevent the assignees gaining access to the estate. The plaintiffs were unhappy with the previous order and paid £5 to have the cause reheard in Chancery. Their appeal was rejected and at a trial in Nottingham the jury gave a verdict for the defendants. However, the plaintiffs were again dissatisfied with the verdict, and moved for a new common law trial in another county, paying a further deposit of £10. It was ordered by the Lord Chancellor that the issue should be referred to the original judge who oversaw the common law trial in Nottingham, to see if it was possible to have the suit reheard. The judge certified that the case was fit to be tried again, and the Lord Chancellor agreed to have the cause reheard at the next assize, either in Nottingham or Suffolk. The complainants chose Suffolk for their new trial and had their £10 deposit returned, but were ordered to pay the defendants their costs for the initial trial. In this second common law trial, the jury again found for the defendants. Upon returning to Chancery, the solicitor for the defendants asked for the remaining purchase money of £2050, plus interest, to be paid to the Clarksons from the

99   Ibid.

other defendant, Rayner. On the opposing side, the solicitor for the plaintiffs again asked for a new trial, which somewhat unsurprisingly was denied.

In an attempt to conclude the situation, the Lord Chancellor referred the matter to a Master to determine what was due to the Clarksons in principal and interest. The Master found that £2815 16s 6d, was due from the defendant Rayner to the Clarksons, and the Lord Chancellor ordered that the report should stand ratified, and once the outstanding balance was paid, the estate was to be assigned over to Rayner from the Clarksons in its entirety.[100] In this example, we again see that such a dispute could be tried in multiple jurisdictions on numerous occasions. It is also clear that the plaintiffs submitted three separate appeals in this case, only one of which was successful. Not only are concepts such as a winning party and a losing party unhelpful, but attempting to define the parties themselves can be problematic. In this case, the plaintiffs were seeking to claim a legal right to an estate, which itself was subject to a mortgage between two opposing parties. As such, this case was not a straightforward example of plaintiffs suing defendants, but rather, the plaintiffs seeking access to the estate in question, which was ultimately denied. In this example, it could be explained in terms of the defendants winning the right to the debt, over an external claim on the property.

Conclusion

It is important not to assume that decrees provide a form of narrative closure to Chancery suits, especially in cases involving bankruptcy, whereby the identification, collection, and redistribution of a bankrupt's assets was often ongoing. Modern conceptions such as one single party suing another – A vs B – are unhelpful, and we need to remove ourselves from such preconceived ideas when analysing enrolled decrees. We have seen throughout this chapter that the parties within a suit, whether plaintiffs or defendants, were not a homogenous group. Often, such parties contained both creditors and debtors, and there were competing claims on sole or multiple estates. While there was obviously a spectrum of success and failure throughout Chancery, the concept of a 'winning' or 'losing' party cannot be clarified and quantified to any meaningful degree. In the vast majority of cases, it is difficult, and in many instances incorrect, to attempt to assign such labels to parties. This analysis can be taken a step further by assessing the concept of blame, as while the appropriation of costs to unsuccessful individuals can give an indication of wrongdoing, often such parties were simply unable to prove that they held a right to equitable relief within the jurisdiction of Chancery.

100   AALT, C78/1653, no.5 [34], 'Jeffreys v Clarkson' (1704).

While the broader aim of Chancery was to uncover and understand the fundamental complaints brought before the court in order to render an appropriate equitable judgment, this chapter has added further evidence to demonstrate that the court was not one where the procedures were focused on finalising a case, but mediating in social and financial disputes.[101] With an increasing case load, the court was placed in a difficult position, as the practical limitations of time, expense, and a lack of judicial staff, led to increased delays and complaints about inefficiency and a lack of finality in the decision-making process. As such, the court acted as an arbitrator, assessing each individual claim and attempting to render a fair and equitable judgment for financial transactions.

When discussing decisions relating to legal rights to land, Edith Henderson has argued that the language used in decrees is 'more than a little puzzling or confused, suggesting that the Chancellors themselves may not have been entirely sure what they were doing'.[102] With a high proportion of cases referred to Chancery Masters, we gain an insight into how the court attempted to identify and categorise failure. Ultimately, it was the court's oral narrative that was transcribed verbatim, and it is important to keep this process in mind when we attempt to unravel these complex cases that came before a judge. Undertaking this task reveals specific aspects of the bankruptcy process which are not obvious, or attainable, at other stages of proceeding. The most prominent of these can be seen in the appeals process, as we see that credit networks had already been formed, and were so complicated in their very existence that it required the expertise and formal authority of the court to untangle such webs. As Tawny Paul has shown, 'just as credit involved networks of people and relationships of trust, so did failure'.[103] While we might expect legal proceedings to be straightforward, executed for a sole purpose, or concluded in a simple manner, this is simply not the case in bankruptcy suits that had been executed in Chancery.

This raises questions about the aims and motivations of those involved in Chancery cases, and particularly the reasons why such individuals would have invested the necessary time, expense, and costs associated with pushing a case forward to a final decree, and subsequently having the order enrolled. In terms of failure, the chapter provides a different angle to the proceeding chapters. If the bankrupt had failed – economically, legally, and morally – but there was no clearly defined winner or loser in the outcome of a case, could either side be said to have failed or succeeded? Furthermore, if the commission of bankruptcy had failed to come to a satisfactory conclusion, and the overarching authority of the court was enacted to provide remedies for such failure, could the debt-recovery process be seen to have concluded and have been successful in the recovery of

101   Horwitz, A Guide to Chancery Equity Records, pp. 9–10.
102   Henderson, 'Legal Rights to Land in the Early Chancery', p. 117.
103   Paul, The Poverty of Disaster, p. 60.

debts? The methodology employed throughout the book does not allow for the background of individual actors to be investigated in detail, or for the contextualisation of the wider bankruptcy regime. However, future research could be undertaken in order to conceptualise the broader picture of financial and personal failure within the trading community, demonstrating how Chancery litigation was just one element of wider dispute resolution taking place in early modern England.

Conclusion

This book has examined bankruptcy as a social construct, which needs to be understood – rather than measured – in order to highlight changing attitudes, assumptions, and narratives concerning financial failure. The multifaceted nature of economic and personal failure has been highlighted throughout, demonstrating how failure was not just a legal and financial state of being, but came to rely on circulating knowledge and moral judgements about a wide range of individuals involved in the debt-recovery process. By focusing on everyday interactions and the ways in which individuals used the court for their own benefit, the book has shown how notions of failure filtered outwards into wider society, and implicated a range of creditors, debtors, trading partners, family members, and middlemen in a complex network of exchange.

Between 1674 and 1750, England was a society in significant transformation. The Commercial and Financial Revolutions coincided with a dramatic increase in the use and extension of credit, both domestically and internationally. Bankrupts traded in substantial amounts of stock and goods which made them comfortably part of the aspiring middle sort of early modern England. However, these individuals became increasingly dependent upon the market, and although their businesses often retained ownership of capital assets – such as houses, workshops, and shops – they were reliant on credit to maintain their raw materials and trading stock.[1] While Tawny Paul has argued that insecurity became a 'defining feature of commercial experience', Paul Langford has stated that because of the unlimited nature of commercial liability, bankruptcy was seen as a 'nightmare' for the middling sort throughout the eighteenth century.[2] Despite these significant social and economic changes, the legislature failed to keep pace with the realities of the marketplace, which complicated the ways in which the sixteenth and seventeenth century bankruptcy statutes were interpreted. With a growing case load and an increased burden of interpretation, the courts became more flexible in their application of specific stipulations: the trading distinction was interpreted liberally, statutory defined acts of bankruptcy were vastly extended, and the £100 threshold became outdated,

---

1 Henry French, *The Middling Sort of People in Provincial England 1600–1750* (Oxford, 2007), p. 26.
2 Tawny Paul, *The Poverty of Disaster: Debt and Insecurity in Eighteenth-Century Britain* (Cambridge, 2019), p. 4; Paul Langford, *A Polite and Commercial People: England 1727–1783* (Oxford, 1989), p. 76.

meaning a wider range of individuals were liable to proceedings. Coupled with the introduction of new legislation in 1706 – and the simultaneous introduction of discharging a bankrupt from future liability and making fraudulent concealment a capital offence – the complexities of the operation of bankruptcy required the overarching authority of the court in order to complete or repair the system.[3] With a significant rise in the number of bankruptcies occurring at the outset of the Industrial Revolution, these issues continued in England, Europe, and America well into the modern period.[4]

Alexandra Shepard, Judith Spicksley, Emily Kadens, and Margot Finn have demonstrated the numerous ways in which the assessment of reputation was becoming unstable and difficult to quantify throughout this period.[5] How those involved in bankruptcy procedure attempted to look back and appraise the actions and words of those who failed has provided practical examples of the process of appraisal in action. The complexity of Chancery cases highlights the inability to effectively judge the personal, financial, and emotional demise of an individual prior to the initiation of a commission of bankruptcy. In contrast to the work of Craig Muldrew, who presents credit and debt recovery in too simplistic a manner, I have argued that the formal authority of Chancery was needed in order to maintain and uphold a complex system of debt recovery.[6] As such, the book has demonstrated the importance of utilising Chancery sources to gain a more nuanced understanding of early modern bankruptcy, as the complex and multifaceted nature of debt recovery has been overlooked, and misunderstood, in the historiography. This is especially true when it comes to a number of international edited collections – particularly the work of Beerbühl – who often assume that European bankruptcy was to be avoided at nearly any cost.[7]

3   4 & 5 Anne I c.4 (1706); 6 Anne c.22 (1707).
4   Julian Hoppit, *Risk and Failure in English Business 1700–1800* (Cambridge, 1987), p. 46.
5   Alexandra Shepard, *Accounting For Oneself: Worth, Status, and the Social Order in Early Modern England* (Oxford, 2015); Alexandra Shepard and Judith Spicksley, 'Worth, Age, and Social Status in Early Modern England', *EHR*, 64 (2011), pp. 493–530; Alexandra Shepard, 'The Worth of Married Women Witnesses in the English Church Courts, 1550–1730', in Cordelia Beattie and Matthew Frank Stevens (eds), *Married Women and the Law in Premodern Northwest Europe* (Woodbridge, 2013), pp. 191–212; Margot Finn, *The Character of Credit: Personal Debt in English Culture, 1740–1914* (Cambridge, 2003; Emily Kadens, 'Pre-Modern Credit Networks and the Limits of Reputation', *Iowa Law Review*, 100 (2015), pp. 2444–2451.
6   Craig Muldrew, *The Economy of Obligation: The Culture of Credit and Social Relations in Early Modern England* (Basingstoke, 1998).
7   Beerbühl, 'Introduction', pp. 9–26; Karl Gratzer and Dieter Stiefel (eds), *History of Insolvency and Bankruptcy From an International Perspective* (Huddinge, 2008); Thomas Max Safley (ed.), *The History of Bankruptcy: Economic, Social and Cultural Implications in Early Modern England* (London, 2013).

The structure of the book has focused on the different stages of proceedings in Chancery, which required a different ordering of language as the case progressed. As such, different sub-themes have emerged in each chapter which enhance our understanding of the multiple meanings attached to failure. The first chapter provided a detailed overview of the development of the equitable jurisdiction of Chancery and the way in which the court conducted its business. This chapter was necessary in order to analyse the roles and duties of officers of the court and legal experts, and the ways in which litigants, defendants, and witnesses interacted with the emerging Chancery bureaucracy of the period. In contrast to the work of Andy Wood, who has undertaken a multi-court analysis in order to 'cull' sources from multiple stages of proceeding, I have argued that scholars must pay close attention to the procedures of the court, and especially to the people and processes that went into creating the documents which have survived.[8] As the legal requirements of the court altered as the suit progressed, we can only understand how bankruptcy – or indeed any type of suit – was litigated by pausing and analysing each stage of proceeding in isolation. Legal evidence does not emerge from a vacuum, and by paying close attention to the ways in which these documents were created and used in the court, we can begin to analyse widely held attitudes, perceptions, and contemporary language surrounding failure. Promulgating such a methodology has wider ramifications for the use and classification of legal documents by historians, as scholars must be attuned to the types of documents they are using as evidence, and from which jurisdiction and phase of the legal process they have been taken.

Chapters two and three analysed the pleadings – bills of complaint and their subsequent answers – stage of proceeding. The second chapter built upon the seminal work of Julian Hoppit by moving away from a quantitative approach to bankruptcy, and instead focusing on the reasons why those involved in a commission of bankruptcy sought redress from the court.[9] Rather than approaching the language utilised in these documents as 'stories' or other such fictional accounts – as seen in the works of Laura Gowing, Margaret Hunt, Sara Butler, and others – constructed to be plausible or believable to the court, the chapter focused on the specific details provided in the surviving documentation.[10] Undertaking this approach provided a greater understanding

---

8   Andy Wood, 'Fear, Hatred and the Hidden Injuries of Class in Early Modern England', *Journal of Social History*, 39 (2006), pp. 803–826.

9   Hoppit, *Risk and Failure in English Business;* see also Louis Levinthal, 'The Early History of Bankruptcy Law', *University of Pennsylvania Law Review*, 66 (1918), pp. 223–250.

10   Laura Gowing, *Domestic Dangers: Women, Words and Sex in Early Modern London* (Oxford, 1998); Margaret R. Hunt, 'Wives and Marital "Rights" in the Court of Exchequer in the Early Eighteenth Century' in Paul Griffiths and Mark S. R. Jenner (eds), *Londinopolis: Essays in the Cultural and Social History of Early Modern London* (Manchester, 2000), pp.107–129, p.113; Sara M. Butler, 'The Law as a Weapon in Marital Disputes: Evidence

of bankruptcy procedure by illustrating particular instances, and specific examples, of how a commission of bankruptcy broke down. When we analyse the failure of a system, it often yields the most interesting information about the nature of that system.[11] With regard to bankruptcy procedure, there were three distinct disparities between the legal ideals established in legal commentary and parliamentary statutes and day-to-day procedure.

First, an informal version of discharge was occurring before 1706, demonstrating that legal scholars have overestimated the importance of this statutory creation.[12] Secondly, multiple suits were executed accusing individuals of manipulating the legal process for their own benefit and to the detriment of others, highlighting the ways in which bankruptcy procedure could be exploited. Finally, the chapter demonstrates how a bankrupt could initiate proceedings and take direct aim at their personal treatment. The combination of these discrepancies problematises the notion of delegated conscience and failure within the court, as well as the authority which has been given to statute law. We have seen instances of the bankrupt acting as a plaintiff – often alongside assignees – and of creditors being on either side of a dispute. In this manner, while the bankrupt had economically failed, and the debt-recovery process had legally failed, it was the defendants in these cases who were seen to have morally failed. Taken in isolation, individual cases grant us insights into the ways in which individuals dealt with specific issues and managed to circumnavigate problems within a commission of bankruptcy. Collectively, they demonstrate that the ideals established in the statutes did not always conform neatly to the practical realities of procedure. The picture we get is not one of a single failure, or even of a sole issue to be decided by the court, but complex and interconnected issues of debt recovery. Ultimately, the historiography of bankruptcy has not paid attention to the specificities of such discrepancies, and this chapter has added a further layer of complexity to failure, and the litigation of bankruptcy in Chancery.

The third chapter examined the body of cases in greater detail, and placed such an analysis within the existing scholarship surrounding circulating judgements, and assessments of trustworthiness and credibility, particularly in relation to the works of Muldrew and Shepard.[13] The chapter discussed the degree to

---

from the Late Medieval Court of Chancery, 1424–1529', *Journal of British Studies*, 43 (2004), pp. 291–316.

11   Karl N. Llewetjtren and E. Adamson Hoebel, *The Cheyenne Way: Conflict and Case Law in Primitive Jurisprudence* (Norman, 1941).

12   Charles Jordan Tabb, 'The Historical Evolution of the Bankruptcy Discharge', *American Bankruptcy Law Journal*, 65 (1991), pp. 325–371; John C. McCoid II, 'Discharge: The Most Important Development in Bankruptcy History', *American Bankruptcy Law Journal*, 70 (1996), pp. 163–193; Beerbühl, 'Introduction', pp. 9–26.

13   Muldrew, *The Economy of Obligation*; Shepard, *Accounting For Oneself*.

which commissions of bankruptcy, and knowledge of the individual actions of a bankrupt, were widely known to those within the trading community. Analysing the narrative in pleadings surrounding a dynamic series of events which led to an individual failure has shown how those involved in bankruptcy proceedings began to judge the demise of an individual. Pleadings provide a clear, chronological description of the path that the commission of bankruptcy had taken, and the specific details of how this procedure had failed. As such, the ambiguities surrounding certain aspects of the timing of failure became amplified in Chancery, as time itself became a contested concept. This chapter illuminates specific aspects regarding the temporality of trade, both in terms of individual actions influencing future dealings as well as an analysis of the past, and credible activities of debtors. Such analysis has greatly enhanced our understanding of bankruptcy procedure and the numerous characteristics of failure that were applied by those seeking to look back and appraise the actions and words of creditors and debtors, in a complex web of credit arrangements.

The fourth chapter turned to the evidentiary stage of proceeding, and foregrounds the important recent work of Frances Dolan, and the need to 'recast mediation as collaboration' and interpret depositions as a form of evidence in their entirety.[14] This is in stark contrast to the work of scholars who employ various technical manoeuvres in order to try to recover the 'authentic voice' of deponents.[15] As this stage of proceeding provided a platform for witnesses to describe, comment, and critique an individual failure, we can see the use and presentation of evaluative language within these documents. By analysing particular words and phrases, it is possible to highlight the narratives constructed in the discussion surrounding economic, physical, psychological, and emotional failure. The construction of emotional language, for example, was another way in which individuals judged reputation and creditworthiness, as emotional displays and descriptions became a by-product of unconscionable actions and immoral behaviour. By paying close attention to the procedure put in place to interrogate witnesses, this chapter showed that Chancery was not only a court that was utilised to maintain the bankruptcy process, but it was also an institution which helped to create such narratives. In doing so,

---

14   Frances E. Dolan, *True Relations: Reading, Literature, and Evidence in Seventeenth-Century England* (Philadelphia, 2013), p. 118.

15   Miranda Chaytor, 'Husband(ry): Narratives of Rape in the Seventeenth Century', *Gender and History*, 7 (1995), p. 401, n. 1; Garthine Walker, 'Rereading Rape and Sexual Violence in Early Modern England, *Gender and History*, 10 (1998), p. 20, n. 4; Garthine Walker, *Crime, Gender and Social Order in Early Modern England* (Cambridge, 2003), p. xv; Bernard Capp, *When Gossips Meet: Women, Family and Neighbourhood in Early Modern England* (Oxford, 2003), p. vii; Laura Gowing, *Common Bodies: Women, Touch and Power in Seventeenth-Century England* (New Haven, 2003), p. 210, n. 1; Gowing, *Domestic Dangers*, pp. 45–46.

we see how economic knowledge concerning failure was created, shared, and disseminated throughout the wider community. The words used to denote failure and decline mirrored wider conceptions of morality, credibility, and ethical behaviour, as bankrupts were depicted as descending from a respectable position to that of an untrustworthy individual. Witnesses maintained a degree of agency over the words and phrases they used, which highlights the multitude of ways in which those involved in a suit discussed and debated such failures. Ultimately, this chapter illuminates wider social norms and values concerning bankruptcy, as well as informing us of how similarities in the construction of narrative – such as between insanity, melancholy, emotional responses, and financial failure – were utilised in a legal setting.

Chapter five focused on the final stage of proceeding in Chancery by analysing a set of enrolled decrees. This chapter demonstrates that Chancery suits were rarely concluded in a definitive manner, as often the collection and distribution of the bankrupt's estate was ongoing. I argue that common notions – traditionally employed by social historians of the law – of attempting to establish a clearly identifiable winner and loser are misguided, and in many circumstances incorrect. Enrolled decrees cannot be expected to provide a form of narrative closure to a case, as very often the parties within a suit – i.e. defendants or plaintiffs – were not a homogenous group, and individuals received different outcomes and varying degrees of success. This analysis was taken a step further by assessing the concept of blame, as while the appropriation of costs to the unsuccessful party can give an indication of wrongdoing, often such parties were simply unable to prove that they held a right to equitable relief within the jurisdiction of Chancery. In contrast to the previous chapters which focused on the narrative of plaintiffs, defendants, and witnesses, this chapter analysed the narrative of the court in its decision-making processes. Credit networks within bankruptcy suits had already been formed, and were so complicated that they required the expertise and formal authority of the court to untangle such webs. Only by unravelling these complex, multifaceted, and vehemently debated cases can we reveal the specificities of how bankruptcy was litigated and decided within the court. As such, the way in which equitable principles of justice were applied in order to identify and establish failure demonstrates how the court mediated in social and economic disputes.

Overall, the book has not attempted to come to a complete and comprehensive understanding of pre-modern bankruptcy, which would require undertaking a multi-court analysis. Similarly, the aim was not to provide a historical analysis of the equitable jurisdiction of Chancery. Because of the statutory stipulations applied to bankruptcy, the discussion of failure was not representative of the broader debt-recovery process and networks of credit. The 'extreme' measure of bankruptcy procedure was limited to merchants and traders and involved vast amounts of credit and debt which was litigated in one central equity court.[16] While debtors were commonplace, only a fraction could enter a commission of bankruptcy.[17] Furthermore, the sample of cases was not representative of the wider operation of bankruptcy, as the vast majority would have been conducted and completed without the need of recourse to Chancery. While chapters two and three utilised a sample of 228 cases, there are a further 743 unexamined cases which are easily identifiable from an online search of The National Archives' database. There is certainly scope to undertake further work and attempt to come to a fuller understanding of early modern bankruptcy. For example, it would be possible to analyse the way in which judges and juries grappled with specific issues of fact in bankruptcy proceedings, or to follow cases into other equitable jurisdictions, such as the court of Exchequer. This holds the potential to see how and why those involved in a commission of bankruptcy sought the aid and assistance of other courts, which came to work alongside Chancery as its case load expanded. It would also be possible to analyse broader cases relating to debt-recovery to see if the same conceptions of failure were applied to the state of being indebted, and whether cultures of appraisal and narratives of obligation were discussed in the same manner.

The book has added to the growing scholarship on how women came to interact with the court as creditors, debtors, investors, plaintiffs, defendants, and perhaps most importantly, witnesses. As Tawny Paul has argued, 'while men faced failure as a consequence of a broad set of factors, for women, debt insecurity was a routine feature of life cycle status'.[18] When discussing marriage ideals, Katie Barclay and Emily Ireland have claimed that 'equity allowed actions that expressly altered, and sometimes contravened, the theoretical unity of husband and wife. Chancery was, therefore, a site where women could not only exercise agency within a patriarchal legal system but also reshape the contract of marriage'.[19] Chancery certainly provided a platform for women to provide detailed accounts of their own lives, and this book has provided a preliminary step towards a more nuanced interpretation of a gendered approach to debt recovery and failure, demonstrating how, when, and why certain women interacted with the process in Chancery.

But again, there are opportunities to expand our knowledge of how women came to be active agents in bankruptcy proceedings. Marjorie McIntosh has

---

16   Alexander Wakelam, *Credit and Debt in Eighteenth Century England: An Economic History of Debtors' Prisons* (London, 2020), p. 34.
17   W. J. Jones, 'The Foundations of English Bankruptcy: Statutes and Commissions in the Early Modern Period', *Transactions of the American Philosophical Society*, 69 (1979), p. 36.
18   Paul, *The Poverty of Disaster*, p. 79.
19   Katie Barclay and Emily Ireland, 'The Household as a Space of the Law in Eighteenth-Century England', *Law and History*, 7 (2020), pp. 98–126, p. 100.

shown how women were seen to be within the scope of the early statutes, and so could be declared bankrupts.[20] However, both reported cases and archival material relating to female bankrupts are exceptionally rare. Discussing cases involving married women bankrupts, Karen Pearlston has suggested that due to the limited number of suits, they cannot inform us 'about trends in terms of the development of bankruptcy, insolvency, or debtor-creditor relations in the narrow sense'.[21] Within my sample, only three cases identified women as bankrupts. *Pollard v Launder* (1725) was discussed in chapter three and centred around the perceived credibility of three siblings and co-partners, Henry, Mary, and Elizabeth Brunsell.[22] Similarly, in *Streare v Hume* (1750), the bankrupt Catherine Hume was described as a grocer and a mercer, and was accused of fraudulently executing a pretended bill of sale to her daughter.[23] *Pope v Pope* (1710–1711) was not discussed in the book, but concerned the will of Richard Pope, whose widow was described as a mercer and was declared a bankrupt after his death.[24] However, across all three suits, there was limited background information provided about their individual failures, meaning that a detailed analysis of these women was not possible. William Jones has stated that 'Women appear as bankrupts, occasionally as partners but more commonly as widows who had assumed a shop or trade'.[25] Ultimately, the book has provided a preliminary analysis of how women were more actively involved in bankruptcy proceedings than has previously been assumed, providing a platform for future research.

The methodology applied throughout will encourage economic, social, and cultural historians to reassess the manner in which they use legal documents, both within and outside Chancery. By analysing the narratives presented at the different stages of proceeding, it has been possible to highlight the multiple meanings of words and phrases used to describe and denote failure, providing further insights into the social and cultural meanings of debt collection. Both legal and cultural terms were utilised in order to appraise an individual's actions, worth, and credibility, demonstrating the criteria used by early modern people to judge what they deemed to be respectable and credible actions in relation to the repayment of debts on the one hand, and fraudulent and criminal activity on the other. Indeed, debt and debt recovery are undoubtedly one of

---

20   See Marjorie Mcintosh, 'The Benefits and Drawbacks of Femme Sole Status in England, 1300–1630', *Journal of British Studies*, 44 (2005), pp. 410–438.

21   Karen Pearlston, 'Married Women Bankrupts in the Age of Coverture', *Law and Social Inquiry*, 34 (2009), pp. 265–299, p. 295.

22   TNA, C11/291/33, 'Pollard v Launder' (1725).

23   TNA, C11/1637/23, 'Steare v Hume' (1750), Bill of Complaint.

24   TNA, C6/362/42, 'Pope v Pope' (1710–1711), Bill of Complaint.

25   Jones, 'The Foundations of English Bankruptcy', p. 24.

the great topics of contemporary society, and the book provides new evidence of the language of debt and failure inherited by modern British – and even Western – society.

During a contemporary period of 'small government', there is a public interest in the degree to which state institutions are seen to intervene in private individual finance to maintain the economy. While absconding and the inability to force debtors into making repayments remains a universal issue, there is a growing demand to better understand indebtedness, and to treat debtors amicably and with compassion. Jukka Kilpi's work on the morality of bankruptcy emerged out of the economic downturn of the 1980s and 1990s. Kilpi argues that the fundamental ethical principle of bankruptcy is that insolvents have essentially failed to keep their promise of repayment.[26] Since the global financial crisis of 2008, several scholar-activists have promulgated a radical reconceptualisation of the concepts of credit, debt, and the mechanisms for enforcing repayment. As the anthropologist David Graeber explained:

> the remarkable thing about the statement 'one has to pay one's debts' is that even according to standard economic theory, it isn't true. A lender is supposed to accept a certain degree of risk. If all loans, no matter how idiotic, were still retrievable – if there were no bankruptcy laws, for instance – the results would be disastrous. What reason would lenders have not to make a stupid loan? ... the reason it's so powerful is that it's not actually an economic statement: it's a moral judgement. After all, isn't paying one's debts what morality is supposed to be all about? Giving people what is due to them. Accepting one's responsibilities. Fulfilling one's obligations to others, just as one would expect them to fulfil their obligations to you. What could be a more obvious example of shirking one's responsibilities than reneging on a promise or refusing to pay a debt?[27]

While the early modern period rested upon a credit-based economy, modern nations are built upon consumer credit and deficit spending. But while debt has become a central issue in global politics, Graeber claims that 'nobody seems to know exactly what it is, or how to think about it'. The ambiguity surrounding the concept of indebtedness and a lack of consensus on how to utilise public and private institutions in order to enforce contracts provides the basis of its pervasive power.[28]

While the legislation and operation of bankruptcy in England became a model for American bankruptcy law, similar issues remain in both countries.[29]

---

26   Jukka Kilpi, *The Ethics of Bankruptcy* (London, 1998), p. i.
27   David Graeber, *Debt: The First 5,000 Years* (London, 2014), pp. 3–4.
28   Ibid., pp. 4–5.
29   Tabb, 'The Historical Evolution of the Bankruptcy Discharge', pp. 325–371.

Despite the 1787 constitution charging the government with creating a federal bankruptcy law, America took a remarkably long time to establish a law of bankruptcy, as all attempts were rejected on 'moral grounds' until 1898.[30] Indeed, while it is still not a crime to be in debt – and official debtors' prisons have long been outlawed – there has been a resurgence in the incarceration of individuals for failures to pay debts, most commonly in the form of court fines.[31] Despite bankruptcy laws being created as a way to stabilise the economy, enforce contracts, and return entrepreneurial spirit to the marketplace, it is possible to see a society in which poverty is increasingly becoming criminalised. Andrew Ross has argued that as bankruptcy laws still overwhelmingly favour creditors, there should be a stronger appetite to cancel prevailing and unmanageable debts. If this is not possible, then Ross claims that there is a need to foreground public debate and increase the involvement of ordinary people in discussions surrounding the moral landscape of debt recovery: 'though we may be more and more aware of the irresponsibility and fraud of big creditors who won't pay their own debts, and who offload all their risky loans to others, we still accept that it is immoral to fail to repay our debts to them'.[32] While debt and morality remain intricately linked, the ways in which such judgements are made in relation to social and cultural norms – both in the present and the past – remain unclear and open to interpretation.

Analysing the numerous meanings and conceptualisations of failure has shown how the complexities of bankruptcy procedure upset the flow of knowledge and circulating judgements about others in the trading environment. Failure was described and debated not just in economic terms, but came to rely on a combination of social, community, and religious values which led to individual bankruptcies. Ultimately, analysing complex bankruptcy cases has illuminated contemporary understandings of what was considered right and wrong, honourable and deceitful, and criminal and compassionate within the moral landscape of debt recovery during the seventeenth and eighteenth centuries. Highlighting how a range of individuals from the past made use of

30   Graeber, *Debt*, p. 16.
31   Ibid., p. 17; Andrew Ross, *Creditocracy: And the Case for Debt Refusal* (London, 2013), pp. 91–92; American Civil Liberties Union, 'In For A Penny: The Rise of America's New Debtors' Prisons' (2010), <https://www.aclu.org/wp-content/uploads/legal-documents/InForAPenny_web.pdf> (accessed 03/03/2024); In England, the *Guardian* newspaper has published several articles on the increase of homeless individuals being fined, given criminal convictions, and imprisoned under Vagrancy Acts or through local authorities imposing Public Spaces Protection Orders; for indicative examples, see Patrick Greenfield and Sarah Marsh 'Hundreds of homeless people fined and imprisoned in England and Wales', The Guardian, 20 May 2018; Tom Wall, 'Thousands of Homeless People Arrested Under Archaic Vagrancy Act', The Guardian, 2 April 2023.
32   Ross, *Creditocracy*, p. 22.

Chancery in an attempt to overcome and repair misfortunes has provided a platform to demonstrate how the effective – or otherwise – navigation of legal processes can provide lessons on how to deal compassionately with debtors in modern society, removing the stigma surrounding indebtedness.

Appendix One: Sample of Cases for Each Chapter

Chapter	Number of Cases	Series
One	-	
Two	228	C5–C12
Three	228	C5–C12
Four	54	C11, C12, C21, C22, C128
Five	43	C78, C79
Total:	325	13

Appendix Two: Table of Pleadings

Year	Number of Cases	Bills of Complaint	Copy Bills	Answers
1674–1699	46	18	12	65
1700	7	3	2	8
1705	5	4	1	6
1710	9	7		10
1715	12	12		13
1720	28	28		30
1725	24	22		24
1730	27	24		41
1735	25	27		42
1740	17	13		23
1745	16	13		20
1750	12	13		11
Total	228	184	15	293

Bibliography

Unprinted Primary Sources

The National Archives, Kew

C6: 385/80, 398/95, 369/77, 385/45, 402/51, 419/88, 404/40, 416/12, 401/61, 409/19, 407/28, 383/6, 373/10, 416/14, 378/46, 327/24, 388/51, 381/30, 388/52, 405/57, 380/58, 394/37, 407/32, 382/69, 381/15, 381/42, 415/77, 384/70, 373/38, 313/16, 387/74, 361/42, 419/54, 411/26, 393/8, 378/53, 395/41, 400/29, 400/38, 378/62, 318/30, 402/70, 376/24, 391/16, 376/19, 417/69, 387/45, 365/48, 383/73, 417/68, 380/74, 407/80, 412/17, 379/39, 378/47, 384/116, 377/36, 411/44, 410/41, 368/90, 418/6, 412/74, 362/42, 382/21, 374/46, 360/26

C7: 602/30

C8: 456/39

C11: 1347/21, 2792/30, 381/37, 2346/20, 1166/26, 664/30, 1703/5, 1386/23, 1386/48, 2631/26, 1790/18, 261/56, 2215/13, 465/14, 717/4, 1713/48, 34/35, 31/29, 2284/114, 2646/21, 853/62, 703/34, 1310/26, 34/37, 1727/12, 2369/72, 1710/1, 1420/31, 844/17, 36/30, 1418/24, 250/14, 1992/19, 1752/22, 1991/38, 2370/46, 38/15, 2650/28, 1194/33, 2575/1, 1451/15, 1450/12, 291/33, 1240/30, 1451/10, 270/22, 314/7, 1761/14, 776/70, 2730/158, 2731/55, 2287/48, 62/3, 2386/10, 1760/31, 2173/13, 1791/26, 770/20, 2615/15, 2282/27, 1451/21, 2729/147, 1791/24, 1142/11, 2177/45, 1485/10, 2037/17, 1272/35, 365/89, 82/24, 1823/26, 1695/3, 313/16, 2034/33, 500/8, 1488/35, 1489/7, 2427/32, 2426/18, 2426/38, 1486/28, 1931/30, 2712/2, 1318/33, 1485/5, 1488/41, 2032/16, 2736/52, 696/28, 2279/4, 2585/12, 2706/31, 2445/22, 787/38, 1876/28, 858/49, 521/10, 520/51, 2318/33, 2318/32, 1523/19, 2785/28, 520/13, 263/27, 618/21, 2445/40, 948/1, 1044/14, 2693/23, 1047/34, 617/46, 1259/1, 1885/10, 1524/18, 2739/13, 2182/39, 1885/12, 1281/30, 1525/26, 1522/11, 1038/24, 2300/22, 954/17, 1061/21, 1254/28, 947/27, 2465/25, 2082/26, 2467/49, 2293/24, 142/1, 807/16, 1884/8, 2465/28, 541/15, 382/70, 1061/3, 143/2, 1829/16, 813/6, 1559/44, 1939/6, 1599/1, 560/8, 1884/39, 1609/14, 1295/1, 1884/10, 819/11, 2489/4, 812/19, 380/5, 873/34, 2336/30, 561/23, 1615/33, 2103/1, 560/5, 2103/30, 1876/28, 1637/23, 587/2, 1643/27, 1642/30,

1645/9, 1641/30, 1636/17, 1640/30, 1642/22, 1641/23, 2508/6, 2197/33, 549/27, 552/25, 555/35, 899/7, 2763/35, 877/7, 2762/22, 2769/14, 2302/19, 2774/6, 2769/5, 897/3, 1368/4, 1931/30, 412/20, 1928/12, 2315/10, 938/7, 1355/16, 1931/3, 1934/7, 1931/5, 1876/28, 948/1, 2318/32, 2785/28, 2318/33, 1929/21, 1934/9, 947/27, 954/17, 2790/23, 2790/24, 2323/13, 1939/25, 2336/30, 1939/6, 2331/17, 2791/3, 1168/23, 1353/21, 2331/23, 798/15, 549/21

C12:   1122/39, 1115/5

C22:   900/3, 78/27, 1048/22, 599/49, 27/16, 27/7, 27/2, 369/13, 370/17, 929/1, 941/7, 655/52, 78/27, 221/33, 615/13, 219/28

C31:   103, 104, 105

C33:   375, 377, 379, 385, 383, 387, 389, 391

C38:   504

C78:   758, 910, 920, 1991, 916, 793, 2062, 957, 784, 2011, 1485, 1653, 1484, 1428, 1719, 1346, 1658, 1584, 1396, 1591, 1402, 1795, 1701, 1724, 1812, 1742, 1816, 1811, 1814, 2075, 1747, 2065, 1761, 1797, 2067, 1833, 1837, 1814

C79:   78, 80, 15, 63

C103:   9

C104:   263, 78, 80, 79, 77, 201, 253, 221, 264, 249, 215, 226, 206, 241, 208, 207

C105:   18

C107:   112, 23, 197, 211, 201, 172, 32

C108:   316

C110:   185

C111:   207, 202, 166

C113:   106

C120:   854

C124:   874/23, 1020/1, 321/1

C128:   24, 15, 13, 10

C276:   6

Printed Primary Sources

A Collection of Interrogatories for the Examination of Witnesses in Courts of Equity. As Settled by the Most Eminent Counsel (Dublin, 1791).

A Succinct Digest of the Laws Relating to Bankrupts (Dublin, 1791).

A True Narrative of that Grand Jesuite Father Andrews (London, 1679).

Animadversions On Capt. Wilkinson's Information (London, 1682).

Animadversions Upon the Present Laws of England (London, 1750).

Antinomus, Nomius, *Observations on the State of Bankrupts: Under the Present Laws. In a letter to a Member of Parliament* (London, 1760).

Baxter, Richard, *The Signs and Causes of Melancholy* (London, 1716, originally 1670).

Blackstone, William, *Commentaries on the Laws of England,* (4 vols, London, 1857).

Burrill, Alexander, *A Law Dictionary and Glossary* (New York, 1859).

Carr, William, *Pluto Furens and Vinctus, or, The Raging Devil Bound a Modern Farse* (Amsterdam, 1669).

Christian, Edward, *The Origin, Progress, and Present Practice of the Bankrupt Law, Both in England and Ireland* (London, 1818).

Considerations Upon Commissions of Bankrupts (London, 1727).

Cook, Aurelian, *Titus Britannicus: An Essay of History Royal: In the Life and Reign of His Late Sacred Majesty, Charles II* (London, 1685).

Davies, Thomas, *The Laws Relating to Bankrupts* (London, 1744).

Defoe, Daniel, *The Complete English Tradesman* (London, 1726).

Donaldson, James, *The Undoubted Art of Thriving* (Edinburgh, 1700).

Dornford, Josiah, *Seven Letters to the Lords and Commons of Great Britain, Upon the Impolicy, Inhumanity, and Injustice, of Our Present Mode of Arresting the Bodies of Debtors* (London, 1786).

Ellesby, James, *A Caution Against Ill Company* (London, 1705).

England and Wales Court of Chancery, *A Collection of Such of the Orders Heretofore Used in Chauncery* (London, 1649).

Finch, Heneage, Earl of Nottingham, *Manual of Chancery Practice*, and *Prolegomena of Chancery and Equity*, D. E. C. Yale (ed.) (Cambridge: Cambridge University Press, 1965).

Fitzsimmonds, Joshua, *Free and Candid Disquisitions, On the Nature and Execution of the Laws of England, Both in Civil and Criminal Affairs* (London, 1751).

Fuller, Thomas ed., *Gnomologia: Adagies and Proverbs; Wise Sentences and Witty Sayings, Ancient and Modern, Foreign and British* (London, 1732).

Gent, Thomas, *Divine Justice and Mercy Displayed* (York, 1772).

Goodinge, Thomas, *The Law Against Bankrupts* (London, 1726).

Goodwin, Phillip, *Dies Dominicus Redivivus; OR; The Lords Day Enlivened* (London, 1654).

Green, Edward, *The Spirit of the Bankrupt Laws Wherein are Principally Considered, the Authority and Power of the Commissioners* (London, 1767).

Hargrave, Francis ed., *A Collection of Tracts Relative to the Law of England* (London, 1787).

Henry, Matthew, *An Exposition on the Old and New Testament* (London, 1737).

London Evening Post, 14 December 1736.

Maddock, Henry, *A Treatise on the Principles and Practice of the Court of Chancery* (London, 1837).

Malynes, Gerard, Consuetudo, *Vel, Lex Mercatoria: Or, The Ancient Law-Merchant* (London, 1686).

Montagu, B., *A Summary of the Law of Composition with Creditors* (London, 1823).

Observations on the Dilatory and Expensive Proceedings in the Court of Chancery (London, 1701).

Parkes, Joseph, *A History of the Court of Chancery* (London, 1828).

Pepys, Samuel, *The Diary of Samuel Pepys*, Henry B. Wheatley (ed.) (London, 1904).

Percy, James, *This Book Makes Appear the Claim, Pedigree and Proceedings of James Percy Now Claimant to the Earldom of Northumberland* (London, 1680).

Philostratus, Philodemius, *The Seasonable Observations on a Late Book Intitvled A System of the Law* (London, 1654).

Pollock, Frederick (ed.), *The Table Talk of John Selden* (London, 1927).

Reading, John, *A Gvide to the Holy City* (Oxford, 1651).

Rowe, Nicholas, *Jane Shore: A Tragedy, In Five Acts* (1714).

Rule, Gilbert, *A Vindication of the Presbyterians of Scotland* (London, 1692).

Smith, Humphry, *The Divine Authority, and Usefulness, of Ecclesiastical Censures, Asserted* (Exeter, 1708).

Spedding, J., Ellis, R. L. and Heath, D. D., eds, *The Works of Francis Bacon*, 15 volumes (New York: Garrett, 1968).

Swift, Jonathan, *A Tale of a Tub*, 12th edn (Edinburgh, 1750).

The Case of the Sworn Clerks, and Waiting Clerks of the Six Clerks Office (London, 1749?).

The Country-Mans Counsellour, Or, Every Man Made His Own Lawyer (London, 1682).

The Cry of Blood; Or, The Horrid Sin of Murther Display'd (1692).

The Law For and Against Bankrupts (York, 1743).

The Practical Register in Chancery (London, 1714).

To the Honourable House of Commons, Assembled in Parliament, the Humble Petition of Divers Persons of Several Callings Who Keep the Markets in London in Behalf of Themselves and Hundreds More (London?, 1689).

Turner, Samuel, *Costs and Present Practice of the Court of Chancery* (London, 1795).

Vernon, John *The Compleat Comptinghouse* (London, 1678).

Watts, Isaac, *Discourses of the Love of God* (London, 1729).

West, William, *The Second Part of Symboleography* (London, 1627).

Wood, Anthony, *Athenae Oxonienses an Exact History of all the Writers and Bishops who have had their Education in the Most Ancient and Famous University of Oxford* (London, 1692).

Secondary Sources

Allen, C. K., *Law in the Making* (Oxford, 1958).

Andrew, Donna T. and McGowen, Randall, *The Perreaus and Mrs. Rudd: Forgery and Betrayal in Eighteenth-Century London* (Berkeley, 2001).

Andrews, Jonathan, 'The (un)Dress of the Mad Poor in England, c.1650–1850. Part I', *History of Psychiatry*, 18 (2007), pp. 5–24.

– – 'The (un)Dress of the Mad Poor in England, c.1650–1850. Part II', *History of Psychiatry*, 18 (2007), pp. 131–115.

Andrews, Jonathan and Scull, Andrew, *Customers and Patrons of the Mad-Trade: The Management of Lunacy in Eighteenth-Century London* (Berkeley, 2002).

Anstey, Peter R. (ed.), *The Idea of Principles in Early Modern Thought: Interdisciplinary Perspectives* (London, 2017).

Antunes, Cátia and Miranda, Susana Münch, 'Going Bust: Some Reflections on Colonial Bankruptcies', *Itinerario*, 43 (2019), pp. 47–62.

Appleby, Joyce, *Economic Thought and Ideology in Seventeenth-Century England* (New Jersey, 1978).

Bailey, Joanne, 'Voices in Court: Lawyers' or Litigants'?', *Historical Research*, 74 (2001), pp. 392–408.

Bailey, Merridee L., '"Most Hevynesse and Sorowe": The Presence of Emotions in the Late Medieval and Early Modern Court of Chancery', *LHR*, 37 (2019), pp. 1–28.

Bailey, Merridee and Knight, Kimberley-Joy, 'Writing Histories of Law and Emotion', *The Journal of Legal History*, 38 (2017), pp. 117–129.

Bailey, Victor, 'Bibliographical Essay: Crime, Criminal Justice and Authority in England', *Bulletin of the Society for the Study of Labour History*, 40 (1980), pp. 36–46.

Baker, J. H., *An Introduction to English Legal History* (Oxford, 2019).

– –, 'The Common Lawyers and the Chancery: 1616', *Irish Jurist*, 4 (1969), pp. 368–392.

– – (ed.), *The Oxford History of the Laws of England* (Oxford, 2010).

– – 'Why the History of English Law Has Not Been Finished', *Cambridge Law Journal*, 59 (2000), pp. 62–84.

Barbour, Willard, 'Some Aspects of Fifteenth-Century Chancery', *Harvard Law Review*, 31 (1918), pp. 834–859.

Barclay, Katie, *Men on Trial: Performing Emotion, Embodiment and Identity in Ireland, 1800–1845* (Manchester, 2018).

Barclay, Katie and Ireland, Emily, 'The Household as a Space of the Law in Eighteenth-Century England', *Law and History*, 7 (2020), pp. 98–126.

Barclay, Katie and Milka, Amy (eds), *Cultural Histories of Law, Media and Emotion* (New York, 2022).

Barker, Hannah, *Family and Business During the Industrial Revolution* (Oxford, 2017).

Barthes, Roland, 'The Reality Effect' reprinted in *The Rustle of Language*, trans. Richard Howard (Oxford: Basil Blackwell, 1986, originally 1968).

Beattie, Cordelia, 'A Piece of the Puzzle: Women and the Law as Viewed from the Late Medieval Court of Chancery', *Journal of British Studies*, 58 (2019), pp. 751–767.

Beattie, Cordelia and Stevens, Matthew Frank (eds), *Married Women and the Law in Premodern Northwest Europe* (Woodbridge, 2013).

Beattie, J. M., *Crime and the Courts in England 1660–1800* (Oxford, 1986).

Beier, A. L., Cannadine, David, and Rosenheim, James (eds), *The First Modern Society: Essays in English History in Honour of Lawrence Stone* (Cambridge, 1989).

Bellany, Alastair and Cogswell, Thomas, *The Murder of King James I* (New Haven, 2015).

Bennett, W. Lance and Feldman, Martha S., *Reconstructing Reality in the Courtroom* (London, 1981).

Ben-Porath, Yoram, 'The F-Connection: Families, Friends, and Firms and the Organization of Exchange', *Population and Development Review*, 6 (1980), pp. 1–30.

Beresford, M. W., 'The Decree Rolls of Chancery as a Source for Economic History, 1547–c. 1700', *EHR*, 32 (1979), pp. 1–10.

Biancalana, Joseph, 'Testamentary Cases in Fifteenth-Century Chancery', *LHR*, 76 (2008), pp. 283–306.

Birks, Michael, 'The Perfecting of Orders in Chancery', *Cambridge Law Journal*, 13 (1955), pp. 101–112.

Birks, Peter (ed.), *The Life of the Law: Proceedings of the Tenth British Legal History Conference, Oxford 1991* (London, 1993).

Bossy, John (ed.), *Disputes and Settlements: Law and Human Relations in the West* (Cambridge, 1983).

Bottomley, Sean, 'Patent Cases in the Court of Chancery, 1714–58', *The Journal of Legal History*, 35 (2014), pp. 27–43.

Bound, Fay, '"An Angry and Malicious Mind"? Narratives of Slander at the Church Courts of York, c.1660–c.1760', *History Workshop Journal*, 56 (2003), pp. 59–77.

Bourke, Joanna, 'Fear and Anxiety: Writing About Emotion in Modern History', *History Workshop Journal*, 55 (2003), pp. 111–133.

Braddick, Michael J., and Withington, Phil (eds), *Popular Culture and Political Agency in Early Modern England and Ireland: Essays in Honour of John Walter* (Woodbridge, 2017).

Brealey, Peter, 'The Charitable Corporation for the Relief of Industrious Poor: Philanthropy, Profit and Sleaze in London, 1707–1733', *History*, 98 (2013), pp. 708–729.

Brewer, John, *The Sinews of Power: War, Money and the English State, 1688–1783* (London, 1989).

Brewer, John and Hellmuth, Eckhart (eds), *Rethinking Leviathan: The Eighteenth-Century State in Britain and Germany* (Oxford, 1999).

Brooks, Christopher W., *Law, Politics and Society in Early Modern England* (Cambridge, 2008).

– – *Lawyers, Litigation and English Society Since 1450* (London, 1998).

– – *Pettyfoggers and Vipers of the Commonwealth: The 'Lower Branch' of the Legal Profession in Early Modern England* (Cambridge, 1986).

Brooks, Christopher and Lobban Michael (eds), *Communities and Courts in Britain, 1150–1900* (London, 1997).

Broomhall, Susan (ed.), *Authority, Gender and Emotions in Late Medieval and Early Modern England* (Basingstoke, 2015).

– – *Early Modern Emotions: An Introduction* (London, 2017).

Brown, R. L., 'The Minters of Wapping: The History of a Debtors' Sanctuary in Eighteenth century East London', *East London Papers*, 14 (1972), pp. 77–86.

Burke, Peter and Porter Roy (eds), *The Social History of Language* (Cambridge, 1987).

Burley, K. H., 'An Essex Clothier of the Eighteenth Century', *EHR*, 11 (1958), pp. 289–301.

Bush, Jonathan A. and Wijffels, Alain Alexandre (eds), *Learning the Law: Teaching and the Transmission of Law in England, 1150–1900* (London, 1999).

Butler, Sara M., 'The Law as a Weapon in Marital Disputes: Evidence from the Late Medieval Court of Chancery, 1424–1529', *Journal of British Studies*, 43 (2004), pp. 291–316.

Capern, Amanda, 'Maternity and Justice in the Early Modern English Court of Chancery', *Journal of British Studies*, 58 (2019), pp. 701–716.

Capern, Amanda, McDonagh, Briony, and Aston, Jennifer (eds), *Women and the Land 1500–1900* (Woodbridge, 2019).

Capp, Bernard, *When Gossips Meet: Women, Family and Neighbourhood in Early Modern England* (Oxford, 2003).

Carlos Ann M., and Neal, Larry, 'Women Investors in Early Capital Markets, 1720–1725', *Financial History Review*, 11 (2004), pp. 197–224.

Carlos, Ann M., Kosack, Edward, and Penarrieta, Luis Castro, 'Bankruptcy Discharge and the Emergence of Debtor Rights in Eighteenth Century England', *Enterprise & Society*, 20 (2019), pp. 475–506.

Carne, W. L., 'A Sketch of the History of the High Court of Chancery From the Chancellorship of Wolsey to that of Lord Nottingham', *The Virginia Law Register*, 13 (1927), pp. 391–421.

Chadwick, Mary, 'Relationality, Community and Collaboration in Seventeenth-Century Chancery Court Records', *The Seventeenth Century*, 38 (2023), pp. 833–852.

Chaytor, Miranda, 'Husband(ry): Narratives of Rape in the Seventeenth Century', *Gender and History*, 7 (1995), pp. 378–407.

Churches, Christine, 'Business at Law: Retrieving Commercial Disputes From Eighteenth-Century Chancery', *The Historical Journal*, 43 (2000), pp. 937–954.

– – '"Equity Against a Purchaser Shall Not Be": A Seventeenth-Century Case Study in Landholding and Indebtedness', *Parergon*, 11 (1993), pp. 69–87.

– – 'False Friends, Spiteful Enemies: A Community at Law in Early Modern England', *Historical Research*, 71 (1998), pp. 52–74.

– – '"The Most Unconvincing Testimony": The Genesis and the Historical Usefulness of the Country Depositions in Chancery', *The Seventeenth Century*, 11 (1996), pp. 209–227.

Cioni, Maria L., *Women and the Law in Elizabethan England With Particular Reference to the Court of Chancery*, PhD Thesis (London, 1985, Originally 1974).

Clayton, Mary, 'The Wealth of Riches to be Found in the Court of Chancery: The Equity Pleadings Database', *Archives: The Journal of the British Records Association*, 28 (2003), pp. 25–31.

Cockburn, J. S., *A History of English Assizes 1558–1714* (Cambridge, 1974).

– – ed., *Crime in England 1550–1800* (London, 1977).

Cohen, Jay, 'The History of Imprisonment for Debt and its Relation to the Development of Discharge in Bankruptcy', *The Journal of Legal History*, 3 (1982), pp. 153–171.

Collins, Aidan, 'Bankrupt Traders in the Court of Chancery, 1674–1750', *Eighteenth-Century Studies*, 55 (2021), pp. 65–82.

– – 'Narratives of Bankruptcy, Failure, and Decline in the Court of Chancery, 1678–1750', *Cultural and Social History*, 19 (2022), pp. 1–17.

– – 'The Interconnected Nature of Family Indebtedness: The Halliday Family of Frome, Somerset (1733–1752)', *Enterprise and Society* (open access online, 2023), pp. 1–27.

Cordes, Albrecht and Beerbühl, Margrit Schulte (eds), *Dealing With Economic Failure: Between Norm and Practice (15th to 21st Century)* (New York, 2016).

Corens, Liesbeth, Peters, Kate and Walsham, Alexandra (eds), *Archives and Information in the Early Modern World* (Oxford, 2018).

Davis, Natalie Zemon, *Fiction in the Archives: Pardon Tales and Their Tellers in Sixteenth-Century France* (Stanford, 1987).

Dickson, Peter, *The Financial Revolution in England: A Study in the Development of Public Credit, 1688–1756* (London, 1967).

Ditz, Toby, 'Shipwrecked; or, Masculinity Imperiled: Mercantile Representations of Failure and the Gendered Self in Eighteenth-Century Philadelphia', *The Journal of American History* 81 (1994), pp. 51–80.

Dolan, Frances E., *Dangerous Familiars: Representations of Domestic Crime in England 1550–1700* (London, 1994).

– – *True Relations: Reading, Literature, and Evidence in Seventeenth-Century England* (Philadelphia, 2013).

Donato, Flora Di, *The Analysis of Legal Cases: A Narrative Approach* (London, 2020).

Downes, Stephanie, Holloway, Sally and Randles, Sarah (eds), *Feeling Things: Objects and Emotions Through History* (Oxford, 2018).

Duffy, Ian P. H., *Bankruptcy and Insolvency in London During the Industrial Revolution* (London, 1985).

– – 'English Bankrupts, 1571–1861', *The American Journal of Legal History*, 24 (1980), pp. 283–305.

Dyer, Christopher and Richardson, Catherine (eds), *William Dugdale, Historian, 1605–1686: His life, His Writings and His County* (Woodbridge, 2009).

Dyson, Matthew and Ibbetson, David (eds), *Law and Legal Process: Substantive Law and Procedure in English Legal History* (Cambridge, 2013).

Earle, Peter, *Sailors: English Merchant Seamen 1650–1775* (London, 1998).

– – *The Making of the English Middle Class: Business, Society and Family Life in London, 1660–1730* (London, 1989).

Erickson, Amy, 'Coverture and Capitalism', *History Workshop Journal*, 59 (2005), pp. 1–16.

– – 'Married Women's Occupations in Eighteenth-Century London', *Continuity and Change*, 23 (2008), pp. 267–307.

– – *Women and Property in Early Modern England* (London, 1993).

Fianu, Kouky and Guth, DeLloyd J. (eds), *Écrit et Pouvoir dans les Chancelleries Médiévales: Espace Français, Espace Anglais* (Louvain-La-Neuve, 1997).

Finn, Margot, *The Character of Credit: Personal Debt in English Culture, 1740–1914* (Cambridge, 2003).

Fisher, John F., 'Chancery and the Emergence of Standard Written English in the Fifteenth Century', *Speculum: A Journal of Medieval Studies*, 52 (1977), pp. 870–899.

Fletcher, Ian F., *The Law of Insolvency* (London, 2017).

Fontaine, Laurence, *The Moral Economy: Poverty, Credit, And Trust In Early Modern Europe* (Cambridge, 2014).

Forestier, Albane, 'Risk, Kinship and Personal Relationships in Late Eighteenth-Century West Indian Trade: The Commercial Network of Tobin & Pinney', *Business History*, 52 (2010), pp. 912–931.

Foster, David, 'Construction and Execution of Trusts in Chancery, c.1660–1750', *The Journal of Legal History*, 40 (2019), pp. 270–297.

Fox, Adam (ed.), *The Experience of Authority in Early Modern England* (Basingstoke, 1996).

Francis, Clinton W., 'Practice, Strategy, and Institution: Debt Collection in the English Common-Law Courts, 1740–1840', *Northwestern University Law Review*, 80 (1986), pp. 807–955.

French, Henry, *The Middling Sort of People in Provincial England 1600–1750* (Oxford: Oxford University Press, 2007).

French, Henry and Barry, Jonathan, *Identity and Agency in England, 1500–1800* (Basingstoke, 2004).

Friedman, Lawrence M. and Niemira, Thadeus F., 'The Concept of the "Trader" in Early Bankruptcy Law', *Saint Louis University Law Journal*, 5 (1958), pp. 223–249.

Gaskill, Malcolm, 'Reporting Murder: Fiction in the Archives in Early Modern England', *Social History*, 23 (1998), pp. 1–30.

Gatrell, V. A. C., Lenman, Bruce and Parker, Geoffrey (eds), *Crime and the Law: The Social History of Crime in Western Europe Since 1500* (London, 1980).

Gauci, Perry, *The Politics of Trade: The Overseas Merchant in State and Society, 1660–1720* (Oxford, 2001).

Getzler, Joshua, 'Chancery Reform and Law Reform', *LHR*, 22 (2004), pp. 601–608.

Ginzburg, Carlo, *The Cheese and the Worms: The Cosmos of a Sixteenth-Century Miller*, trans. John and Anne Tedeschi (London, 1976).

Glennie, Paul and Thrift, Nigel, 'Reworking E. P. Thompson's "Time, Work-Discipline and Industrial Capitalism"', *Time and Society*, 5 (1996), pp. 275–300.

– – *Shaping the Day: A History of Timekeeping in England and Wales 1300–1800* (Oxford, 2009).

Gómez-Arostegui, H. Tomás, 'What History Teaches Us About Copyright Injunctions and the Inadequate-Remedy-at-Law Requirement', *Southern California Law Review*, 81 (2008), pp. 1197–1280.

Goodich, Michael (ed.), *Voices From the Bench: the Narratives of Lesser Folk in Medieval Trials* (Basingstoke, 2006).

Gordon, W. M. and Fergus, T. D. (eds), *Legal History in the Making: Proceedings of the Ninth British Legal History Conference*, Glasgow 1989 (London, 1991).

Gowing, Laura, *Common Bodies: Women, Touch and Power in Seventeenth-Century England* (New Haven, 2003).

– – *Domestic Dangers: Women, Words and Sex in Early Modern London* (Oxford, 1998).

– – 'Girls on Forms: Apprenticing Young Women in Seventeenth-Century London', *Journal of British Studies*, 55 (2016), pp. 447–473.

Gowland, Angus, 'The Problem of Early Modern Melancholy', *Past and Present*, 191 (2006), pp. 77–120.

Graeber, David, *Debt: The First 5,000 Years* (London, 2014).

Graham, Aaron and Walsh, Patrick (eds), *The British Fiscal-Military States, 1660–c.1783.* (London, 2016).

Gratzer, Karl and Stiefel, Dieter (eds), *History of Insolvency and Bankruptcy From an International Perspective* (Huddinge, 2008).

Griffin, Carl J. and McDonagh, Briony (eds), *Remembering Protest in Britain Since 1500: Memory, Materiality and the Landscape* (Cham, 2018).

Griffiths, Paul and Jenner, Mark S. R. (eds), *Londinopolis: Essays in the Cultural and Social History of Early Modern London* (Manchester, 2000).

Hadfield, Andrew and Healy, Simon, 'Edmund Spenser and Chancery in 1597', *Law and Humanities*, 6 (2012), pp. 57–64.

Haggerty, Sheryllynne, *Merely for Money'? Business Culture in the British Atlantic 1750–1815* (Liverpool, 2012).

– – *The British-Atlantic Trading Community 1760–1810: Men, Women, and the Distribution of Goods* (Leiden, 2006).

– – '"You Promise Well and Perform as Badly:" The Failure of the "Implicit Contract of Family" in the Scottish Atlantic', *International Journal of Maritime History*, 23 (2011), pp. 267–282.

Hamilton, Douglas, 'Local Connections, Global Ambitions: Creating a Transoceanic Network in the Eighteenth-Century British Atlantic Empire', *International Journal of Maritime History*, 23 (2011), pp. 283–300.

Hamilton, Marsha, 'Commerce around the Edges: Atlantic Trade Networks among Boston's Scottish Merchants', *International Journal of Maritime History*, 23 (2011), pp. 301–326.

Hancock, David, 'The Trouble with Networks; Managing the Scots' Early Modern Madeira Trade', *Business History Review* 79 (2005), pp. 467–491.

Haskett, Timothy S., 'The Medieval English Court of Chancery', *LHR*, 14 (1996), pp. 245–313.

Haude, Sigrun and Zook, Melinda S. (eds), *Challenging Orthodoxies: The Social and Cultural Worlds of Early Modern Women* (Surrey, 2014).

Hedlund, Richard, 'The Theological Foundations of Equity's Conscience', *Oxford Journal of Law and Religion*, 4 (2015), pp. 119–140.

Helmholz, R. H., *The Ius Commune in England: Four Studies* (Oxford, 2001).

Henderson, Edith G., *Foundations of English Administrative Law: Certiorari and Mandamus in the Seventeenth Century* (Cambridge, 1963).

– – 'Legal Rights to Land in the Early Chancery', *The American Journal of Legal History*, 26 (1982), pp. 97–122.

Herrup, Cynthia B., *A House in Gross Disorder: Sex, Law and the 2nd Earl of Castlehaven* (Oxford, 1999).

Hertzler, James R., 'The Abuse and Outlawing of Sanctuary for Debt in Seventeenth-Century England', *The Historical Journal*, 14 (1971), pp. 467–477.

Heward, Edmund, *Masters in Ordinary* (Chichester, 1990).

Hindle, Steve, 'Below Stairs at Arbury Hall: Sir Richard Newdigate and his Household Staff, c.1670–1710', *Historical Research*, 85 (2012), pp. 71–88.

Hindle, Steve, Shepard, Alexandra and Walter, John (eds), *Remaking Social History: Social Relations and Social Change in Early Modern England* (Woodbridge, 2013).

Hitchcock, Tim, *Down and Out in Eighteenth-Century London* (London, 2004).

Hofri-Winogradow, Adam, 'Parents, Children and Property in Late Eighteenth-Century Chancery', *Oxford Journal of Legal Studies*, 32 (2012), pp. 741–769.

Holdsworth, W. S., *A History of English Law* (16 vols, London, 1926–1966).

Holmes, Geoffrey, *Augustan England: Professions, State and Society, 1680–1730* (London, 1982).

Hoppit, Julian, *Risk and Failure in English Business 1700–1800* (Cambridge, 1987).

Horsefield, J. Keith, 'The "Stop of the Exchequer" Revisited', *EHR*, 35 (1982), pp. 511–528.

Horwitz, Henry, *A Guide to Chancery Equity Records and Proceedings 1600–1800* (Kew, 1995).

– – 'Chancery's "Younger Sister": The Court of Exchequer and its Equity Jurisdiction, 1649–1841', *Historical Research*, 72 (1999), pp. 160–182.

– – *Exchequer Equity Records and Proceedings, 1649–1841* (Kew, 2001).

– – 'Record-Keepers in the Court of Chancery and Their "Record" of Accomplishment in the Seventeenth and Eighteenth Centuries', *Historical Research*, 70 (1997), pp. 34–51.

Horwitz, Henry and Polden, Patrick, 'Continuity or Change in the Court of Chancery in the Seventeenth and Eighteenth Centuries?', *Journal of British Studies*, 35 (1996), pp. 24–57.

Hubbard, Eleanor, *Englishmen at Sea: Labor and the Nation at the Dawn of Empire, 1570–1630* (New Haven, 2021).

Hunt, Margaret, *The Middling Sort: Commerce, Gender, and the Family in England, 1680–1780* (London, 1996).

– – 'Time-Management, Writing, and Accounting in the Eighteenth-Century English Trading Family: A Bourgeois Enlightenment', *Business and Economic History*, 18 (1989), pp. 150–159.

Ingram, Allan (ed.), *The Madhouse of Language: Writing and Reading Madness in the Eighteenth Century* (London, 1991).

– – *Voices of Madness: Four Pamphlets, 1683–1796* (Thrupp Stroud, 1997).

Innes, Joanna, *Inferior Politics: Social Problems and Social Policies in Eighteenth-Century Britain* (Oxford, 2009).

Innes, Joanna and Styles, John, 'The Crime Wave: Writing on Crime and Criminal Justice in England', *Journal of British Studies*, 25 (1988), pp. 380–435.

Ives, E. W., 'English Law and English Society', *History*, 61 (1981), pp. 50–60.

Jarrett, Sadie, 'Credibility in the Court of Chancery: Salesbury v Bagot, 1671–1677', *The Seventeenth Century*, 36 (2019), pp. 1–26.

Johnson, Tom, 'The Preconstruction of Witness Testimony: Law and Social Discourse in England before the Reformation', *LHR*, 32 (2014), pp. 127–147.

Jones, N. G., 'The Use Upon a Use in Equity Revisited', *Cambrian Law Review*, 33 (2002), pp. 67–80.

– – 'Trusts for Secrecy: The Case of John Dudley, Duke of Northumberland', *The Cambridge Law Journal*, 54 (1995), pp. 545–551.

– – 'Tyrrel's Case (1557) and the Use Upon a Use', *The Journal of Legal History*, 14 (1993), pp. 75–93.

– – 'Wills, Trusts and Trusting from the Statute of Uses to Lord Nottingham', *The Journal of Legal History*, 31 (2010), pp. 273–298.

Jones, Sophie H. and Talbott, Siobhan, 'Sole Traders? The Role of the Extended Family in Eighteenth-Century Atlantic Business Networks', *Enterprise and Society*, 23 (2021), pp. 1–30.

Jones, W. J., 'Conflict or Collaboration? Chancery Attitudes in the Reign of Elizabeth I', *The American Journal of Legal History*, 5 (1961), pp. 12–54.

– – *The Elizabethan Court of Chancery* (Oxford, 1967).

– – 'The Foundations of English Bankruptcy: Statutes and Commissions in the Early Modern Period', *Transactions of the American Philosophical Society*, 69 (1979), pp. 1–63.

Kadens, Emily, 'Pre-Modern Credit Networks and the Limits of Reputation', *Iowa Law Review*, 100 (2015), pp. 2429–2507.

– – 'The Last Bankrupt Hanged: Balancing Incentives in the Development of Bankruptcy Law', *Duke Law Journal*, 59 (2010), pp. 1229–1319.

– – 'The Pitkin Affair: A Study of Fraud in Early English Bankruptcy', *American Bankruptcy Law Journal*, 84 (2010), pp. 483–570.

Kilpi, Jukka, *The Ethics of Bankruptcy* (London, 1998).

Kippen, Kim and Woods, Lori (eds), *Worth and Repute: Valuing Gender in Late Medieval and Early Modern Europe: Essays in Honour of Barbara Todd* (Toronto, 2011).

Kleinig, John, 'Criminal Liability for Failures to Act', *Law and Contemporary Problems*, 49 (1986), pp. 161–180.

Klinck, Dennis, *Conscience, Equity and the Court of Chancery in Early Modern England* (London, 2010).

– – 'Imagining Equity in Early Modern England', *Canadian Bar Review*, 84 (2005), pp. 217–247.

– – 'Lord Nottingham and the Conscience of Equity', *Journal of the History of Ideas*, 67 (2006), pp. 123–147.

– – 'Lord Nottingham's "Certain Measures"', *LHR*, 28 (2010), pp. 711–748.

Klinck, Dennis and Mirella, Loris, 'Tracing the Imprint of the Chancellor's Foot in Contemporary Canadian Judicial Discourse', *Canadian Journal of Law and Society*, 13 (1998), pp. 63–98.

Kuen, Thomas, 'Reading Microhistory: The Example of Giovanni and Lusanna', *Journal of Modern History*, 61 (1989), pp. 512–535.

Ladurie, Emmanuel Le Roy, *Montaillou: Cathars and Catholics in a French Village*, trans. Barbara Bray (New York, 1978).

Langford, Paul, *A Polite and Commercial People: England 1727–1783* (Oxford, 1989).

Law, Jonathan and Martin, Elizabeth A. (eds), *Oxford Dictionary of Law* (Oxford, 2014).

Lee, W. R. and Hudson, Pat (eds), *Women's Work and the Family Economy in Historical Perspective* (Manchester, 1990).

Lemmings David (ed.), *The British and Their Laws in the Eighteenth Century* (Woodbridge, 2005).

Lester, Markham V., *Victorian Insolvency: Bankruptcy, Imprisonment for Debt, and Company Winding-up in Nineteenth-Century England* (Oxford, 1995).

Levinthal, Louis, 'The Early History of Bankruptcy Law', *University of Pennsylvania Law Review and American Law Register*, 66 (1918), pp. 223–250.

Lewis, Andrew and Lobban, Michael (eds), *Law and History* (Oxford, 2004).

Liapi, Lena, *Roguery in Print: Crime and Culture in Early Modern London* (Woodbridge, 2019).

Lipovsky, Caroline, 'Storytelling in Legal Settings: A Case Study from a Crown Prosecutor's Opening Statement', *Australian Review of Applied Linguistics*, 40 (2017), pp. 71–91.

Llewetjtren, Karl N. and Hoebel, E. Adamson, *The Cheyenne Way: Conflict and Case Law in Primitive Jurisprudence* (Norman, 1941).

Lobban, Michael, 'Preparing for Fusion: Reforming the Nineteenth-Century Court of Chancery (part 1)', *LHR*, 22 (2004), pp. 389–427.

– – 'Preparing for Fusion: Reforming the Nineteenth-Century Court of Chancery (part 2)', *LHR*, 22 (Autumn, 2004), pp. 565–599.

– – 'The Chancellor, the Chancery, and the History of Law Reform', *LHR*, 22 (2004), pp. 615–617.

– – *The Common Law and English Jurisprudence, 1760–1850* (Oxford, 1991).

Lobban, Michael, Begiato, Joanne, and Green, Adrian (eds), *Law, Lawyers, and Litigants in Early Modern England: Essays in Memory of Christopher W. Brooks* (Cambridge, 2019).

MacDonald, Michael, *Mystical Bedlam: Madness, Anxiety, and Healing in Seventeenth Century England* (Cambridge, 1981).

Macfarlane, Alan, 'Equity and Conscience', *Oxford Journal of Legal Studies*, 27 (2007), pp. 659–681.

– – *Witchcraft in Tudor and Stuart England: A Regional and Comparative Study* (London, 1970).

Macnair, Mike, 'Development of Uses and Trusts: Contract or Property, and European Influences and Images', *Studi Urbinati, A – Scienze Giuridiche, Politiche Ed Economiche*, 66 (2016), pp. 305–333.

Macnair, M. R. T., *The Law of Proof in Early Modern Equity* (Berlin, 1999).

Macneil, Ian R., 'Contracts: Adjustment of Long-Term Economic Relations Under Classical, Neo-Classical, and Relational Contract Law', *Northwestern University Law Review*, 72 (1978), pp. 854–905.

Maitland, F. W., *Equity, Also the Forms of Action at Common Law: Two Course of Lectures* (Cambridge, 1929).

Mann, Bruce H., *Republic of Debtors: Bankruptcy in the Age of American Independence* (Cambridge, 2002).

Marriner, Sheila, 'English Bankruptcy Records and Statistics Before 1850', *EHR*, 33 (1980), pp. 351–366.

Mason, Rebecca, 'Women, Marital Status, and Law: The Marital Spectrum in Seventeenth-Century Glasgow', *Journal of British Studies*, 58 (2019), pp. 787–804.

McCoid II, John C., 'Discharge: The Most Important Development in Bankruptcy History', *American Bankruptcy Law Journal*, 70 (1996), pp. 163–193.

McCusker, John J. and Morgan, Kenneth (eds), *The Early Modern Atlantic Economy* (Cambridge, 2000).

McIntosh, Marjorie, 'The Benefits and Drawbacks of Femme Sole Status in England, 1300–1630', *Journal of British Studies*, 44 (2005), pp. 410–438.

McNairn, Jeffrey L., '"The Common Sympathies of our Nature": Moral Sentiments, Emotional Economies, and Imprisonment for Debt in Upper Canada', *Social History*, 49 (2016), pp. 49–72.

McShane, Angela and Walker, Garthine (eds), *The Extraordinary and the Everyday in Early Modern England: Essays in Celebration of the Work of Bernard Capp* (Basingstoke, 2010).

Mitchell, Charles and Mitchell, Paul (eds), *Landmark Cases in Equity* (Oxford, 2012).

Muldrew, Craig, '"A mutual Assent of Her Mind"?: Women, Debt, Litigation and Contract in Early Modern England', *History Workshop Journal*, 55 (2003), pp. 47–71.

– – 'Credit and the Courts: Debt Litigation in a Seventeenth-Century Urban Community', *EHR*, 46 (1993), pp. 23–38.

– – '"Hard food for Midas": Cash and its Social Value in Early Modern England', *Past & Present*, 170 (2001), pp. 78–120.

– – 'The Culture of Reconciliation: Community and the Settlement of Economic Disputes in Early Modern England', *The Historical Journal*, 39 (1996), pp. 915–942.

– – *The Economy of Obligation: The Culture of Credit and Social Relations in Early Modern England* (Basingstoke, 1998).

Musson, Anthony (ed.), *Expectations of the Law in the Middle Ages* (Woodbridge, 2001).

Neal, Larry, '*I Am Not Master of Events': The Speculations of John Law and Lord Londonerry in the Mississippi and South Sea Bubbles* (New Haven, 2012).

Newman, Simon P., *Embodied History: The Lives of the Poor in Early Philadelphia* (Philadelphia, 2003).

Oldham, James, *English Common Law in the Age of Mansfield* (Chapel Hill, 2004).

Orlin, Lena Cowen, *Locating Privacy in Tudor England* (Oxford, 2007).

Paul, John, 'Bankruptcy and Capital Punishment in the 18th and 19th Centuries' (16 January 2009). Available at SSRN: https://ssrn.com/abstract=1329067

Paul, Tawny, The Poverty of Disaster: Debt and Insecurity in Eighteenth-Century Britain (Cambridge, 2019), pp. 1–6.

Pearlston, Karen, 'Married Women Bankrupts in the Age of Coverture', *Law and Social Inquiry*, 34 (2009), pp. 265–299.

Phillips, Nicola, *The Profligate Son: Or, a True Story of Family Conflict, Fashionable Vice, and Financial Ruin in Regency England* (Oxford, 2013).

Plank, Thomas E., 'The Constitutional Limits of Bankruptcy', *Tennessee Law Review*, 63 (1996), pp. 487–584.

Pollock, Linda, 'Anger and the Negotiation of Relationships in Early Modern England', *Historical Journal*, 47 (2004), pp. 567–590.

Porter, Jonathan, *Representing Reality: Discourse, Rhetoric and Social Construction* (London, 1996).

Porter, Roy (ed.), *Medicine in the Enlightenment* (Amsterdam, 1995).

– – *Mind-Forg'd Manacles: A History of Madness from the Restoration to the Regency* (London, 1987).

Posner, Eric A., 'A Theory of Contract Law Under Conditions of Radical Judicial Error', *Northwestern University Law Review*, 94 (2000), pp. 749–774.

Prest, Wilfrid and Anleu, Sharyn Roach (eds), *Litigation Past and Present* (Sydney, 2004).

Quilter, Michael, 'Daniel Defoe: Bankrupt and Bankruptcy Reformer', *The Journal of Legal History*, 25 (2004), pp. 53–73.

Quinn, Stephen, 'Gold, Silver, and the Glorious Revolution: Arbitrage Between Bills of Exchange and Bullion', *EHR*, 49 (1996), pp. 473–490.

– – 'Goldsmith-Banking: Mutual Acceptance and Interbanker Clearing in Restoration London', *Explorations in Economic History*, 34 (1997), pp. 411–432.

Radzinowicz, Leon, *A History of English Criminal Law and its Administration from 1750* (5 vols, London, 1948–1990).

Reay, Barry (ed), *Popular Culture in Seventeenth Century England* (London, 1985).

Richard, Jessica, *The Romance of Gambling in the Eighteenth-Century British Novel* (London, 2011).

Robertson, Kellie and Uebel, Michael (eds), *The Middle Ages at Work: Practicing Labor in Late Medieval England* (Basingstoke, 2004).

Rosenwein, Barbara H., 'Worrying About Emotions in History', *American Historical Review*, 107 (2002), pp. 821–845.

Rosenwein, Barbara H. and Cristiani, Riccardo, *What is the History of Emotions?* (Malden, 2018).

Roseveare, Henry, *The Financial Revolution 1660–1760* (London, 1991).

Ross, Andrew, *Creditocracy: And the Case for Debt Refusal* (London, 2013).

Rubinstein, Amnon, *Jurisdiction and Illegality: A Study in Public Law* (Oxford, 1965).

Rushton, Peter, 'Lunatics and Idiots: Mental Disability, the Community, and the Poor Law in North-east England, 1600–1800', *Medical History*, 32 (1988), pp. 34–50.

Safley, Thomas Max (ed.), *The History of Bankruptcy: Economic, Social and Cultural Implications in Early Modern England* (London, 2013).

Samaha, Joel, *Law and Order in Historical Perspective: The Case of Elizabethan Essex* (New York, 1974).

Sandage, Scott A., *Born Losers: A History of Failure in America* (Cambridge, 2005).

Scheppele, Kim Lane, 'Foreword: Telling Stories', *Michigan Law Review*, 87 'Legal Storytelling' (1989), pp. 2073–2098.

Selgin, George, 'Those Dishonest Goldsmiths', *Financial History Review*, 19 (2012), pp. 269–288.

Sgard, Jérôme, 'Courts at Work: Bankruptcy Statutes, Majority Rule and Private Contracting in England (17th–18th Century)', *Journal of Comparative Economics*, 44 (2016), pp. 450–460.

Shapiro, Barbara J., *A Culture of Fact: England, 1550–1720* (Ithaca, 2000).

– – *Probability and Certainty in Seventeenth-Century England: A Study of the Relationship between Natural Science, Religion, History, Law, and Literature* (Princeton, 1983).

Sharpe, J. A., *Crime in Early Modern England 1550–1750* (London, 1999).

– – *Crime in Seventeenth-Century England* (Cambridge, 1983).

– – 'The History of Crime in Late Medieval and Early Modern England: A Review of the Field', *Social History*, 7 (1982), pp. 187–203.

Shepard, Alexandra, *Accounting For Oneself: Worth, Status, and the Social Order in Early Modern England* (Oxford, 2015).

– – 'Worthless Witnesses? Marginal Voices and Women's Legal Agency in Early Modern England', *Journal of British Studies*, 58 (2019), pp. 717–734.

Shepard, Alexandra and Spicksley, Judith, 'Worth, Age, and Social Status in Early Modern England', *EHR*, 64 (2011), pp. 493–530.

Shepard, Alexandra and Stretton, Tim, 'Women Negotiating the Boundaries of Justice in Britain, 1300–1700: An Introduction', *Journal of British Studies*, 58 (2019), pp. 677–683.

Simonton, Deborah (ed.), *The Routledge History Handbook of Gender and the Urban Experience* (London, 2017).

Simpson, A. W. B., *A History of the Common Law of Contract: The Rise of the Action of Assumpsit* (Oxford, 1975).

Smith, David A., 'The Error of Young Cyrus: The Bill of Conformity and Jacobean Kingship, 1603–1624', *LHR*, 28 (2010), pp. 307–341.

Sogner, Sølvi (ed.), *Fact Fiction and Forensic Evidence* (Oslo, 1997).

Speake, Jennifer (ed.), *Oxford Dictionary of Proverbs* (Oxford, 2015).

Stearns, Peter N. and Stearns, Carol Z., 'Emotionology: Clarifying the History of Emotions and Emotional Standards', *American Historical Review*, 90 (1985), pp. 813–836.

Steinmetz, William (ed.), *Private Law and Social Inequality in the Industrial Age: Comparing Legal Cultures in Britain, France, Germany and the United States* (Oxford, 2000).

Stirk, Nigel, 'Arresting Ambiguity: The Shifting Geographies of a London Debtors' Sanctuary in the Eighteenth Century', *Social History*, 25 (2000), pp. 316–329.

– – 'Fugitive Meanings: The Literary Construction of a London Debtors' Sanctuary in the Eighteenth Century', *British Journal for Eighteenth-Century Studies*, 24 (2001), pp. 175–188.

Stoler, Ann Laura, 'Colonial Archives and the Arts of Governance', *Archival Science*, 2 (2002), pp. 87–109.

Stone, Lawrence, *Broken Lives: Separation and Divorce in England 1660–1857* (Oxford, 1993).

– – *Road to Divorce in England 1530–1987* (Oxford, 1990).

Stretton, Tim, 'Women, Legal Records, and the Problem of the Lawyer's Hand', *Journal of British Studies*, 58 (2019), pp. 684–700.

Styles, John, *The Dress of the People: Everyday Fashion in Eighteenth-Century England* (New Haven, 2007).

Tabb, Charles Jordan, 'The Historical Evolution of the Bankruptcy Discharge', *American Bankruptcy Law Journal*, 65 (1991), pp. 325–371.

Tadmor, Naomi, *Family and Friends in Eighteenth-Century England: Household, Kinship and Patronage* (Cambridge, 2001).

Talbott, Siobhan, *Conflict, Commerce and Franco-Scottish Relations, 1560–1713* (London, 2014).

– – *Knowledge, Information and Business Education in the British Atlantic World, 1620–1760* (Oxford University Press, forthcoming 2024)

Triantis, Alexander J. and Triantis, George G., 'Timing Problems in Contract Breach Decisions', *The Journal of Law and Economics*, 41 (1998), pp. 163–208.

Trivellato, Francesca, *The Familiarity of Strangers: The Sephardic Diaspora, Livorno, and Cross-Cultural Trade in the Early Modern Period* (New Haven, 2009).

Tucker, P., 'The Early History of the Court of Chancery: A Comparative Study', *The English Historical Review*, 115 (2000), pp. 791–811.

Wakelam, Alexander, *Credit and Debt in Eighteenth Century England: An Economic History of Debtors' Prisons* (London, 2020).

Walker, Claire and Kerr, Heather (eds), *'Fama' and Her Sisters: Gossip and Rumour in Early Modern Europe* (Turnhour, 2015).

Walker, Garthine, *Crime, Gender and Social Order in Early Modern England* (Cambridge, 2003).

– – 'Rereading Rape and Sexual Violence in Early Modern England', *Gender and History*, 10 (1998), pp. 1–25.

Weisberg, Robert, 'Commercial Morality, the Merchant Character, and the History of the Voidable Preference', *Stanford Law Review*, 39 (1986), pp. 3–137.

Wennerlind, Carl, *Casualties of Credit: The English Financial Revolution, 1620–1720* (Cambridge, 2011).

Wilson, Adrian (ed.), *Rethinking Social History: English Society 1570–1920 and its Interpretation* (Manchester, 1993).

Wilson, Lee B, *Bonds of Empire: The English Origins of Slave Law in South Carolina and British Plantation America, 1660–1783* (Cambridge, 2011).

Winter, Mabel, *Banking, Projecting and Politicking in Early Modern England: The Rise and Fall of Thompson and Company 1671–1678* (Cham, 2022).

– – 'The Collapse of Thompson and Company: Credit, Reputation and Risk in Early Modern England', *Social History*, 45 (2020), pp. 145–166.

White, Hayden, *Tropics of Discourse: Essays in Cultural Criticism* (Baltimore, 1978).

White, Jerry, *Mansions of Misery: A Biography of the Marshalsea Debtors' Prison* (London, 2016).

Whyte, Nicola, 'Landscape, Memory and Custom: Parish Identities c.1550–1700', *Social History*, 32 (2007), pp. 166–186.

Wood, Andy, 'Fear, Hatred and the Hidden Injuries of Class in Early Modern England', *Journal of Social History*, 39 (2006), pp. 803–826.

– – '"Some Banglyng About the Customes": Popular Memory and the Experience of Defeat in a Sussex Village, 1549–1640', *Rural History*, 25 (2014), pp. 1–14.

– – 'Subordination, Solidarity and the Limits of Popular Agency in a Yorkshire Valley, c.1596–1615' *Past and Present*, 193 (2006), pp. 41–72.

– – *The 1549 Rebellions and the Making of Early Modern England* (Cambridge, 2007).

Woodfine, Philip, 'Debtors, Prisons, and Petitions in Eighteenth-Century England', *Eighteenth-Century Life*, 30 (2006), pp. 1–31.

Worthen, Hannah, McDonagh, Briony and Capern, Amanda, 'Gender, Property and Succession in the Early Modern English Aristocracy: The Case of Martha Janes and her Illegitimate Children', *Women's History Review*, 30 (2019), pp. 1–20.

Wrightson, Keith, *Earthly Necessities: Economic Lives in Early Modern Britain, 1470–1750* (London, 2002).

Yale, D. E. C. (ed.), *Lord Chancellor Nottingham's Chancery Cases* (2 vols, London, 1957).

Yorke, Philip C., *The Life and Correspondence of Philip York, Earl of Hardwicke, Lord High Chancellor of Great Britain* (3 vols, New York, 1977, originally 1913).

Unpublished Theses

Bailey, Joanne, 'Breaking the Conjugal Vows: Marriage and Marriage Breakdown in the North of England' (Unpublished PhD dissertation, University of Exeter, 1999).

Nantes, Robert 'English Bankrupts 1732–1831: A Social Account' (Unpublished PhD dissertation, University of Exeter, 2020).

Web-based Sources

American Civil Liberties Union, 'In For A Penny: The Rise of America's New Debtors' Prisons' (2010), <https://www.aclu.org/wp-content/uploads/legal-documents/InForAPenny_web.pdf>

Lexis+ UK, <https://plus.lexis.com/uk/legalresearch?crid=73313ee8–5f61–499e-a173-e2ac3efecf21>

Oxford Dictionary of National Biography (Oxford University Press), <https://www.oxforddnb.com>

TNA, Online Discovery, <https://discovery.nationalarchives.gov.uk>

United Kingdom House of Lords Decisions, <http://www.bailii.org/uk/cases/UKHL/>

University of Houston: Anglo-American Legal Tradition, 'Chancery Final Decrees', <http://aalt.law.uh.edu/C78_79.html>

Index

PEOPLE, MARKETS, GOODS:
ECONOMIES AND SOCIETIES IN HISTORY

Previously published